THE **ROUGH GUIDE TO**

BRUSSELS

Forthcoming titles include

The Algarve • The Bahamas • Cambodia
Caribbean Islands • Costa Brava
New York Restaurants • South America • Zanzibar

Forthcoming reference guides include

Children's Books • Online Travel • Videogaming
Weather

Rough Guides online

www.roughguides.com

Rough Guide Credits

Text editor: Ruth Blackmore and Claire Saunders
Series editor: Mark Ellingham
Production: Rachel Holmes
Cartography: Maxine Repath

Publishing Information

This second edition published November 2001
by Rough Guides Ltd,
62–70 Shorts Gardens, London, WC2H 9AH

Distributed by the Penguin Group:

Penguin Books Ltd, 80 Strand, London WC2R ORL
Penguin Putnam, Inc. 375 Hudson Street, New York 10014, USA
Penguin Books Australia Ltd, 487 Maroondah Highway,
PO Box 257, Ringwood, Victoria 3134, Australia
Penguin Books Canada Ltd, 10 Alcorn Avenue,
Toronto, Ontario, Canada M4V 1E4
Penguin Books (NZ) Ltd,
182–190 Wairau Road, Auckland 10, New Zealand

Typeset in Bembo and Helvetica to an original design by Henry Iles.
Printed in Spain by Graphy Cems.

THE ROUGH GUIDE TO

BRUSSELS

by Martin Dunford and Phil Lee

with additional contributions by
Eric Drosin

We set out to do something different when the first Rough Guide was published in 1982. Mark Ellingham, just out of university, was travelling in Greece. He brought along the popular guides of the day, but found they were all lacking in some way. They were either strong on ruins and museums but went on for pages without mentioning a beach or taverna. Or they were so conscious of the need to save money that they lost sight of Greece's cultural and historical significance. Also, none of the books told him anything about Greece's contemporary life – its politics, its culture, its people, and how they lived.

So with no job in prospect, Mark decided to write his own guidebook, one which aimed to provide practical information that was second to none, detailing the best beaches and the hottest clubs and restaurants, while also giving hard-hitting accounts of every sight, both famous and obscure, and providing up-to-the-minute information on contemporary culture. It was a guide that encouraged independent travellers to find the best of Greece, and was a great success, getting shortlisted for the Thomas Cook travel guide award, and encouraging Mark, along with three friends, to expand the series.

The Rough Guide list grew rapidly and the letters flooded in, indicating a much broader readership than had been anticipated, but one which uniformly appreciated the Rough Guide mix of practical detail and humour, irreverence and enthusiasm. Things haven't changed. The same four friends who began the series are still the caretakers of the Rough Guide mission today: to provide the most reliable, up-to-date and entertaining information to independent-minded travellers of all ages, on all budgets.

We now publish more than 150 titles and have offices in London and New York. The travel guides are written and researched by a dedicated team of more than 100 authors, based in Britain, Europe, the USA and Australia. We have also created a unique series of phrasebooks to accompany the travel series, along with an acclaimed series of music guides, and a best-selling pocket guide to the Internet and World Wide Web. We also publish comprehensive travel information on our Web site: www.roughguides.com

Help us update

We've gone to a lot of trouble to ensure that this Rough Guide is as up to date and accurate as possible. However, things do change. All suggestions, comments and corrections are much appreciated, and we'll send a copy of the next edition (or any other Rough Guide if you prefer) for the best letters.

Please mark letters "Rough Guide Brussels Update" and send to:

Rough Guides, 62–70 Shorts Gardens, London, WC2H 9AH, or Rough Guides, 4th Floor, 345 Hudson St, New York NY 10014.

Or send email to: mail@roughguides.co.uk
Online updates about this book can be found on Rough Guides' Web site (see opposite)

The authors

Martin Dunford is a co-founder of Rough Guides. He has authored the Rough Guides to Belgium, Brussels, Holland, Amsterdam, New York, Rome and Italy – places he still visits when not attending home matches of Charlton Athletic and training to fulfil his ambition of sailing around the world. He lives in southeast London but dreams of living in Belgium.

Phil Lee has worked as a freelance author with Rough Guides for over ten years. Previous books include the Rough Guides to Norway, Belgium and Luxembourg, Mallorca and Menorca, and Canada. He has also written extensively for magazines and newspapers. He lives in Nottingham where he was born and raised.

Acknowledgements

Phil Lee would like to thank both Ailsa Uys of Tourism Flanders-Brussels and Françoise Scheepers of the Belgian Tourist Office – Brussels & Ardennes for all their help and efficient assistance. Thanks also to Rachel Holmes for typesetting, Maxine Repath for cartography and Brian Priestley for proofreading.

Readers' letters

Thanks to all the people who wrote in with comments on the previous edition of this guide, in particular: Annik Altruy, Charles Booth, Sylvia Chen, Yannick Chevalier, Barry Dawson, Ted Freeman, Linda Gibbs, Ivor Grote, Luna Hawxwell, Peter Howard, D. Jennings, Jacquie Mowbray, Jim Reese, Dena Seki, Suzy Sumner, K. Tipping, Ewan Turner, Marie-Louise Vanherk and I. Williams.

ACKNOWLEDGEMENTS

CONTENTS

Listings

Contexts

MAP LIST

Introduction

mongst Europeans, Brussels is best known as the home of the EU, which, given recent developments, is something of a poisoned chalice. But in fact, the EU neither dominates nor defines Brussels, merely forming one layer of a city that has become, in postwar years at least, a thriving, cosmopolitan metropolis. It's a vibrant and fascinating place, with architecture and museums to rank among the best of Europe's capitals, not to mention a superb restaurant scene and an energetic nightlife. Moreover, most of the key attractions are crowded into a centre that is small enough to be absorbed over a few days, its boundaries largely defined by a ring of boulevards known as the "petit ring".

The layout of this city centre embodies historic class divisions. For centuries, the ruling class has lived in the Upper Town, an area of wide boulevards and grand mansions which looks down on the maze of tangled streets that characterize the Lower Town, traditionally home to shopkeepers and workers. This fundamental class divide has in recent decades been further complicated by discord between Belgium's two main linguistic groups, the Walloons (the French-speakers) and the Flemish (basically Dutch-speakers). As a cumbersome compromise, the city is Belgium's only officially **bilingual** region and by law all road signs, street names and virtually all published information must be in both languages, even though French-speakers make up nearly eighty percent of Brussels' population. As if this was not complex enough, since the 1960s the city has become much more ethnically diverse, with communities of immigrants from North Africa, Turkey, the Mediterranean and Belgium's former colonies as well as European administrators, diplomats and business people, now comprising a quarter of the population.

Each of these communities leads a very separate, distinct existence and this is reflected in the number and variety of affordable ethnic restaurants. But, even without these, Brussels would still be a wonderful place to **eat**: its gastronomic reputation rivals that of Paris and London, and though restaurants are rarely inexpensive, there is great-value food to be had in many of the **bars**. The bars themselves can be sumptuous, basic, traditional or very fashionable – and one of the city's real pleasures. Another pleasure is **shopping**: Belgian chocolates and lace are de rigueur, but it's also hard to resist the charms of the city's designer clothes shops and antique markets, not to mention the numerous specialist shops devoted to anything and everything from comic books to costume jewellery.

Many of the city's best bars and restaurants are dotted round the city centre, within the petit ring, and this is where you'll find the key sights. The **Lower Town** centres on the Grand-Place, one of Europe's most magnificent squares, boasting a superb ensemble of Baroque guildhouses and an imposing Gothic town hall, while the **Upper Town** weighs in with a splendid cathedral and a fine art museum of international standing, the Musées Royaux des Beaux Arts. Few visitors stray beyond the petit ring, but there are delights here too, principally in **St Gilles** and **Ixelles**, two *communes* (or boroughs) just to the south of the centre, whose streets are studded with fanciful Art Nouveau residences, including the old home and studio of Victor Horta, the style's prime exponent.

Belgium is such a small country, and the rail network so fast and efficient, that Brussels also makes a feasible base for many other day-trips. In Chapter Eight, we've selected five prime destinations, all within an hour's travelling time – the battlefield at **Waterloo**, the abbey ruins of **Villers-la-Ville** and a trio of fascinating Flemish towns: **Antwerp**, **Ghent** and **Bruges**.

Climate

Brussels – and Belgium – enjoys a fairly standard temperate climate, with warm, if mild, summers and cold winters,

	C°	RAINFALL
	AVERAGE DAILY	AVERAGE MONTHLY
		MM
Jan	1	66
Feb	4	61
March	7	53
April	11	60
May	13	55
June	18	76
July	19	95
Aug	18	80
Sept	17	63
Oct	12	83
Nov	7	75
Dec	3	88

without much snow. The warmest months are usually June, July and August, the coldest December and January, when short daylight hours and weak sunlight can make the weather seem colder (and wetter) than it actually is. Rain is always a possibility, even in summer, which actually sees a greater degree of rainfall than autumn or winter. Warm days in April and May, when the light has the clarity of springtime, are especially appealing.

THE GUIDE

THE GUIDE

Introducing the City

Visitors to **Brussels** are often surprised by the raw vitality of the **city centre**. It's not neat and tidy, and many of the old tenement houses are shabby and bruised, but there's a buzz about the place that's hard to resist and it's here you'll find the majority of the city's sights and attractions, restaurants and bars. The centre is also surprisingly compact, sitting neatly within the rough pentagon of boulevards that enclose it – the **petit ring** – which follows the course of the fourteenth-century city walls, running from place Rogier in the north round to Porte de Hal in the south. The city centre is itself divided into two main areas. The larger, westerly portion comprises the Lower Town, built for the working and lower-middle classes and fanning out from the Grand-Place, while up on the hill to the east lies the much smaller Upper Town, the traditional home of the Francophile upper classes. Broadly speaking, the boundary between the two zones follows the busy boulevard which swings through the centre under several names – Berlaimont, L'Impératrice and L'Empereur.

The Brussels area telephone code is ℡02, but note that it has to be dialled even for local calls. From abroad, omit the "0".

The **Grand-Place**, with its exquisite guildhouses and town hall, is the unquestionable centre of Brussels, a focus for tourists and locals alike. It's surrounded by the **Lower Town**, whose cramped and populous quarters are bisected by a major north–south boulevard, variously named Adolphe Max, Anspach and Lemonnier. The Lower Town is at its most beguiling to the northwest of the Grand-Place: the area is a cobweb of quaint, narrow lanes and tiny squares, on one of which stands the sturdy church of **Ste Catherine**, while on another sits the beautiful **St Jean Baptiste au Béguinage**. By comparison, the streets to the north of the Grand-Place are of less immediate appeal, with dreary **rue Neuve**, a pedestrianized street of mainstream shops and department stores, leading up to the clumping skyscrapers that surround the place Rogier and the **Gare du Nord**. This is an uninviting part of the city, but relief is at hand in the precise if bedraggled Habsburg symmetries of the **place des Martyrs** and at the Belgian Comic Strip Centre, the **Centre Belge de la Bande Dessinée**. To the south of the Grand-Place lie the old working-class streets of the **Marolles** district and the depressed and predominantly immigrant area in the vicinity of the **Gare du Midi**.

Quite different in feel from the rest of the city centre, the **Upper Town** is a self-consciously planned, more monumental quarter, with statuesque buildings lining wide boulevards and squares. Appropriately, it's the home of the Belgian parliament and government departments, formal parks and the **Palais Royal**. More promisingly, it also accommodates the **Cathedral**, a fine Gothic edifice with wonderful stained-glass windows, the superb **Musées Royaux des Beaux Arts**, arguably Belgium's best collection of fine art, and some of the city's swishest shops clustered around the charming **place du Grand Sablon**. There's also the preposterous bulk of the **Palais de Justice**, which lords it over the rest of the city, commanding views that on clear days reach way across the suburbs.

Brussels by no means ends with the petit ring. Léopold II pushed the city limits out beyond the course of the old walls, grabbing land from the surrounding communes to create the irregular boundaries that survive today. To the **east**, he sequestered a rough rectangle of land where he laid out **Parc Léopold** and across which he ploughed two wide boulevards – Belliard and La Loi. These were designed to provide an imperial approach to the **Parc du Cinquantenaire**, whose self-glorifying and over-sized monuments were erected to celebrate Belgium's golden jubilee and now house three large if rather turgid museums – the pick is the **Musées Royaux d'Art et d'Histoire**. The boulevards were soon colonized by the city's bourgeoisie, but in the last few years they have been displaced by the brash concrete and glass tower blocks of the **EU Quarter**, among which is the flashy new **European Parliament**.

All prices in this book are given in **euros**, the new currency replacing the Belgian Franc from January 1, 2002. The exchange rate is fixed at one Euro to 40.34 Belgian Francs.

South of the city centre is the animated and cosmopolitan district of **St Gilles**, while neighbouring **Ixelles** has become the favoured hangout of the arty and the cool, its streets nurturing a handful of designer stores and a growing number of chic bars and restaurants. These two communes also boast much of the best of the city's **Art Nouveau** architecture. Ixelles is bisected by **avenue Louise**, a prosperous corridor that's actually considered part of the city centre – and is home to the enjoyable **Musée Constantin Meunier**.

Further out, to the **southwest** of the city centre, lies the gritty suburb of **Anderlecht**, famous for its soccer team and also worth a visit for its Gueuze brewery and the fascinating Erasmus house, one-time residence of Desiderius Erasmus, who lodged here in 1521. Adjacent to this area is **Koekelberg**, the site of the Basilique du Sacré Coeur, another whopping pile built by Léopold II. Also nearby is the *commune* of **Jette**, site of the **Musée René Magritte**. To the **north** of the city centre, beyond the tough districts of St Josse and Schaerbeek, is **Laeken**, city residence of the Belgian royal family, and **Heysel**, with its notorious soccer stadium and the **Atomium**, a clumsy leftover from the 1958 World Fair.

In Brussels, the languages of the French- and Flemish-speaking communities have parity. This means that every instance of the written word, from road signs to the yellow pages, has to appear in both languages. Visitors soon adjust, but on arrival this can be very confusing, especially with regard to the names of the city's three main train stations: Bruxelles-Nord (in Flemish it's Brussel-Noord), Bruxelles-Centrale (Brussel-Centraal), and, most bewildering of the lot, Bruxelles-Midi (Brussel-Zuid). Note that for simplicity we've used the French version of street names and sights.

Arrival

Brussels is easy to reach by plane, with flights arriving at its airport from every corner of the globe. In addition, the city is on the main routes heading inland from the Channel ports and is well connected by train to major cities across Europe, including direct from London via the Channel Tunnel. Brussels itself has a good public transport system, which puts the main **points of arrival** – its airport, train and bus stations – within easy reach of the city centre.

BY AIR

Planes land at Brussels' **international airport** in Zaventem, 13km northeast of the city centre (Map 1, G1). There are two **tourist information desks** in the arrivals hall. One is Info Tourisme (daily 6am–9pm), which has a reasonable range of information on Brussels and its surroundings and shares its space with Espace Wallonie, representing OPT, the Wallonian tourist board; the other is Destination Belgium (daily 6.30am–9.30pm), where the emphasis is on the Flemish-speaking regions. Destination Belgium (but not Info Tourisme) will make hotel reservations on your behalf any-where in Belgium, a service that is provided free – you just pay a percentage of the room rate as a deposit and this is then subtracted from your final hotel bill. In addition, the arrivals hall has all the **facilities** you would expect of a major airport, notably bureaux de change, a bank, a post office and ATMs.

From the airport, **trains** run every fifteen minutes to the city's three main stations. The journey time to Bruxelles-Centrale (the nearest station to the Grand-Place; Map 3, E6) is about twenty minutes; the cost is €2.35 one-way, and tickets can be bought from the ticket office in the airport-complex train station. If the ticket office is closed, you can pay the ticket inspector on the train at no extra charge, but there is a small surcharge if the office is open and you still choose to pay the inspector. Trains run from around 5am until midnight; after that you'll need to take a **taxi** into the city centre – reckon on paying around €34.70 for the trip. Finally, there's an hourly **bus** service (6am–11pm) from the airport's bus station through the city's northeastern suburbs to the Gare du Nord; the journey takes about 35 minutes – much longer during rush hour.

ARRIVAL: BY AIR

BY TRAIN

Brussels has three main **train stations** – Bruxelles-Nord, Bruxelles-Centrale and Bruxelles-Midi. Almost all **domestic** trains stop at all three, but the majority of **international** services only stop at Bruxelles-Midi, including Eurostar trains from London and Thalys express trains from Amsterdam, Paris, Cologne and Aachen. **Bruxelles-Centrale** (Map 3, E6) is, as its name suggests, the most central of the stations, a five-minute walk from the Grand-Place; **Bruxelles-Nord** (Map 3, F1) lies amongst the bristling tower blocks of the business area just north of the main ring road; and **Bruxelles-Midi** (Map 3, A10) is located in a depressed area just to the south of the city centre. Note that on bus timetables and on maps of the city transit system, Bruxelles-Nord appears as "Gare du Nord", Bruxelles-Centrale as "Gare Centrale" and Bruxelles-Midi as "Gare du Midi". The former name stands for the mainline train station while the latter signifies the métro stop. If you arrive late at night, it's best to take a taxi to your hotel or hostel – and you should certainly avoid the streets around Bruxelles-Midi.

If you need to **transfer from one of the city's three main train stations** to another, then simply jump on the next available mainline train. There are services between the three stations every ten minutes or so; the journey only takes minutes and all you'll have to do (at most) is swap platforms. In addition, Bruxelles-Midi and Bruxelles-Nord are linked by underground tram – the **prémétro** – with several services shuttling underneath the city centre between these two stations. Thus, there are two ways to reach the Grand-Place (Map 3, D6) from either Bruxelles-Nord or Bruxelles-Midi: either take a mainline train to Bruxelles-Centrale, or take the prémétro to the Bourse station; from either it's a brief walk to the Grand-Place.

BY BUS

Most **international bus** services to Brussels, including
those from Britain, are operated by Eurolines, whose terminal is in the Bruxelles-Nord station complex (Map 3, F1).
Belgium's comprehensive rail network means that it's
unlikely that you'll arrive in the city by **long-distance
domestic bus**, but if you do, Bruxelles-Nord is the main
terminal for these services too.

Information and maps

Aside from the offices at the airport, there are two
tourist information offices in the city, both located
right in the centre. The main one is the **BI-TC**
(Bruxelles International – Tourisme et Congrès), in the
Hôtel de Ville on the Grand-Place (Map 3, D6;
May–Sept daily 9am–6pm; Oct–Dec & March–April
Mon–Sat 9am–6pm, Sun 10am–2pm; Jan & Feb Mon–Sat
9am–6pm; ☎02 513 89 40, ℻513 83 20, ⓦwww.tib.be),
which handles information on the city only. It stocks a
wide range of handouts, including free city maps, has
details of up-and-coming events and concerts and sells a
variety of general- and specialist-interest guides, the most
useful of which is the detailed *Brussels Guide and Map*
(€2). In addition, the BI-TC issues a list of all the city's
(recognized) hotels, and makes **hotel reservations** for
free – the deposit is subtracted from your final hotel bill.
This is especially attractive as the BI-TC can often offer
substantial discounts on published rates. It can help with
public transport, too: the BI-TC sells the 24-hour *carte
d'un jour* pass (see below) and issues free public transport

INFROMATION AND MAPS

maps. Finally, the BI-TC offers several **package deals**, combining public transport and admission into certain sights, though frankly these aren't especially enticing. Probably the best is the **Tourist Passport** (€7.45), which entitles bearers to free use of the city's public transport network for two days and offers modest discounts at a variety of attractions, though you do have to work fairly hard to recover your outlay.

The Bulletin (€2.35), the city's main English-language weekly, contains an excellent entertainment listings section, detailing what's on and where. The magazine is on sale at most downtown newsagents. The BI-TC also provides *The Bulletin*'s listings section – "What's On" – for free.

The city centre's second tourist office, the **Belgian tourist information centre**, footsteps from the Grand-Place at rue Marché aux Herbes 63 (Map 3, D6; July & Aug Mon–Fri 9am–7pm, Sat & Sun 9am–1pm & 2–7pm; May, June, Sept & Oct Mon–Fri 9am–6pm, Sat & Sun 9am–1pm & 2–6pm; Nov–April Mon–Fri 9am–6pm, Sat 9am–1pm & 2–6pm, Sun 9am–1pm; ⓣ02 504 03 90, ⓕ504 02 70), provides information on the whole of Belgium. They do stock a few brochures on Brussels, but this is not their main concern – they leave the city largely to the BI-TC. They also operate a hotel room reservation service, but again it's for the rest of Belgium, not Brussels.

If you need a large city **map**, buy the *Girault Gilbert* map, which comes complete with an index. It's available at most city-centre souvenir shops, newsagents and book-shops, but at prices that range from €4.95 to €7.45: as you might expect, the souvenir shops near the Grand-Place tend to up the ante.

BRUSSELS ON THE INTERNET

Tintin

Ⓦwww.tintin.be

Blistering barnacles! Anything you've ever wanted to know.

Anderlecht football team

Ⓦwww.rsca.be

'Ere we go, the thrilling fields of Anderlecht.

Beer

Ⓦwww.belgianstyle.com

More encouragement, if you need it.

Lace

Ⓦwww.belgian-lace.com

Examples of lacy bits for all occasions.

Magritte

Ⓦwww.virtuo.be

More than 300 pics in this library and not just bowler hats.

Tourist Information

Ⓦwww.brusselsdiscovery.com

Straight from the tourist board's mouth. Well presented and organized, and full of practical information.

City transport

The easiest way to get around the city centre, within the petit ring, is to **walk**, but, to get from one side of the centre to the other, or to reach some of the outlying attractions, you will need to use **public transport**. Operated by STIB (information line ☎02 515 20 00, Ⓦwww.stib.be), the urban system runs on an integrated mixture of bus, tram, underground tram (prémétro) and métro lines that covers the city comprehensively. It's a user-friendly network, with every station carrying métro-system diagrams and with timetables posted at most bus and tram stops.

TICKETS

Tickets are fairly cheap. A single ticket costs €1.35, a strip of five €5.95, and a strip of ten €8.90, available either from tram or bus drivers, métro kiosks, or from newsagents displaying the STIB sign. These can be used on any part of the STIB system. Tickets can also be obtained from automatic machines at all métro stations. A go-as-you-please *carte d'un jour*, for €3.60, allows for 24 hours of city-wide travel on public transport.

MÉTRO, TRAMS AND TRAINS

The **métro** system consists of two underground train lines – lines #1 and #2. Line #1 runs west–east through the centre, and splits into two branches (#1A and #1B) at either end to serve the city's suburbs. Line #2 circles the centre, its route roughly following that of the petit ring up above. Brussels has a substantial **tram** system serving the city centre and the suburbs. These trams are at their speediest when they go underground to form what is sometimes called the **prémétro**, part of the system which runs underneath the heart of the city from Bruxelles-Nord, through De Brouckère and Bourse, to Bruxelles-Midi, Porte de Hal and on underneath St Gilles.

There is a métro map at the back of this guide. The symbol Ⓜ is used throughout the book to denote a métro station.

At the **beginning of each journey**, you're trusted to stamp your ticket yourself, either in the machines provided on each and every métro station concourse or in the machines located inside every tram and bus. After that, the ticket is valid for an hour, during which you can get on and off as many trams, métros and buses as you like. The system can seem open to abuse, as ticket controls at the métro stations are almost non-existent and you can get on at the back of any tram without ever showing a ticket. But bear in mind that there are roving inspectors who impose heavy on-the-spot fines for anyone caught without a valid ticket. Finally, remember that doors on métros, trams and buses have to be opened manually.

STIB **route maps** are available free from the BI-TC tourist office and from major métro stations. The STIB has information kiosks at Porte de Namur, Rogier and Midi métro stations. Amongst the multitude of routes, times of operation and frequency vary considerably, but key parts of the system operate from 6am until midnight. Lone travellers should avoid the métro late at night.

In addition to the STIB network there are **local trains**, run by Belgian Railways, which connect different parts of the inner city and the outskirts, though unless you're living and working here, you're unlikely to need to use them. These trains use the city's three main stations, as well as four smaller ones – Bruxelles-Chapelle, Bruxelles-Quartier Léopold, Bruxelles-Schuman and Bruxelles-Congrès.

BUSES

STIB **buses** supplement the trams and métro. In particular, they provide a limited and sporadic **night bus** service on major routes – often just one bus operating on a route between midnight and around 4am. In addition, **De Lijn** (☎02 526 28 28) runs buses from the city to the Flemish-speaking communities that surround the capital, whilst **TEC** (☏010/230 53 53) operates services to the French-speaking areas. Many of these buses run from – or at least call in at – the Gare du Nord complex. Both De Lijn and TEC also run services to other Belgian cities, but they can take up to four times longer than the train.

TAXIS

Taxis don't cruise the streets, but can be picked up at stands around the city – notably on Bourse (Map 3, D6), De Brouckère (Map 3, D4) and Porte de Namur (Map 3, F9), at train stations and outside the smarter hotels. There is a fixed **tariff** consisting of two main elements – a fixed charge of €2.35 (€4.20 at night) and the price per km (€1 inside the city). If you can't find a taxi, phone Taxis Verts (☏02 349 49 49), Taxis Orange (☏02 349 43 43), or Autolux (☏02 411 12 21).

GUIDED TOURS

Guided tours are big business in Brussels and the BI-TC has details of – and takes bookings for – about twenty operators. On offer is everything from a quick stroll or bus ride round the city centre to themed visits – following, for example, in the footsteps of René Magritte or visiting the pick of the city's Art Nouveau buildings. As a general rule, the more predictable tours can be booked on the day, while the more exotic tours need to be booked ahead of time: the BI-TC normally requires at least two weeks' advance notice. Among the many more straightforward options, **De Boeck**, rue de la Colline 8 (☏02 513 77 44, ⊛www.brussels-city-tours.com), operates a breathless, three-hour bus tour round the city and its major sights for €19.85 (students €17.85) between twice and four times daily. They also run the rather more agreeable Visit Brussels Line, a hop-on, hop-off bus service which loops round the city visiting twelve of its principal sights daily between 10am and 6pm. Tickets, valid for 24 hours, cost €12.15 (students €11.15).

More promising still, **Chatterbus**, rue des Thuyas 12 (☎02 673 18 35, @chatterbus@skynet.be), runs well-regarded walking tours throughout the summer, with their first-rate "Brussels through the Ages" tour lasting about three hours and costing €7.45. Chatterbus also operates French-only excursions devoted to a particular theme, for example Baroque Brussels or Belgian beers. Another rec-ommendation is **ARAU** (Atelier de Recherche et d'Action Urbaines), boulevard Adolphe Max 55 (☎02 219 33 45), a heritage action group which provides tours exploring the city's architecture, with particular emphasis on Art Nouveau. Their English-language, three-hour, Art Nouveau bus tour runs at the weekend (times vary), from March through to December, and costs €14.90. Most of their other tours – including a fascinating excursion into the Marolles district – are in French.

Cyclists are catered for by **Pro Vélo**, rue de Londres 15 (☎02 502 73 55, ⊜02 502 86 41, @provelo@skynet.be); they operate several half-day cycle tours round the city and its environs and also offer an evening city-centre excursion. The charge is €7.45 per tour, with bike rental costing an extra €4.95.

GUIDED TOURS

The Grand-Place

The **Grand-Place**, one of Europe's most beautiful squares, is tucked away amid the tangle of ancient cobbled lanes that lies at the heart of Brussels. It's the Gothic magnificence of the **Hôtel de Ville** – the town hall – which first draws the eye, but in its shadow is an exquisite sequence of late seventeenth-century guildhouses, whose gilded facades with their columns, scrolled gables and dainty sculptures encapsulate the Baroque ideals of exuberance and complexity. There's no better place to get the flavour of Brussels' past, and, as you nurse a coffee watching the crowds from one of the pavement cafés, its Eurocapital present.

**The area covered by this chapter is
shown in detail on colour map 4.**

Originally marshland, the Grand-Place was drained in the twelfth century, and by 1350 a covered market for bread, meat and textiles had appeared, born of an economic boom underpinned by a flourishing cloth industry. The market was so successful that it soon expanded beyond the boundaries of the square – hence the names of the warren of narrow streets around it: rues au Beurre and des Bouchers, marchés aux Herbes, aux Poulets and aux

Fromages. On the square itself, the city's merchants built themselves their headquarters, the guildhouses that cemented the Grand-Place's role as the commercial hub of the emergent city.

In the fifteenth century, with the building of the Hôtel de Ville, the square took on a civic and political function too, with the ruling dukes descending from their Upper Town residence to hold audiences and organize tournaments. Official decrees and pronouncements were also read here, and rough justice was meted out with public executions. In 1482, however, Brussels, along with the rest of the Low Countries, became a fiefdom of the **Habsburgs** and the city was effectively demoted. In addition, the role of the Grand-Place was transformed by that most Catholic of Habsburgs, **Philip II of Spain** (1555–98), who turned the square's public executions into religious events as he strove to crush the city's Protestants. These were the opening shots of a bitter religious war that was to rack the Low Countries for the next hundred years. Initially, the repression cowed the city, but in 1565 the Protestant guildsmen and their apprentices struck back with widespread rioting. Shortly afterwards, an enraged Philip dispatched a massive Spanish army to crush his heretical subjects, and in anticipation of its arrival, thousands fled the city and, as the local economy collapsed, many more died of famine.

From Tuesday to Sunday from March to the end of October, there's a modest flower and plant market on the Grand-Place (8am–6pm). For more on markets, see p.248.

Religious conflict dogged the city for another twenty years, but when the Habsburgs finally captured the town in 1585 they were surprisingly generous, granting a general amnesty and promising to honour ancient municipal privileges. The city's economy revived and the Grand-Place resumed its role as a commercial centre. Of the square's medieval buildings, however, only parts of the Hôtel de Ville and one guildhouse survive today, the consequence of a 36-hour **French artillery bombardment** which pretty much razed Brussels to the ground in 1695.

Unperturbed, the city's **guilds** swiftly had their headquarters rebuilt, using their control of the municipal council both to impose regulations on the sort of construction that was permitted and to ward off the Habsburg governor's notions of a royal – as distinct from bourgeois – main square. The council was not to be trifled with. In an early example of urban planning, it decreed "(We) hereby forbid the owners to build houses on the lower market [ie the Grand-Place] without the model of the facade . . . first being presented to the Council . . . Any construction erected contrary to this provision shall be demolished at the expense of the offender." By these means, the guilds were able to create a homogeneous Grand-Place, choosing to rebuild in a distinctive and flamboyant Baroque which made the square more ornate and more imposing than before. This magisterial self-confidence was, in fact, misplaced, and the factories that were soon to render the guilds obsolete were already colonizing parts of the city. The industrialization of the city effectively becalmed the Grand-Place, and hence it has survived pretty much intact to this day.

THE HÔTEL DE VILLE

Map 4, C4. Guided tours (40 min) in English April–Sept on Tues & Wed at 3.15pm & Sun at 12.15pm; Oct–March on Tues & Wed at 3.15pm; €2.50. Ⓜ Bourse.

From the south side of the Grand-Place, the newly scrubbed and polished **Hôtel de Ville** dominates the proceedings, its 96-metre spire soaring high above two long series of robust windows, whose straight lines are mitigated by fancy tracery, striking gargoyles, solid statuettes and an arcaded gallery. The town hall dates from the beginning of the fifteenth century when the town council decided to build itself a mansion that adequately reflected its wealth and power. The first part to be completed was the **east wing** – and the original entrance is marked by the twin lions of the Lion Staircase, though the animals were only added in 1770. Work started on the **west wing** in 1444 and continued until 1480. Despite the gap, the wings are of very similar style, and you have to look hard to notice that the later wing is slightly shorter than its neighbour, allegedly at the insistence of Charles the Bold who – for some unknown reason – refused to have the adjacent rue de la Tête d'Or narrowed. The niches were left empty and the statues you see now – which represent leading figures from the city's past – are modern, part of a heavy-handed nineteenth-century refurbishment.

By any standard, the **tower** of the Hôtel de Ville is quite extraordinary, its remarkably slender appearance the work of Jan van Ruysbroeck, the leading spire specialist of the day, who also played a leading role in the building of the cathedral (see p.49) and SS. Pierre et Guidon in Anderlecht (see p.110). Ruysbroeck had the lower section built square to support the weight above, choosing a design that blended seamlessly with the elaborately carved facade on either side – or almost: look carefully and you'll see that the main entrance is slightly out of kilter. Ruysbroeck used the old belfry porch as the base for the new tower, hence the mis-alignment, a deliberate decision and not a miscalculation prompting the architect's suicide, as legend would have it. Above the cornice protrudes an octagonal extension where the basic design of narrow windows flanked by pencil-thin columns and pinnacles is repeated up as far as the pyramid-shaped **spire**, a delicate affair surmounted by a gilded figure of **St Michael**, protector of Christians in

THE HEALTH OF CHARLES II

Philip IV of Spain (1605–65) had no less than fourteen children, but only one of his sons – Charles II (1661–1700) – reached his twenties. With women banned from the succession, the hapless, sickly Charles became king at the tender age of four and, much to everyone's surprise, survived to adulthood. After his first marriage in 1679, there were great hopes that he would be able to sire an heir, but none arrived, probably because Charles suffered from premature ejaculation. A second marriage, twenty years later, was equally fruitless and, as it became increasingly clear Charles was unable to procreate, Europe focused on what was to happen when Charles died and the Spanish royal line died out. Every ambassador to the Spanish court wrote long missives home about the health of Charles, no one more so than the English representative, Stanhope, who painted an especially gloomy picture: "He (Charles) has a ravenous stomach and swallows all he eats whole, for his nether jaw stands out so much that his two rows of teeth cannot meet…His weak stomach not being able to digest the food, he voids it in the same (whole) manner."

In the autumn of 1700, it was clear that Charles was dying and his doctors went to work in earnest, replacing his pillows with freshly killed pigeons and covering his chest with animal entrails. Surprise, surprise, this didn't work and Charles died on the first of November, his death leading directly to the War of the Spanish Succession (1701–14).

general and of soldiers in particular. The tower is off-limits and **guided tours** are confined to a string of lavish official rooms used for receptions and town council meetings. The most dazzling of these is the sixteenth-century **Council Chamber**, decorated with gilt moulding, faded tapestries and an oak floor inlaid with ebony. The entrance chamber at the top of the first flight of stairs is also of interest for its assortment of royal portraits. The Empress Maria Theresa of Austria is pictured side-saddle with her little feet (of which she was inordinately proud) poking out from her fancy lacy dress, while a gallant-looking **Charles II** sits astride his handsome steed, courtesy of Jan van Orley. This must have stretched Orley's imagination to the limit: Charles, the last of the Spanish Habsburgs, was – according to the historian J. H. Elliott – "a rachitic and feeble-minded weakling, the last stunted sprig of a degenerate line". Tours begin at the reception desk off the interior quadrangle; be prepared for the guides' overly reverential script.

THE GUILDHOUSES

Flanking and facing the Hôtel de Ville are the **guildhouses** that give the Grand-Place its character, their slender, gilded facades swirling with exuberant, self-publicizing carvings and sculptures. Decorated with semicircular arches and classical motifs, scrollwork, supple bas-reliefs and statuettes, they represent the apotheosis of **Italian–Flemish architecture**, a melding of two stylistic traditions first introduced into the Low Countries by artists and architects returning from Italy in the early seventeenth century. Each guildhouse has a name, usually derived from one of the statues, symbols or architectural quirks decorating its facade – and the more interesting are described below.

On the west side of the square, at the end of the row, stands **no. 1: Roi d'Espagne** (Map 4, C3). This particularly fine building, which was once the headquarters of the guild of bakers, is named after the bust of Charles II (see opposite) on the upper storey. Charles is flanked by a Moorish and a Native American prisoner, symbolic trophies of war. Balanced on the balustrade are allegorical statues of Energy, Fire, Water, Wind, Wheat and Prudence, presumably meant to represent the elements necessary for baking the ideal loaf. The guildhouse now holds the most famous of the square's bars, *Le Roy d'Espagne*, a surreal, though somewhat dingy, affair with animal bladders and marionettes hanging from the ceiling – and repro halberds in the toilets.

All of the cafés lining the Grand-Place charge premium rates, but the most comfortable and appealing is *La Brouette*, at nos. 2–3, with its tasteful repro furniture and fittings. Its first floor offers an attractive view of the square, but, like everywhere else on the Grand-Place, it's best visited early in the morning before about 10am, when the tourists arrive in force.

Nos. 2–3: Maison de la Brouette was the tallow makers' guildhouse, but it takes its name from the wheelbarrows etched into the cartouches. The figure at the top is St Gilles, the guild's patron saint.

Next door, the three lower storeys of the **Maison du Sac, at no. 4**, escaped the French bombardment of 1695. It was constructed for the carpenters and coopers, with the upper storeys being appropriately designed by a cabinet-maker, and featuring pilasters and caryatids which resemble the ornate legs of Baroque furniture.

The **Maison de la Louve, at no. 5**, also survived the French artillery, and was originally home to the influential archers' guild. The pilastered facade is studded with sanctimonious representations of concepts such as Peace and Discord, and the medallions just beneath the pediment carry the likenesses of four Roman emperors set above allegorical motifs indicating their particular attributes. Thus, Trajan is above the Sun, a symbol of Truth; Tiberius with a net and cage for Falsehood; Augustus and the globe of Peace; and Julius Caesar with a bleeding heart for Disunity. Above the door, there's a charming bas-relief of the Roman she-wolf suckling Romulus and Remus, while the pediment holds a relief of Apollo firing at a python; right on top the Phoenix rises from the ashes.

The **Maison du Cornet, at no. 6**, headquarters of the boatmen's guild, is a fanciful creation of 1697 sporting a top storey resembling the stern of a ship. Charles II makes another appearance here – it's his head in the medallion, flanked by representations of the four winds and of a pair of sailors.

The house of the haberdashers' guild, the **Maison du Renard at no. 7**, displays animated cherubs in bas-relief playing at haberdashery on the ground floor, while a scrawny, gilded fox – after which the house is named – squats above the door. Up on the third storey a statue of Justice proclaims the guild's honest intentions, and is flanked by statues symbolizing the four continents, suggesting the guild's designs on world markets – an aim to which St Nicolas, patron saint of merchants, glinting above, clearly gives his blessing.

On the south side of the square, beside the Hôtel de Ville, the arcaded **Maison de l'Etoile (no.8)** is a nineteenth-century rebuilding of the medieval home of the city magistrate. In the arcaded gallery, the exploits of one **Everard 't Serclaes** are commemorated: in 1356 the Francophile Count of Flanders attempted to seize power from the Duke of Brabant, occupying the magistrate's house and flying his standard from the roof. 'T Serclaes scaled the building, replaced Flanders' standard with that of the Duke of Brabant, and went on to lead the recapturing of the city, events represented in bas-relief above a reclining statue of 't Serclaes. His effigy is polished smooth from the long-standing superstition that good luck will come to those who stroke it – surprising really as 't Serclaes was ultimately hacked to death by the count's mates in 1388.

Next door, the mansion that takes its name from the ostentatious swan on the facade, the **Maison du Cygne, at no. 9**, once housed a bar where Karl Marx regularly met up with

Engels during his exile in Belgium. It was in Brussels in February 1848 that they wrote the Communist Manifesto, only to be deported as political undesirables the following month. Appropriately enough, the Belgian Workers' Party was founded here in 1885, though nowadays the building shelters one of the city's more exclusive restaurants (see p.180).

The **Maison de l'Arbre d'Or, at no. 10**, is the only house on the Grand-Place still to be owned by a guild – the brewers' – not that the equestrian figure stuck on top gives any clues: the original effigy – of one of the city's Habsburg governors – dropped off and the present statue, picturing the eighteenth-century aristocrat Charles of Lorraine, was moved here simply to fill the gap. Inside, the small and mundane **Musée de la Brasserie** (daily 10am–5pm; €2.50) has various bits of brewing paraphernalia; a beer is included in the price of admission.

The seven guildhouses **(nos. 13–19)** that fill out the east side of the Grand-Place have been subsumed within one grand edifice, the **Maison des Ducs de Brabant,** named after the nineteen busts of dukes of Brabant that grace the facade's pilasters. This building, perhaps more than any other on the Grand-Place, has the flavour of the aristocracy, as distinct from the bourgeoisie, and needless to say, it was much admired by the city's Habsburg governors. At no. 13 there's another museum – the **Musée du Cacao et du Chocolat** (Tues–Sun 10am–5pm; €5), but the exhibits are scanty and uninformative.

The guildhouses and private mansions **(nos. 20–39)** running along the north side of the Grand-Place are not as distinguished as their neighbours, though the **Maison du Pigeon (nos. 26–27)**, the painters' guildhouse, is of interest as the house where Victor Hugo spent some time during his exile from France – he was expelled after the French insurrection of 1848. The house also bears four unusual masks in the manner of the green man of Romano-Celtic folklore. The adjacent **Maison des Tailleurs (nos. 24–25)** is appealing too; the old headquarters of the tailors' guild, it is adorned by a pious bust of St Barbara, their patron saint.

MAISON DU ROI AND THE MUSÉE DE LA VILLE DE BRUXELLES

Map 4, D3. Tues–Fri 10am–5pm, Sat & Sun 10am–1pm; €2.50. Ⓜ Bourse.

Much of the northern side of the Grand-Place is taken up by the late nineteenth-century **Maison du Roi**, a fairly faithful reconstruction of the palatial Gothic structure commissioned by Charles V in 1515. The emperor had a point to make: the Hôtel de Ville was an assertion of municipal independence and Charles wanted to emphasize imperial power by erecting his own building directly opposite. With its angular lines, spiky pinnacles and lacy stonework, the original Maison du Roi was an impressive building, but although its replacement, which was completed in the 1890s, is still fairly grand, the arcaded galleries – which were an addition – interrupt the flow of the design. Charles spared no expense in the earlier construction. When it turned out that the ground was too marshy to support the edifice, the architects began again, sinking piles deep into the ground and stretching cattle hides between them to keep the stagnant water at bay.

Despite its name, no sovereign has ever taken up residence in the Maison du Roi, though this was where the Habsburgs sometimes stayed when they visited the city. They also installed their tax men and law courts here, and used it to hold their more important prisoners – the counts of Egmont and Hoorn (see p.75) spent their last night in the Maison du Roi before being beheaded outside in the Grand-Place. The building was also used as a sort of royal changing room: the future Philip II donned his armour here before joining a joust held in the Grand-Place, and the Archdukes Albert and Isabella dressed up inside before appearing on the balcony to shoot down a symbolic target that made them honorary members of the guild of crossbowmen.

The building now holds the **Musée de la Ville de Bruxelles**, a wide-ranging but patchy collection whose best sections feature medieval fine and applied art – not that you'll glean much from the scanty (French and Flemish) labelling.

To the **left of the entrance**, there's a room full of Gothic sculpture retrieved from various city buildings. Pride of place goes to the eight prophets, complete with heavy beards and eccentric headgear, who once decorated the porch of the Hôtel de Ville. Two rooms further on you'll find a small but charming sample of eighteenth-century glazed earthenware, for which the city was once internationally famous. The finest work is by Philippe Mombaers (1724–54), whose workshop, on rue de Laeken, is credited with developing table decorations in the form of vegetables or animals – hence the splendid turkey, cod-fish, duck and cabbage soup tureens and casse-role dishes.

The first of the rooms to the **right of the entrance** boasts superb **altarpieces** – or retables – the intricacy of which was a Brussels speciality, with the city producing hundreds of them from the end of the fourteenth century until the economic slump of the 1640s. Their manufacture was similar to a production line with panel- and cabinet-makers, wood carvers, painters and goldsmiths (for the gild-ing) working on several altarpieces at any one time. The standard format was to create a series of mini-tableaux illus-trating Biblical scenes, with the characters wearing medieval gear in a medieval landscape. It's the extraordinary detail that impresses: look closely at the niche carvings on the whop-ping **Saluzzo altarpiece** (*The Life of the Virgin and the Infant*

Christ) of 1505 and you'll spy the candle-sticks, embroidered pillowcase and carefully draped coverlet of Mary's bedroom in the *Annunciation* scene, while the adjacent Nativity panel comes complete with a set of cute little angels. Up above, in a swirling, phantasmagorical landscape (of what look like climbing toadstools), is the *Shepherds Hear the Good News*. Also in this room is Pieter Bruegel the Elder's *Wedding Procession*, a good-natured scene with country folk walking to church to the accompaniment of bagpipes.

The second room to the right is devoted to four large-scale **tapestries** from the sixteenth and seventeenth centuries. The earliest of the four – from 1516 – relates the legend of *Notre Dame du Sablon*, the tedious tale of the transfer of a much revered statue of the Virgin from Antwerp to Brussels (see p.76) – though fortunately the tapestry is much better than the story. A second tapestry, dating from 1580, tells the Arthurian legend of Tristan and Isolde, but easily the most striking is the *Solemn Funeral of the Roman Consul Decius Mus*, based on drawings by Rubens. Decius was a heroic figure who had won a decisive victory against the Samnites, thus securing Roman control of Italy in the third century BC. In this extraordinary painting, he is shown laid out on a chaise-longue and surrounded by classical figures of muscular men and fleshy women. Even inanimate objects join in the general mourning – with the lion head of the chaise-longue, for instance, glancing sorrowfully at the onlooker.

The museum's upper floors are less diverting. The first floor has scale models of the city and various sections on aspects of its development, and the second continues in the same vein. On the second floor also is a goodly sample of the Manneken Pis's (see p.30) vast wardrobe – around one hundred sickeningly saccharine costumes ranging from Mickey Mouse to a maharajah, all of them gifts from various visiting dignitaries.

MAISON DU ROI AND THE MUSÉE DE LA VILLE DE BRUXELLES

TAPESTRY MANUFACTURE AND DESIGN

Tapestry manufacture in Brussels began in the middle of the fifteenth century and soon came under the control of a small clique of manufacturers who imposed a rigorous system of quality control. From 1528 every tapestry made in Brussels had to bear the town's trademark – two "Bs" enclosed in a red shield. Brussels' tapestries were famous for their lavish raw materials – especially gold thread – and this also served to keep control of the industry in the hands of the few. Only rarely were weavers able to accumulate enough money to buy their materials, never mind their own looms.

The first great period of Brussels tapestry-making lasted until the middle of the sixteenth century, when religious conflict overwhelmed the city and many of its Protestant-inclined weavers migrated north to rival workshops. There was a partial revival at the beginning of the seventeenth century, but later the French occupation and the shrinking of the Spanish market led to diminishing production, with the industry finally fizzling out in 1794.

Tapestry production was a cross between embroidery and ordinary weaving. It consisted of interlacing a wool weft above and below the strings of a vertical linen "chain", a process similar to weaving. However, the weaver had to stop to change colour, requiring as many shuttles for the weft as he had colours, as in embroidery. The design of a tapestry was taken from a painting to which the weaver made constant reference. Standard-size tapestries took six months to make and were produced exclusively for the very wealthy, the most important of whom would often insist on the use of gold and silver thread and the employment of the most famous artists of the day for the preparatory painting. Amongst many, Pieter Paul Rubens, Jacob Jordaens and David Teniers all had tapestry commissions.

AROUND THE GRAND-PLACE — THE MANNEKEN PIS

In the 1890s, burgomaster **Charles Buls** spearheaded a campaign to preserve the city's ancient buildings. One of his rewards was to have a street named after him, and this runs south from the Grand-Place in between the Maison de l'Étoile and the Hôtel de Ville to the corner of **rue des Brasseurs** (the first on the left), scene of a bizarre incident in 1873 when the French Symbolist poet Paul Verlaine shot his fellow poet and lover Arthur Rimbaud. This rash act earned him a two-year prison sentence — and all because Rimbaud had dashed from Paris to dissuade him from joining the Spanish army.

Moving on, you come to **rue de la Violette**, the second turn on the left, and here at no. 6 the **Musée de Costume et de la Dentelle** (Map 4, C5; Thurs, Fri, Mon & Tues 10am–12.30pm & 1.30–5pm, Sat & Sun 2–4.30pm; €2.50) focuses firmly on costume, showcasing temporary exhibitions of varying quality. The museum rambles over three small floors and most of the exhibitions carry multilingual labelling. The permanent collection is modest (to say the least), but is redeemed on the top floor by four wooden cupboards, which hold drawer after drawer of lace illustrating the work of all the principal centres of manufacture. Lace became an important Brussels product in the seventeenth century, and by the nineteenth century, when the industry reached its peak, the city had ten thousand lacemakers, all of them women. The lace made here was renowned for the intricacy of its designs and was in demand worldwide, bought by the rich to embellish their clothes. Nowadays lace is still made in Brussels, though on a much smaller scale - and it's still very expensive.

F. Rubbrecht on the Grand-Place - at no. 23 – has a first-rate assortment of handmade lace. See p.246 for further details and other outlets.

From the foot of rue de la Violette, **rue de l'Étuve** runs south to the **Manneken Pis** (Map 4, B6), a diminutive statue of a pissing urchin stuck high up in a shrine-like affair protected from the hoards of tourists by an iron fence. The Manneken is supposed to embody the "irreverent spirit" of the city, or at least that is reputed to have been the intention of Jérôme Duquesnoy when he cast the original bronze statue in the 1600s to replace the medieval stone fountain that stood here before. It's likely that Duquesnoy invented the Manneken Pis, whose popularity blossomed during the sombre, priest-dominated years following the Thirty Years' War, but it's possible his bronze replaced an earlier stone version of ancient provenance. There are all sorts of folkloric tales about its origins, from lost aristocratic children recovered when they were taking a pee, to peasant lads putting out dangerous fires and – least likely of the lot – boys slashing on the city's enemies from the trees and putting them to flight. As a talisman, it has certainly attracted the attention of thieves, notably in 1817 when a French ex-convict swiped it before breaking it into pieces. The thief and the smashed Manneken were apprehended, the former publicly branded on the Grand-Place and sentenced to a life of forced labour, while the fragments of the latter were used to create the mould in which the present-day Manneken was cast. It's long been the custom for visiting VIPs to donate a costume, and the little chap is regularly kitted out in different tackle – often military or folkloric gear, from C&W stetsons and chaps to golfers' plus fours and Donald Duck and Mickey Mouse outfits.

At the Manneken Pis, your best bet is to double back to the Grand-Place before starting to explore the Lower Town – as outlined in the next chapter.

The Lower Town

The **Lower Town** is the commercial centre of Brussels, a bustling quarter that's home to most of the city's best restaurants, shops and hotels. It fans out from the Grand-Place, north, south and west to the boulevards of the petit ring, and east as far as the foot of the ridge which marks the start of the Upper Town (see Chapter 4), along the line of boulevards Berlaimont, L'Impératrice and L'Empereur. The layout of the heart of the Lower Town remains essentially medieval – a labyrinth of narrow, cobbled lanes and alleys whose names mostly reveal their original purpose as markets: rue du Marché aux Fromages, for example. This medieval street pattern is interrupted by the boulevards that were inserted during the nineteenth century – part of a drive to modernize the city. At the same time the River Senne was covered over and hundreds of culs-de-sac were eliminated. The boulevards, however, done little to disturb the jostle and jangle that give the Lower Town its character, with almost every street crimped by tall and angular town houses. There's nothing neat and tidy about all of this, but that's what makes Brussels so intriguing – dilapidated terraces stand next to prestigious mansions and the whole district is dotted with superb buildings: everything from beautiful Baroque churches through to Art Nouveau department stores.

NORTHWEST OF THE GRAND-PLACE

Arguably the most diverting part of the Lower Town, the jumble of narrow streets and pocket-sized squares that spreads **northwest of the Grand-Place** to **place Ste Catherine** is crowded by the elegant, though often down-at-heel, town houses of the late nineteenth-century bour-geoisie. Pockets of stylish fashionability poke out here and there and the district has lots of great bars. There are also a couple of especially fine buildings, the Victorian **Bourse** and the Baroque church of **St Jean Baptiste au Béguinage**.

The area covered by this chapter is shown
in detail on colour maps 3, 4 and 5.

The Church of St Nicholas

Map 5, G8. Mon–Fri 8am–6.30pm, Sat 9am–6pm & Sun 9am–7.30pm; free. Ⓜ Bourse.

Walking northwest out of the Grand-Place along rue au Beurre, you come across the pint-sized church of **St Nicholas** on the right-hand side. It dates from the twelfth century, but has been heavily restored on several occasions, most recently in the 1950s, when parts of the outer shell were reconstructed in a plain Gothic style. The church is dedicated to St Nicholas of Bari, the patron saint of sailors, or, as he's better known, Santa Claus. The church is unusual in so far as the three aisles of the nave were built at an angle to the chancel, in order to avoid a stream. It also carries a memento of the French bombardment of 1695 in the cannon ball embedded high up in the third pillar on the left of the nave. Otherwise, the gloomy church hardly sets the pulse racing, although – among a scattering of *objets d'art* – there's a handsome, gilded copper reliquary shrine near the entrance. The shrine was made in Germany in the nineteenth century to honour a group of Catholics martyred by Protestants in Gorinchem in the Netherlands in 1572.

Maison Dandoy, at rue au Beurre 31, is something of a city institution, a long-established confectioner's whose tasty specialities are macaroons and "spekuloos", a sugary brown, cinnamon-flavoured biscuit that's prepared in a variety of traditional and intricate moulds.

The Bourse and place St Géry

Opposite the church and newly cleaned and polished, rises the grandiose **Bourse** (Map 5, F8), formerly the home of the city's stock exchange, a Neoclassical structure of 1873 caked with fruit, fronds, languishing nudes and frolicking putti. This breezily self-confident structure sports a host of allegorical figures (Industry, Navigation, Asia, Africa, etc) which both reflect the preoccupations of the nineteenth-century Belgian bourgeoisie and, in their easy self-satisfaction, imply that wealth and pleasure are synonymous. The Bourse is flanked by sterling town houses, the setting for two of the city's more famous cafés, the Art Nouveau *Falstaff* (see p.200), on the south side at rue Henri Maus 17–23, and the fin-de-siècle *Le Cirio* (see p.199) on the other side at rue de la Bourse 18. In front of *Le Cirio* are the glassed-in foundations of a medieval church and convent, unearthed by archeologists in the 1980s and now known rather grandly as **Bruxella 1238** (Map 5, F8). There are occasional guided tours of the site, although these are only of specialist interest – the tourist office on the Grand-Place can give you times.

The square in front of the Bourse – **place de la Bourse** – is little more than an unsightly, heavily trafficked pause along boulevard Anspach, but the streets on the other side of the boulevard have more appeal, with tiny **place St Géry** (Map 5, C8) crowded by high-sided tenements, whose stone balconies and wrought-iron grilles hark back to the days of bustles and parasols. The square is thought to occupy the site of the sixth-century chapel from which the medieval city grew, but this is a matter of conjecture – no archeological evidence has ever been unearthed and the only clue to the city's early history is in its name, literally "settlement in the marshes". Place St Géry has one specific attraction in the refurbished, late nineteenth-century covered market, the **Halles St Géry**, an airy, glass, brick and iron edifice. The elegance of the structure is, however, obscured by a huge stone fountain plonked right in the middle – and moved here from the town of Grimbergen to the north of Brussels apparently for decorative reasons.

Rue Antoine Dansaert and place Ste Catherine

From place St Géry, it's a couple of minutes' stroll north to **rue Antoine Dansaert** (Map 5, C6), where the most innovative and stylish of the city's **fashion designers** have set up shop amongst the dilapidated old houses that stretch up towards place du Nouveau Marché aux Grains. Amongst several outstanding boutiques on this street, three of the best are Nicole Cadine, at no. 28, Oliver Strelli, at no. 46, and Via Della Spiga, at no. 44, which sells everything from locally designed gear to Westwood, McQueen and Paul Smith. Stijl, at no. 74, showcases a bevy of big-name designers too, and there's strikingly original furniture at Max, whose two shops face each other across the street at nos. 90 and 103.

Turning right off rue Antoine Dansaert, place du Nouveau Marché aux Grains leads straight into **place Ste Catherine** (Map 5, C5), which is, despite its dishevelled appearance, at the heart of one of the city's most fashionable districts, not least because of its excellent seafood restaurants. Presiding over the square is the **church of Ste Catherine**, a battered nineteenth-century replacement for the Baroque original, of which the creamy, curvy belfry is the solitary survivor. Venture inside the church and you'll spy – behind the glass screen that closes off most of the nave – a fourteenth-century Black Madonna and Child, a sensually carved stone statuette that was chucked into the Senne by Protestants, but landed rather fortuitously on a clod of peat and was fished out.

Ste Catherine is open daily 8.30am–5.30pm; free.

Quai aux Briques and the parallel quai aux Bois à Brûler extend northwest from place Ste Catherine on either side of a wide and open area that was – until it was filled in – the most central part of the city's main **dock**. Strolling along this open area, you'll pass a motley assortment of nineteenth-century warehouses, shops and bars which maintain an appealing canalside feel – an impression heightened in the early morning when the streets are choked with lorries bearing trays of fish for local restaurants. At the end of the old quays, the fanciful **water fountain** (Map 5, C2), with its lizards and dolphins, honours Burgomaster Anspach, a driving force in the move to modernize the city during the 1880s.

St Jean Baptiste au Béguinage

Map 5, E3. Normally July & Aug Tues–Sat 11am–5pm, Sun 10am–5pm; Sept–June Tues-Fri 10am–5pm, Wed, plus occasional Sat and Sun morning, but currently closed by fire damage; free. Ⓜ Ste Catherine.

Just north of place Ste Catherine, place du Samedi and then rue du Cyprès squeeze through to **place du Béguinage**, a good-looking piazza dominated by **St Jean Baptiste au Béguinage**, a supple, billowing structure dating from the second half of the seventeenth century. This beautiful church is the only building left from the Béguine convent founded here in the thirteenth century. The convent once crowded in on the church, and only since its demolition – and the creation of the star-shaped place du Béguinage in 1855 – has it been possible to view the exterior with any degree of ease. There's a sense of movement in each and every feature, a dynamism of design culminating in three soaring gables where the upper portion of the central tower is decorated with pinnacles that echo those of the Hôtel de Ville. The church's light and spacious interior is lavishly decorated, the white stone columns and arches dripping with solemn-faced cherubs intent on reminding the congregation of their mortality. The nave and aisles are wide and open, offering unobstructed views of the high altar, but you can't fail to notice the enormous wooden pulpit featuring St Dominic preaching against heresy – and trampling a heretic under foot for good measure.

Around the back of the church, a short street takes you through to a slender, tree-lined square framed by the austere Neoclassicism of the **Hospice Pacheco** (no access; Map 5, E2), built to house the destitute in the 1820s. It's a peaceful spot today, but the stern wall that surrounds the complex is a reminder of times when the hospice was more like a prison than a shelter, and draconian rules were imposed with brutal severity. The Senne River once flowed beside the hospice, but is no longer viewable here. By the nineteenth century it had become intolerably polluted – to quote the Brussels writer Camille Lemonnier, "the dumping ground, not only of industry, but also of the houses lining the river: it was not unusual to see the ballooned stomach of a dog mixed pell mell with its own litter..." After an outbreak of cholera in 1866, which killed over 3500 city folk, the river was piped underground and paved over.

From the Hospice Pacheco, it's a five- to ten-minute walk east to the place des Martyrs (see p.39) to the north of the Grand-Place.

NORTH OF THE GRAND-PLACE

The busy streets between the Grand-Place and the Gare du Nord are not especially enticing, though **rue des Bouchers** does heave with restaurants and **rue Neuve** possesses many of the city's biggest shops and stores. The prime architectural sight hereabouts is the **place des Martyrs**, a handsome square built by the Austrian Habsburgs in their pomp, whilst the most interesting attraction is the **Centre Belge de la Bande Dessinée** – the Belgian Comic Strip Centre. Belgian artists and writers produce the best comics in the world – or so they would argue – and the centre samples their work, beginning with the most famous comic strip character of the lot, Tintin, who first appeared as long ago as 1929.

Rue des Bouchers and the Galeries St Hubert

Just to the north of the Grand-Place, the quarter hinging on the pedestrianized **rue des Bouchers** (Map 4, E2) is the city centre's restaurant ghetto, the narrow cobblestone lanes transformed at night into fairy-lit tunnels where restaurants vie for custom with elaborate displays of dull-eyed fish and glistening molluscs. Tucked away down an alley off petite rue des Bouchers, at Impasse Schuddeveld 6, is the **Théâtre Royal de Toone** (Map 4, D3), which puts on puppet plays in the bruxellois dialect – Brusselse Sproek or Marollien (see p.46). It's very much a city institution and there are regular performances from Tuesday to Saturday – as well as an excellent bar.

You'll need to be careful if you're thinking of eating out in one of rue des Bouchers' many restaurants: some charge excessive prices and have poor standards. For recommended places see reviews on p.179.

Footsteps away are the **Galeries St Hubert** (Map 4, E3–F1), whose trio of glass-vaulted galleries – du Roi, de la Reine and the smaller des Princes – cut across rue des Bouchers. Opened by Léopold I in 1847, these galleries were one of Europe's first shopping arcades, and the pastel-painted walls, classical columns and cameo sculptures still retain an air of genteel sophistication.

For further details and/or tickets for the Théâtre Royal de Toone, see p.267. Just beyond the Galeries St Hubert is one of the city's most famous bars, *À La Mort Subite* (see p.205).

Théâtre de la Monnaie and the Hôtel Métropole

Emerging at the north end of the Galerie du Roi, you've a brief walk down rue de l'Écuyer to **place de la Monnaie**, the drab and dreary modern square that's overshadowed by the huge **centre Monnaie** (Map 3, D5), housing offices, shops and the main post office. The only building of interest here is the **Théâtre de la Monnaie** (Map 3, E5), Brussels' opera house, a Neoclassical structure built in 1819 and with an interior added in 1856 to a design by Poelaert, the architect of the Palais de Justice (see p.77). The theatre's real claim to fame, however, is as the starting-point of the revolution against the Dutch in 1830: a nationalistic libretto in Auber's *The Mute Girl of Portici* sent the audience wild, and they poured out into the streets to raise the flag of Brabant, signalling the start of the rebellion. The opera told the tale of an Italian uprising against the Spanish, and with such lines as "To my country I owe my life, To me it will owe its liberty" one of the Dutch censors – of whom there were many – should really have seen what was coming, as a furious King William I pointed out.

On the far side of the centre Monnaie is traffic-choked boulevard Anspach which forks and widens at **place de Brouckère** (Map 3, D4), a busy junction that accommodates the **Hôtel Métropole**, whose splendidly ornate public areas date from 1895 and were once the haunt of the likes of Sarah Bernhardt and Isadora Duncan.

For Théâtre de la Monnaie tickets and
performance information, see p.228.

Rue Neuve and place des Martyrs

From place de la Monnaie, **rue Neuve** (Map 3, E4–F3) forges north, a workaday pedestrianized shopping street that's home to the big chain stores and the City 2 shopping mall. About halfway up, turn east along rue St Michel for the **place des Martyrs** (Map 3, E4), a cool, rational square superimposed on the city by the Habsburgs in the 1770s. Long neglected, the square is very much the worse for wear – work has at last started on a thoroughgoing refurbishment – but there's still no mistaking the architectural elegance of the ensemble, completed in the last years of Austrian control. The only stylistic blip is the nineteenth-century centrepiece, a clumsy representation of the **Fatherland Crowned** rising from an arcaded gallery inscribed with the names of those 445 rebels who died in the Belgian revolution of 1830.

Centre Belge de la Bande Dessinée

Map 3, F4. Tues–Sun 10am–6pm; €6.20. Reference Library Tues–Thurs noon–5pm, Fri noon–6pm, Sat 10am–6pm; no extra charge. Ⓜ Botanique.

Heading east from the place des Martyrs, you'll take about five minutes to walk to the city's only surviving Horta-designed department store, the **Grand Magasin Waucquez**, situated amongst run-down offices and warehouses at rue des Sables 20. Recently restored after lying empty for many years, it's a wonderfully airy, summery construction, with light flooding through the glass and stained glass that encloses the expansive entrance hall. It was completed in 1906, built for a textile tycoon, and exhibits all the classic features of Horta's work (see p.84) – from the soft lines of the ornamentation to the metal grilles, exposed girders and balustrades.

Around the entrance hall is a café, the *Brasserie Horta*, as well as the reference library, bookshop and ticket office of the **Centre Belge de la Bande Dessinée**. The centre's displays are extensive and diverting and though the labelling is in French and Flemish only, an English guidebook is available free at reception. The exhibits begin at the top of the first flight of stairs with a modest section outlining the processes involved in drawing comic strips and cartoon animation. There's also a small auditorium offering non-stop cartoons and documentaries. On the two floors above, the grandly titled "Museum of the Imagination" begins by tracing the development of the Belgian comic strip up until 1960 in broadly chronological order, with an especially interesting section on **Tintin**, the creation of Brussels-born **Georges Remi**, aka Hergé (1907–83). Remi's first efforts (non-Tintin) had been sponsored by a right-wing Catholic journal, *Le XXème Siècle*, and in 1929 when this same paper produced a kids' supplement – *Le Petit Vingtième* – Remi was given his first major break. Remi was responsible for a two-page comic strip and he created *Tintin in the Land of the Soviets*, a didactic tale about the evils of Bolshevism. Tintin's Soviet adventure lasted until May 1930, and the director of *Le XXème Siècle* decided to stage a reception – as a PR stunt – to celebrate Tintin's return. Remi – along with a Tintin lookalike – hopped on a train just east of Brussels and when they pulled into the capital they were mobbed by scores of excited children. Remi and Tintin never looked back. Remi decided on the famous quiff straight away, but other features – the mouth and expressive eyebrows – only came later. His popularity was – and remains – quite phenomenal. *Tintin* has been translated into fifty languages and over twenty million copies of the comic *Le Journal de Tintin*, Remi's own independent creation, have been sold. First published in 1946, this *Journal* also helped to popularize the work of some of the country's most creative cartoonists, including **Willy Vandersteen** and **Edgar-Pierre Jacobs**, whose theatrical compositions and fluent combination of genres – science fiction, fantasy and crime – are displayed in his *Blake and Mortimer*. Belgium's oldest comic-strip paper, the *Spiro Journal*, performed a similar service and was responsible for launching the career of **André Franquin**, the creator of the feckless anti-hero *Gaston Lagaffe*. Sadly, *Spiro* was also where *The Smurfs* first saw light of day, the creation of Peyo, in 1958.

On the top floor, the "Museum of Modern Comic Strips" looks at new trends and themes. The comic strip has long ceased to be primarily aimed at children, but now focuses on the adult (sometimes very adult) market. A series

CENTRE BELGE DE LA BANDE DESSINÉE

of regularly rotated displays ably illustrates some of the best of this new work and there's also a programme of temporary exhibitions.

La Boutique Tintin, just off the Grand-Place at rue de la Colline 13, has all manner of Tintin paraphernalia.

Le Botanique

Map 3, G3.

Heading north from the Centre Belge de la Bande Dessinée along **rue du Marais**, you'll soon hit the petit ring and, on the other side, an attractive **park**, whose carefully manicured woods, lawns and borders are decorated by statues and a tiny lake. The park slopes up to **Le Botanique**, an appealingly grandiose greenhouse dating from 1826. The building once housed the city's botanical gardens, but these were moved out long ago and the place has been turned into a Francophone cultural centre. Despite the proximity of the traffic-congested boulevards of the ring road, it's a pleasant spot, though be warned that dodgy characters haunt its precincts in the evening.

After Le Botanique, an obvious choice is to push on into St Josse (see below), but alternatively, it's a quick walk west to **place Rogier**, from where glistening new office blocks march up **rue du Progrès** to the recently revamped **Gare du Nord** (Map 3, F1).

St Josse

Map 3, H1–3.

The district of **St Josse**, immediately north of Le Botanique, is somewhere you'll probably go only at night, the main attraction being its numerous (and inexpensive) Turkish restaurants. It's a compelling, uncompromisingly foreign neighbourhood, where men while away the hours over glasses of tea in cafés and head-scarved women emerge during the day to shop. Dating from the 1840s, the vast, domed **Église de Ste Marie** (Map 3, H1), standing at the head of rue Royale, is the quarter's landmark, its clumping cupola rising high above its heavy-duty buttresses. However, life centres on **chaussée de Haecht**, joining rue Royale just beyond Le Botanique, packed with restaurants, snack bars and the odd shop selling fruit and veg, Turkish videos, and gimcrackery.

SOUTH OF THE GRAND-PLACE

Few tourists venture into the working-class districts to the **south of the Grand-Place**, either into the dishevelled **Quartier Marolles**, to either side of rue Blaes, or further south to the impoverished immigrant area around the **Gare du Midi**. There are, however, a couple of interesting attractions on the northern periphery of the Quartier Marolles: the beautiful church of **Notre Dame de la Chapelle** and the **Fondation internationale Jacques Brel**, celebrating the country's leading songster – and the district itself has several atmospheric bars and restaurants. In addition, both districts have an excellent **market**.

The Fondation internationale Jacques Brel

Map 4, C7. Tues–Sat 11am–6pm; €5. Ⓜ Gare Centrale.
Strolling south from the Grand-Place along rue de l'Etuve, turn left up rue du Lombard and you'll soon reach **place Saint Jean** (Map 4, D6), where the memorial in the middle of the square commemorates the remarkable **Gabrielle Petit**. Equipped with a formidable – some say photographic – memory, Petit played a leading role in the Resistance

movement during the German occupation of World War I. Caught, she refused to appeal even though as a woman her sentence would almost certainly have been commuted. Instead, she declared that she would show the Germans how a Belgian woman could die. And that is precisely what she did: the Germans shot her by firing squad in 1916.

Just to the south of the square, place de la Vieille-Halle aux Blés holds the **Fondation internationale Jacques Brel**, a small but inventive museum celebrating the life and times of the Belgian singer Jacques Brel (1933–1978). Brel became famous in the 1960s as a singer of mournful *chansons* about death and love. The museum begins with a false lift that actually doesn't move at all – despite the sounds – and beyond you can hear Brel pouring out his feelings on a mock-up stage and in a replica bar with juke box. It's all good fun (if you like this type of music), though the labelling of the exhibits is only in French and Flemish.

From the square, it's a short walk south to **boulevard de l'Empereur**, a busy carriageway that disfigures this part of the centre. Across the boulevard, you'll spy the crumbling brickwork of **La Tour Anneessens** (Map 3, D8), a chunky remnant of the medieval city wall, while to the south gleams the recently restored Notre Dame de la Chapelle.

Notre Dame de la Chapelle

Map 3, D8. June–Sept Mon–Sat 9am–5pm & Sun 11.30–4.30pm; Oct–May daily 12.30–4.30pm; free. Ⓜ Gare Centrale.

The city's oldest church, founded in 1134, **Notre Dame de la Chapelle** is a sprawling, broadly Gothic structure that boasts an attractive if somewhat incongruous Baroque bell tower, added after the French artillery bombardment of 1695 had damaged the original. Inside, the well-proportioned **nave** is supported by heavyweight columns with curly-kale capitals and bathed in light from the huge clerestory windows. The **pulpit** is an extraordinary affair, a flashy, intricately carved hunk featuring Eli in the desert beneath the palm trees. The prophet looks mightily fed up, but then he hasn't realized that there's an angel beside him with manna (bread). Also of note is the statue of **Our Lady of Solitude**, in the second chapel of the north aisle – to the left of the entrance. The Flemings were accustomed to religious statues whose clothing formed part of the original carving. It was the Spaniards who first dressed their statues in finery – and this is an example, gifted to the church by the Spanish Infanta in the 1570s. The church's main claim to fame, however, is the memorial plaque to Pieter Bruegel the Elder. It was made by his son Jan and is located in the fourth chapel off the south aisle; Pieter is supposed to have lived and died just down the street at **rue Haute 132**.

After visiting Notre Dame de la Chapelle, the obvious route is to press on into the Quartier Marolles. However, perhaps a better bet – unless you're heading for the Marolles flea market – is to backtrack to La Tour Anneessens, round the corner from which is rue de Rollebeek (Map 3, D8), a pleasant pedestrianized lane dotted with cafés and restaurants that climbs up to the place du Grand Sablon (see p.77) in the Upper Town.

The Quartier Marolles

Map 3, D8–B10.

South of Notre Dame de la Chapelle, **rue Blaes** (Map 3, D8–C10) together with the less appealing **rue Haute** form the double spine of the **Quartier Marolles**, stacked on the slopes below the Palais de Justice (see p.77). An earthy neighbourhood of run-down housing and cheap, basic restaurants, shops and bars, it's one of the few places in the city where you can still hear older people using the traditional dialect, **Brusselse Sproek** or Marollien. A brand of Flemish which has, over the centuries, been influenced by the languages of the city's overlords, it is now in danger of dying out, and local people have set up an academy to preserve it. They propose – to add to the capital's linguistic complexities – that all newcomers to Brussels should learn one hundred words of the dialect. It's a colourful, ribald language; you could make a start with *dikenek*, "big mouth"; *schieve lavabo*, "idiot" (literally "a twisted toilet"); or *fieu,* "son of a bitch".

The Marolles neighbourhood grew up in the seventeenth century as a centre for artisans working on the nearby mansions of Sablon. Industrialized in the eighteenth century, it remained a thriving working-class district until the 1870s, when the paving-over of the Senne led to the riverside factories closing down and moving out to the suburbs. The workers and their families followed, abandoning Marolles to the old and poor. Today, gentrification is creeping into the district – along rue Blaes dilapidated houses are in the process of being restored, and the occasional restaurant or antique shop has sprouted up among the bars and secondhand clothes shops. **Place du Jeu de Balle** (Map 3, C10), the heart of Marolles, is relatively unchanged, a shabby square surrounded by rough-edged bars that is the scene of the city's best flea market (see "Markets", p.248). The **market** is a daily event (7am–2pm), but it's at its most hectic on Sunday mornings, when the square and the surrounding streets are completely taken over by pile after pile of rusty junk alongside muddles of eccentric bric-à-brac – everything from a chipped buddha, a rococo angel or African idol, to horn-rimmed glasses, a top hat or a stuffed bear.

If you've ventured as far south as the place du Jeu de Balle, then the Gare du Midi area (see below) is within easy walking distance – another ten minutes or so to the west. You're also within comfortable striking distance of the Porte de Hal and St Gilles (see Chapter 80). In addition, boulevard Lemonnier (Map 3, C6–A9) runs straight from the Bourse (see p.33) to the Gare du Midi, but it's a dreary thoroughfare of no particular interest.

Gare du Midi

Map 3, A10. Ⓜ Gare du Midi

Just outside the petit ring, the **Gare du Midi** is now the city's major railway terminal, the terminus of most international services including those operated by Eurostar from the UK. The station has already been expanded and modernized on several occasions, but work continues with the construction of more platforms and facilities. The area round the station is, however, home to many of the city's North African immigrants, a severely depressed and at times seedy quarter with an uneasy undertow by day and sometimes overtly threatening at night. The only good time to visit the district is on a Sunday morning, when a vibrant souk-like **market** is held under the station's rail arches and along boulevard du Midi (see p.248).

GARE DU MIDI

The Upper Town

From the heights of the **Upper Town**, the Francophile ruling class long kept a beady eye on the proletarians down below, and it was here they built their palaces and mansions, churches and parks. Political power is no longer concentrated hereabouts, but the wide avenues and grand architecture of this aristocratic quarter – the bulk of which dates from the late eighteenth and nineteenth centuries – has survived pretty much intact, lending a stately, dignified feel that's markedly different from the bustle of the Lower Town below.

The Lower Town ends and the Upper Town begins at the foot of the sharp **slope** which runs north to south from one end of the city centre to the other, its course marked – in general terms at least – by a traffic-choked boulevard that's variously named Berlaimont, L'Impératrice and L'Empereur. This slope is home to the city's **cathedral**, a splendid Gothic edifice that's recently been restored, but otherwise is little more than an obstacle to be climbed by a series of stairways. Among the latter, the most frequently used are the covered walkway running through the **Galerie Ravenstein** shopping arcade behind the **Gare Centrale**, and the open-air stairway that climbs up through the stodgy, modern buildings of the so-called **Mont des Arts**. Léopold II gave the area its name in anticipation of a fine art museum he intended to build, but the project was never completed, and the land was only properly built upon in the 1950s.

The area covered by this chapter is shown in detail on colour maps 3, 4 and 6.

Above the rigorous layout of the Mont des Arts lie the exuberant **rue Royale** and **rue de la Régence**, which together make up the Upper Town's spine, a suitably smart location for the outstanding **Musées Royaux des Beaux Arts**, probably the best of Belgium's many fine art collections, and the surprisingly low-key **Palais Royal**. Further south, rue de la Régence soon leads to the well-heeled **Sablon** neighbourhood, whose antique shops and chic bars and cafés fan out from the medieval church of **Notre Dame du Sablon**. Beyond this is the monstrous **Palais de Justice**, traditionally one of the city's most disliked buildings.

THE CATHEDRAL

Map 4, I2. Daily 8am–6pm; free. Treasury Mon–Fri 10am–12.30pm & 2–5pm, Sat 10.30am–12.30pm & 2–3.30pm, Sun 2–5pm; €1.25. Crypt Tues–Thurs 10am–noon & 2–5pm; €2.50. Ⓜ Gare Centrale.

It takes only a couple of minutes to walk from the Grand-Place to the east end of rue de la Montagne, where a short slope climbs up to the **Cathedral**, a fine Gothic building whose commanding position has been sorely compromised by a rash of modern office blocks. Begun in 1215, and three hundred years in the making, the cathedral is dedicated jointly to the patron and patroness of Brussels – St Michael the Archangel, and St Gudule, a vague, seventh-century figure whose reputation was based on her gentle determination: despite all sorts of shenanigans, the devil could never put her off her prayers.

The cathedral sports a striking twin-towered, whitestone **facade**, with the central double doorway trimmed by fanciful tracery as well as statues of the Apostles and – on the central column – the Three Wise Men. The facade was erected in the fifteenth century in High Gothic style, but the intensity of the decoration fades away inside with the airy triple-aisled **nave**, completed a century before. Other parts of the interior illustrate several phases of Gothic design, with the chancel being the oldest part of the church, built in stages between 1215 and 1280 in the Early Gothic style. A stairway in the north side-aisle leads down to the Romanesque **crypt**, which gives an inkling as to the layout of the first church built on this site in the eleventh century.

The interior is short on furnishings and fittings, reflecting the combined efforts of the Protestants, who ransacked the church (and stole the shrine of St Gudule) in the middle of the seventeenth century, and the French Republican army, who wrecked the place a century later. Unfortunately, neither of them dismantled the ponderous sculptures that are attached to the columns of the nave – clumsy seventeenth-century representations of the Apostles, which only serve to dent the nave's soaring lines. Another, much more appealing survivor is the massive oak **pulpit**, an extravagant chunk of frippery by the Antwerp sculptor Hendrik Verbruggen. Among several vignettes, the pulpit features Adam and Eve, dressed in rustic gear, being chased from the Garden of Eden, while up above the Virgin Mary stamps on the head of the serpent.

The cathedral also boasts some superb sixteenth-century **stained-glass** windows, beginning above the main doors with the hurly-burly of the *Last Judgement*. Look closely and you'll spy the donor in the lower foreground with an angel on one side and a woman with long blonde hair (symbolising Faith) on the other. Each of the main colours has a symbolic meaning with green representing hope, yellow eternal glory and light blue heaven.

There's more remarkable work in the **transepts**, where the stained glass is distinguished by the extraordinary clarity of the blue backgrounds. These windows are eulogies to the Habsburgs – in the north transept, Charles V kneels alongside his wife beneath a vast triumphal arch as their patron saints present them to God the Father, and in the south transept Charles V's sister, Marie, and her husband, King Louis of Hungary, play out a similar scenario. Both windows were designed by Bernard van Orley (1490–1541), long-time favourite of the royal family and the leading Brussels artist of his day.

Chapelle du Saint Sacrement de Miracle

Just beyond the north transept, flanking the choir, the cathedral treasury is displayed in the Flamboyant Gothic **Chapelle du Saint Sacrement de Miracle**, named after a shameful anti-Semitic legend whose key components were repeated again and again across medieval Christendom. Dating back to the 1360s, this particular version begins with a Jew from a small Flemish town stealing the consecrated Host from his local church. Shortly afterwards, he is murdered in a brawl and his wife moves to Brussels, taking the Host with her. The woman then presents the Host at the synagogue on Good Friday and her fellow Jews stab it with daggers, whereupon it starts to bleed. Terrified, the Jews disperse and the woman tries to save her soul by giving the Host to the city's cathedral – hence this chapel which was built to display the retrieved Host in the 1530s. The four stained-glass **windows of the chapel** retell the tale, a strip cartoon that unfolds above representations of the aristocrats who paid for the windows. The workmanship is delightful – based on designs by van

Orley and his one-time apprentice Michiel van Coxie (1499–1592) – but the effects of this unsavoury legend on the congregation are not hard to imagine.

The **treasury** (*Le trésor*) itself holds a fairly predictable collection of monstrances and reliquaries, but there is a splendid Anglo-Saxon reliquary of the True Cross (Item 5) and a flowing altar painting, *The Legend of Ste Gudule*, by Michiel van Coxie (Item 3). Coxie spent much of his long life churning out religious paintings in the High Renaissance style he picked up when he visited Italy early in his career. Behind the chapel's high altar, which carries a routine nineteenth-century painting of the *Adoration of the Sacrament*, look out also for the more-than-usually ghoulish **skull** of St Elizabeth of Hungary (1207–1231). In her short life, this Hungarian princess managed to squeeze in just about everything you need to get canonised. She was a faithful wife (whose husband died on a Crusade), a devoted mother, and a loyal servant of the church, renouncing the world to become a nun and devote herself to the care of the poor and sick.

Chapelle de Notre-Dame de la Délivrance

Opposite the treasury, next to the south transept, the **Chapelle de Notre-Dame de la Délivrance** dates from the middle of the seventeenth century, its stained glass windows depicting scenes from the life of the Virgin on the upper level with the donors posing down below. The windows were designed by Théodore van Thulden, one of Rubens' pupils, and commissioned by the Infanta Isabella in 1649 – perhaps as spiritual compensation for the drubbing the Habsburgs had recently received from the Dutch, who had secured their independence from Spain the year before.

GALERIE RAVENSTEIN AND THE MUSÉE DU CINÉMA

Just to the south of the cathedral, along boulevard de l'Impératrice, the carrefour de l'Europe roundabout (Map 4, G5) is dominated by the curving, modern stonework of **Le Meridien Hotel** (see p.167), one of the city's more successful modern buildings. Opposite is the **Gare Centrale**, a bleak and somewhat surly Art Deco creation seemingly dug deep into the slope where Lower and Upper Town meet. Behind the station, on the far side of rue Cantersteen, the **Galerie Ravenstein** (Map 6, C1–D1) shopping arcade is traversed by a covered walkway. A classic piece of 1950s design, the arcade carries cheerfully bright decorative panels and an airy atrium equipped with a water fountain. It has, perhaps, seen better days, but its walkway is still an agreeable way to climb up to rue Ravenstein.

The latter is home to the **Palais des Beaux Arts** (Map 6, D2), a severe, low-lying edifice designed by Victor Horta during the 1920s in complete contrast with his flamboyant earlier works. The building holds a theatre and concert hall and hosts numerous temporary exhibitions, mostly of modern and contemporary art. Part of the complex – though it also has its own entrance a few metres up the stairway at the side – accommodates the **Musée du Cinéma** (Map 6, E2; daily 5.30–10.30pm; €2.25), which has displays on the pioneering days of cinema and shows old movies every evening. One projection room presents two silent films with piano accompaniment every night, the other shows three early "talkies".

From the museum, there's a choice of routes: you can either climb the steps up to rue Royale near the Palais Royal (see p.69); or stroll south along rue Ravenstein to the top of Mont des Arts and the Musée des Instruments de Musique – see below.

See Chapter 13 for further details on the city's
classical music, cinema and performing arts.
The Musée Victor Horta is described on p.83.

MONT DES ARTS AND THE PLACE DU MUSÉE

Map 6, B1–C2. Ⓜ Parc.

The wide stone stairway that cuts up through the **Mont
des Arts** also climbs the slope marking the start of the
Upper Town – and thereby serves as an alternative to the
Galerie Ravenstein (see above). The stairs begin on **place
de l'Albertine** (Map 6, B1), where the figure of Queen
Elizabeth, bouquet in hand, stands opposite a statue honouring her husband, **Albert I**, who is depicted in military
gear on his favourite horse. Easily the most popular king
Belgium has ever had, Albert became a national hero for his
determined resistance to the Germans in World War I. He
died in a climbing accident near Namur, in southern
Belgium, in 1934. Flanked by severe 1940s and 1950s government buildings, the stairway leads to a piazza, equipped
with water fountains and gravel footpaths, and then carries
on up to rue Ravenstein, from where there are wide views
over the Lower Town.

At the top of the stairway, on the right, a short flight of
steps leads up to the **place du Musée** (Map 6, C3), a
handsome cobbled square edged by a crisp architectural
ensemble of sober symmetry, subtly adorned by
Neoclassical sculptures – urns, cherubs and so forth. Two
sides of the square date from the nineteenth century and are
now part of the Musées Royaux des Beaux Arts (see p.57),
as is the hole in the middle, which allows light to reach the
museum's subterranean floors. On the north side, however,
are the five salons of the **Appartements de Charles de**

Lorraine (Map 6, C3), all that remain of the lavish palace built for Charles de Lorraine, the Austrian governor-general from 1749 to 1780. The salons reflect Charles's avowed enthusiasm for the Enlightenment: he viewed himself as the epitome of the civilised man and fully supported the reforms of his emperor, Joseph II (1741–90), though these same reforms – especially the move towards a secular society – created pandemonium amongst his fiercely Catholic Flemish and Wallonian subjects. Recently restored, and scheduled to be open to the public in the next couple of years, the salons feature attractive marble floors and a plethora of Rococo decoration, with Greek gods and cherubs scattered everywhere. Charles could never be accused of false modesty: stucco work proclaims the duke's military prowess and celebrates his skills as an alchemist. In case anyone missed the point, the statue of Hercules, just inside the main entrance bears the duke's face.

Charles built his own private chapel next door – he was well-known as a rake, so presumably it was handy for confession – and he decorated it in suitably ornate style, dripping with delicate stucco work and glitzy chandeliers. After his death, no one knew quite what to do with it, but in 1804 the chapel was turned over to the city's Protestants, becoming the **Église Protestante de Bruxelles** (visits by appointment only; ⓣ02 513 23 25).

LE MUSÉE DES INSTRUMENTS DE MUSIQUE (MIM)

Map 6, D3. Tues, Wed & Fri 9.30am–5pm, Thurs 9.30am–8pm, Sat & Sun 10am–5pm. €3.70. ⓦwww.mim.fgov.be. Ⓜ Parc.
Across from the place du Musée, at rue Montagne de la Cour 2, the **Old England building** is a whimsical Art Nouveau confection, all glass and wrought-iron, that started

LE MUSÉE DES INSTRUMENTS DE MUSIQUE (MIM)

life as a store, taking its name from the eponymous British company who had the place built as their Brussels headquarters in 1899. It has recently been refurbished to house **Le Musée des Instruments de Musique**, a prestige development with ninety musical themes – and 1500 instruments – displayed over four floors. It's all very glitzy, the special feature being the infra-red headphones which allow visitors to listen to scores of musical extracts from ancient Greece to the present day. There's a concert hall too – with regular performances on Thursday evenings – and a café on the top floor offering a great view over the city. One particular highlight of the museum is the section dedicated to Adolphe Sax, the Belgian-born inventor of the saxophone. Sax certainly had a vivid imagination – some of his wilder contraptions, like the oddly contorted saxhorn, are quite remarkable.

PLACE ROYALE

Map 6, D4. Ⓜ Parc.

Composed and self-assured, the **place Royale** forms a fitting climax to rue Royale, the dead straight backbone of the Upper Town which runs the 2km north to the suburb of St Josse (see p.42). Precisely symmetrical, the square is framed by late eighteenth-century mansions, each an exercise in architectural restraint, though there's no mistaking their size nor the probable cost of their construction.

Pushing into this understated opulence is the facade of the church of **St Jacques sur Coudenberg** (Sat 10am–6pm, Sun 10–11am; free), a fanciful, 1780s version of a Roman temple with a colourfully frescoed pediment representing Our Lady as Comforter of the Depressed. Indeed, the building was so secular in appearance that the French Revolutionary army had no hesitation in renaming it a Temple of Reason.

The French also destroyed the statue of a Habsburg governor that originally occupied the middle of the square, and its replacement – a dashing equestrian representation of **Godfrey de Bouillon**, one of the leaders of the first Crusade – dates from the 1840s. The statue has Godfrey, all rippling muscles and tree-trunk legs, rushing into battle in a supposedly heroic manner, but the sculptor wasn't quite up to his brief. Godfrey is supposed to be staring determinedly into the distance, but instead it looks as if he needs specs.

Once you've reached the Place Royale, the obvious option is to visit the Musées Royaux des Beaux Arts (see below). But, if that doesn't appeal, there is a choice of walking routes: it's a short stroll south along rue de la Régence to the Sablon neighbourhood (see p.75), one of the city's most engaging quarters; or you can walk round to the Palais Royal (see p.69) and then the fine art of the Musée Charlier (see p.73).

THE MUSÉES ROYAUX DES BEAUX ARTS

Map 6, C4. Tues–Sun 10am–5pm; €5. Ⓜ Trône.

A few metres from place Royale, at the start of rue de la Régence, the **Musées Royaux des Beaux Arts** comprise two museums, one displaying modern art, the other older works. Together they make up Belgium's most satisfying, all-round collection of fine art, with marvellous collections of work by – amongst many – Pieter Bruegel the Elder, Rubens and the surrealists Paul Delvaux and René Magritte.

Both museums are large, and to do them justice you should see them in separate visits. Finding your way around is made easy by the detailed English-language **museum plan** issued with admission. The older paintings – up to the beginning of the nineteenth century – are exhibited in the **Musée d'Art Ancien**, where the **blue** area shows paintings of the fifteenth and sixteenth centuries, including the Bruegels, and the **brown** area concentrates on paintings of the seventeenth and eighteenth centuries, with the collection of Rubens (for which the museum is internationally famous) as the highlight. The **orange** area comprises the small and undistinguished Gallery of Sculptures. The **Musée d'Art Moderne** has a **yellow** area devoted to nineteenth-century works, notably the canvases of Ostend-born James Ensor, and a **green** area, whose eight subterranean levels cover the twentieth century.

The Musée d'Art Ancien also hosts, in the **red** area, a prestigious programme of **temporary exhibitions**. A supplementary admission fee is usually payable and for the most popular you'll need to buy a ticket ahead of time; the ticket may specify the time of admission. The larger exhibitions may cause some disruption to the permanent collection, so treat the room numbers we've given with a little caution. Inevitably, the account below just scratches the surface; the museum's bookshop sells a wide range of detailed texts including a well-illustrated guide to the collections for €14.75.

Musée d'Art Ancien

Well presented, if not exactly well organized, the **Musée d'Art Ancien** is saved from confusion by its colour-coded zones – blue, brown, orange and red. It's a large collection and it's best to start a visit with the **Flemish primitives**.

Rogier van der Weyden and Dieric Bouts

Rooms 11 and 12 hold several paintings by Rogier van der Weyden (1399–1464), the official city painter to Brussels in the middle of the fifteenth century. When it came to portraiture his favourite technique was to highlight the features of his subject – and tokens of rank – against a black background. The *Portrait of the Grand Bâtard de Bourgogne* (Room 11) is a good example, with Anthony, the illegitimate son of Philip the Good, casting a haughty, tight-lipped stare to his right while wearing the chain of the Order of the Golden Fleece and clasping an arrow, the emblem of the guild of archers.

In **Room 13**, the two panels of the *Justice of the Emperor Otto* are the work of Weyden's contemporary, the Leuven-based Dieric Bouts (1410–75). The story was well known: in revenge for refusing her advances, the empress accuses a nobleman of attempting to seduce her. He is executed, but the man's wife remains convinced of his innocence and subsequently proves her point by means of an ordeal by fire in which she holds a red hot iron bar.

Hans Memling and the Master of the Legends of St Lucy and St Barbara

Room 14 has some fine portraits by Hans Memling (1430–94) as well as his softly hued *Martyrdom of St Sebastian*. Legend asserts that Sebastian was an officer in Diocletian's bodyguard until his Christian faith was discovered, at which point he was sentenced to be shot to death by the imperial archers. Left for dead by the bowmen, Sebastian recovered and Diocletian had to send a bunch of assassins to finish him off with cudgels. The tale made Sebastian popular with archers across Western Europe, and Memling's picture – showing the trussed up saint serenely indifferent to the arrows of the firing squad – was commissioned by the guild of archers in Bruges around 1470. In the same room, the Master of the Legend of St Lucy weighs in with a finely detailed and richly allegorical *Madonna with Saints*, where, with the city of Bruges in the background, the Madonna presents the infant Jesus for the adoration of eleven holy women. Decked out in elaborate medieval attire, the women have blank, almost expressionless faces,

MUSÉE D'ART ANCIEN

but each bears a token of her sainthood which would have been easily recognised by a medieval congregation. St Lucy, whose assistance was sought by those with sight problems, holds two eyes in a dish.

In **Room 15**, there's more early Flemish art in the shape of the *Scenes from the Life of St Barbara*, one panel from an original pair by the Master of the Legend of St Barbara. One of the most popular of medieval saints, Barbara, so the story goes, was a woman of great beauty whose father locked her away in a tower to keep her away from her admirers. The imprisoned Barbara became a Christian whereupon her father, Dioscurus, tried to kill her, only to be thwarted by a miracle that placed her out of his reach – a part of the tale that's ingeniously depicted in this painting. Naturally, no self-respecting saint could escape so easily, so later parts of the story have Barbara handed over to the local prince, who tortures her for her faith. Barbara resists and the prince orders Dioscurus to kill her himself, which he does only to be immediately incinerated by a bolt of lightning.

School of Hieronymus Bosch

Moving on, **Room 17** boasts a copy of the Hieronymus Bosch *Temptations of St Anthony* that's in the Museu Nacional in Lisbon. No one is quite sure who painted this triptych – it may or may not have been one of Bosch's apprentices – but it was certainly produced in Holland in the late fifteenth or early sixteenth century. The painting refers to St Anthony, a third-century nobleman who withdrew into the desert, where he endured fifteen years of temptation before settling down into his long stint as a hermit. It was the temptations that interested Bosch – rather than the ascetic steeliness of Anthony – and the central panel has an inconspicuous saint sticking desperately to his prayers surrounded by all manner of fiendish phantoms.

The side panels develop the theme: to the right Anthony is tempted by lust and greed, and on the left Anthony's companions help him back to his shelter after he's been transported through the skies by weird-looking demons.

Cranach, Gerard David, Matsys and Bernard van Orley

Next door, **Room 18** holds works by Martin Luther's friend, the Bavarian artist Lucas Cranach (1472–1553), whose *Adam and Eve* presents a stylized, Renaissance view of the Garden of Eden with an earnest-looking Adam on the other side of the Tree of Knowledge from a coquettish Eve, painted with legs entwined and her teeth marks visible on the apple. **Room 21** displays a couple of panels by Gerard David (1460–1523), a Bruges-based artist whose draughtsmanship may not be of the highest order, but whose paintings do display a tender serenity, as exhibited here in his *Adoration of the Magi* and *Virgin and Child*.

In **Room 22**, Quentin Matsys (1465–1530) is well represented by the *Triptych of the Holy Kindred*. Matsys' work illustrates a turning point in the development of Flemish painting, and in this triptych, which was completed in 1509, Matsys abandons the realistic interiors and landscapes of his Flemish predecessors in favour of the grand columns and porticos of the Renaissance. Notice that each scene is rigorously structured, its characters – all relations of Jesus – assuming lofty, idealized poses.

Room 26 has several works by Bernard van Orley (1488–1541), a long-time favourite of the Habsburg officials in Brussels until his Protestant sympathies put him in the commercial dog house. A versatile artist, Orley produced action-packed paintings of Biblical scenes, often back-dropped by classical buildings in the Renaissance style, as well as cartoon designs for tapestries and stained glass windows. His designs were used for several of the Cathedral's windows (see pp.51-52). The pick of his paint-

MUSÉE D'ART ANCIEN

ings displayed here are the *Haneton Triptych*, whose crowded central panel is an intense vision of the Lamentation, and the *Triptych of the Virtue of Patience*, which tells the tale of Job. At the top of the left-hand panel, Satan challenges God to test Job, his faithful follower. God accepts the challenge and visits calamities on Job – at the bottom of the left-hand panel his sheep are hit by lightning and his animals stolen. Even worse, the fearful central panel shows the roof falling in on Job's family while they are eating and only on the right-hand panel is order restored with God telling Job he has passed the test.

Bruegel

The museum's collection of works by the Bruegel family, notably **Pieter the Elder** (1527–69), is focused on **Room 31**. Although he is often regarded as the finest Netherlandish painter of the sixteenth century, little is known of Pieter the Elder's life, but it's likely he was apprenticed in Antwerp and he certainly moved to Brussels in the early 1560s. He also made at least one long trip to Italy, but judging by his oeuvre, he was – unlike most of his "Belgian" contemporaries – decidedly unimpressed by Italian art. He preferred instead to paint in the Netherlandish tradition and his works often depict crowded Flemish scenes in which are embedded religious or mythical stories. This sympathetic portrayal of everyday life revelled in the seasons and was worked in muted browns, greys and bluey greens with red or yellow highlights. Typifying this approach, and on display here, are the *Adoration of the Magi* and the *Census at Bethlehem* – a scene that his son, Pieter (1564–1638), repeated on several occasions – two particularly absorbing works with the traditionally momentous events happening, almost incidentally, among the bustle of everyday life. The versatile Pieter also dabbled with the lurid imagery of Bosch, whose influence is seen most clearly in the *Fall of the Rebel Angels*, a frantic panel painting which had actually been attributed to Bosch until Bruegel's signature was discovered hidden under the frame. The *Fall of Icarus* is, however, his most haunting work, its mood perfectly captured by Auden in his poem "Musée des Beaux Arts":

> *In Bruegel's Icarus, for instance: how everything turns away*
> *Quite leisurely from the disaster; the ploughman may*
> *Have heard the splash, the forsaken cry,*
> *But for him it was not an important failure; the sun shone*
> *As it had to on the white legs disappearing into the green*
> *Water; and the expensive delicate ship that must have seen*
> *Something amazing, a boy falling out of the sky,*
> *Had somewhere to get to and sailed calmly on.*

Rubens and his contemporaries

Apprenticed in Antwerp, **Rubens** (1577–1640) spent eight years in Italy studying the Renaissance masters before returning home, where he quickly completed a stunning series of paintings for Antwerp Cathedral. His fame spread far and wide and for the rest of his days Rubens was inundated with work, receiving commissions from all over Europe. In **Room 52**, the popular misconception that Rubens painted nothing but chubby nude women and muscular men is dispelled with a sequence of fine portraits, each aristocratic head drawn with great care and attention to detail – in particular, note the exquisite ruffs adorning the Archduke Albert and Isabella. *Studies of a Negro's Head* is likewise wonderfully observed, a preparation for the black magus in the *Adoration of the Magi*, a luminous work that's one of several huge canvases next door in **Room 62**. Here you'll also find the *Ascent to Calvary*, an intensely physical painting, capturing the confusion, agony and strain as Christ struggles on hands and knees under the weight of

MUSÉE D'ART ANCIEN

the cross. There's also the bloodcurdling *Martyrdom of St Lieven*, whose cruel torture – his tongue has just been ripped out and fed to a dog – is watched from on high by cherubs and angels.

Two of Rubens' pupils, Anthony van Dyck (1599–1641) and Jacob Jordaens (1593–1678), also feature in this part of the museum, with the studied portraits of the former dotted along the length of **Room 53** and the big and brassy canvases of Jordaens dominating **Room 57**. Like Rubens, Jordaens had a bulging order-book and for years he and his apprentices churned out paintings by the cartload. His best work is generally agreed to have been completed early on – between about 1620 and 1640 – and there's evidence here in the two versions of the *Satyr and the Peasant*, the earlier work clever and inventive, the second a hastily cobbled together piece that verges on buffoonery.

Close by, in **Room 60**, is a modest sample of Dutch painting, including a couple of sombre and carefully composed Rembrandts (1606–69). One of them – the self-assured *Portrait of Nicolaas van Bambeeck* – was completed in 1641, when the artist was finishing off his famous *Night Watch*, now exhibited in Amsterdam's Rijksmuseum. Rembrandt's pupils are displayed in the same room, principally Nicolaes Maes (1634–93), who is well represented by the delicate *Dreaming Old Woman*. There are also several canvases by Rembrandt's talented contemporary, Frans Hals (1580–1666), notably his charming *Three Children and a Cart drawn by a Goat*.

Musée d'Art Moderne

To reach the **Musée d'Art Moderne** you'll need to use the underground passageway which leads from the main museum entrance to **Level -2** of the yellow area, whose nineteenth-century, mostly Belgian paintings are spread over five small floors – two underground and three above. Another **stairway** on Level -2 leads down to the six subterranean half-floors that constitute the green area of twentieth-century works. The green area is comparatively small and has an international flavour, with the work of Belgian artists – including René Magritte and Paul Delvaux – supplemented by the likes of Dalí, Picasso, Chagall, Henry Moore, Miró, Matisse and Francis Bacon.

Social Realists

Level -2 features the work of the Social Realists, whose paintings and sculptures championed the working class. One of the early figures in this movement was Charles de Groux (1825–70), whose paternalistic *Poor People's Pew* and *Benediction* are typical of his work. Much more talented was Constantin Meunier (1831–1905), who is well represented here by two particularly forceful bronzes, *Firedamp* and the *Iron Worker*. Look out also for the stirring canvases of their mutual friend Eugene Laermans (1864–1940), who shifted from the Realist style into more Expressionistic works, as in the overtly political *Red Flag* and *The Corpse*, a sorrowful vision that is perhaps Laermans' most successful painting.

David and his contemporaries

Skipping the uninspiring nineteenth-century works of **Level −1**, press on up to **Level +1**, where the obvious highlight is Jacques-Louis David's famous *Death of Marat*, a propagandist piece of 1793 showing Jean-Paul Marat, the French revolutionary hero, dying in his bath after being stabbed by Charlotte Corday. David (1748–1825) has given Marat a perfectly proportioned, classical torso and a face which, with its large hooded eyes, looks almost Christ-like, the effect heightened by the flatness of the composition and the emptiness of the background. The dead man clasps a quill in one hand and the letter given him by Corday in the

MUSÉE D'ART MODERNE

other, inscribed "my deepest grief is all it takes to be entitled to your benevolence". The other note, on the wooden
chest, is written by Marat and begins "You will give this
warrant to that mother with the five children, whose husband died for his country". This was David's paean to a fellow revolutionary for, like Marat, he had voted for the exe-
cution of Louis XVI, was a Jacobin – the deadly rivals of
the Girondins, who were supported by Corday – and a
member of the revolutionary Convention, which commissioned this picture. He was also a leading light of the
Neoclassical movement and became the new regime's
Superintendent of the Fine Arts. He did well under
Napoleon, too, but after Waterloo David, along with all the
other regicides, was exiled, ending his days in Brussels.

Symbolism and James Ensor

The Symbolists are clustered on **Level +2** and amongst
them are the disconcerting paintings of Fernand Khnopff
(1858–1921), a founding member of the Les XX art movement (see p.93). Khnopff painted his sister, Marguerite,
again and again, using her refined, almost plastic, beauty to
stir a vague sense of passion – for she's desirable and utterly
unobtainable in equal measure. His haunting *Memories of
Lawn Tennis* is typical of his oeuvre, a work without narra-
tive, a dream-like scene with each of the seven women
bearing the likeness of Marguerite. In *Caresses* Marguerite
pops up once more, this time with the body of a cheetah
pawing sensually at an androgynous youth. Also exhibited
here – and a real surprise – is *Psyche's Wedding*, a delightful
painting by that forerunner of Art Nouveau, the
Englishman Edward Burne-Jones (1833–98). Antoine
Wiertz, who has a museum all to himself near the EU
Parliament building (see p.101), pops up too, his *La Belle
Rosme* a typically disagreeable painting in which the woman
concerned faces a skeleton.

In a separate section on Level +2 is a superb sample of the work of **James Ensor** (1860–1949). Ensor, the son of an English father and Flemish mother, spent nearly all of his long life working in Ostend, his home town. His first paintings were rather sombre portraits and landscapes, but in the early 1880s he switched to a more Impressionistic style, delicately picking out his colours as in *The Lady in Blue*. It is, however, Ensor's use of masks which sets his work apart – ambiguous carnival masks with the sniff of death or perversity. His *Scandalized Masks* of 1883 was his first mask painting, a typically unnerving canvas that works on several levels, whilst his *Skeletons quarrelling for a Kipper* (1891) is one of the most savage and macabre paintings you're ever likely to see.

Impressionism and Post-Impressionism
Pressing on, **Level +3** has a sprinkling of French Impressionists and Post-Impressionists – Monet, Seurat, Gauguin – alongside the studied pointillism of Théo van Rysselberghe (1862–1926), a versatile Brussels artist and founder member of Les XX (see p.93). Henry van de Velde (1863–1957), another member of Les XX, changed his painting style as often as Rysselberghe, but in the late 1880s he was under the influence of Seurat – hence *The Mender*.

Cubists, Expressionists and Fauvists
A **stairway** leads down from yellow-coded Level -2 to the green area, whose six subterranean half-floors (Levels −3 to −8) hold a diverse collection of modern art and sculpture. It's a challenging collection of international dimensions that starts as it means to continue – at the entrance to **Level -3/4** – with a lumpy, uncompromising Henry Moore and an eerie Francis Bacon, *The Pope with Owls*. Beyond lies an assortment of works by Picasso, Braque and Matisse, a Dufy *Port of Marseilles*, and two fanciful paintings by Chagall, one

MUSÉE D'ART MODERNE

of which is the endearingly eccentric *The Frog that Wanted to Make Itself as Big as a Bull*. Another highlight is Léon Spilliaert's evocations of intense loneliness, from monochromatic beaches to empty rooms and train cars. Spilliaert (1881–1946) lived in Ostend, the setting for much of his work, including the piercing *Woman on the Dyke*. Another noteworthy Belgian is Constant Permeke (1886–1952), whose grim and gritty Expressionism is best illustrated by *The Potato Eater* of 1935.

Surrealism – Delvaux and Magritte

Level -5/6 is given over to the Surrealists. There's a fine Dalí, *The Temptation of St Anthony*, a hallucinatory work in which spindly-legged elephants tempt the saint with fleshy women, and a couple of haunting de Chirico paintings of dressmakers' dummies. Amongst the Belgian Surrealists, Paul Delvaux is represented by his trademark themes of ice-cool nudes set against a disintegrating backdrop as well as trains and stations – see the *Evening Train* and the *Public Voice*. Even more elusive is the gallery's collection of paintings by **René Magritte** (1898–1967), perplexing works whose weird, almost photographically realized images and bizarre juxtapositions aim to disconcert. Magritte was the prime mover in Belgian surrealism, developing – by the time he was thirty – an individualistic style that remained fairly constant throughout his entire career. It was not, however, a style that brought him much initial success and, surprising as it may seem today, he remained relatively unknown until the 1950s. The museum has a substantial sample of his work, amongst which two of the more intriguing pieces are the baffling *Secret Player* and the subtly discordant *Empire of Lights*.

The Musée Magritte is covered on p.115.

MUSÉE D'ART MODERNE

Contemporary art

Down on **Level -7/8**, there's some pretty incomprehensible modern stuff, featuring an international range of artists with the displays — and installations - regularly rotated. All the same, you're likely to spot the swirling abstracts of Brussels-born and Paris-based Pierre Alechinsky (b. 1927), as well as the tongue-in-cheek work of Marcel Broodthaers (1924–76), famously his *Red Mussels Casserole*.

THE PALAIS ROYAL

Map 6, F4. Late July to early Sept Tues–Sun 10.30am–4.30pm; free. Ⓜ Trone.

Just to the north of the Musées Royaux des Beaux Arts, around the corner from place Royale, is the long and architecturally repetitive **Palais Royal**, a sombre conversion of some late eighteenth-century town houses begun by King William I, the Dutch royal who ruled both Belgium and the Netherlands from 1815 to 1830. The Belgian rebellion of 1830 polished off the joint kingdom and since then the kings of independent Belgium haven't spent much money on the palace. Indeed, although it remains their official residence, the royals have lived elsewhere (in Laeken, see p.118) for decades and it's hardly surprising, therefore, that the **palace interior** is formal and unwelcoming. It consists of little more than a predictable sequence of opulent rooms — all gilt trimmings, parquet floors, and endless royal portraits, though the tapestries designed by Goya and the magnificent chandeliers of the Throne Room make a visit (just about) worthwhile.

THE MUSÉE DE LA DYNASTIE AND PALAIS COUDENBERG

Map 6, E3. Tues–Sun 10am–6pm. Museum €6.20, Coudenberg €4.95, combined ticket €7.45. Ⓜ Trône.

One of the mansions that makes up the Palais Royal, the **Hôtel Bellevue**, at the corner of place des Palais and rue

BELGIUM'S KINGS

Léopold I (1831–65). Foisted on Belgium by the great powers, Léopold, the first King of the Belgians, was imported from Germany, where he was the prince of Saxe-Coburg – and the uncle of Queen Victoria. Despite lacking a popular mandate, Léopold made a fairly good fist of things, keeping the country neutral as the great powers had ordained.

Léopold II (1865–1909). Energetic and forceful, Léopold II encouraged the urbanisation of his country and promoted its importance as a major industrial power. He was also the man responsible for landing Brussels with such pompous monuments as the Palais de Justice and for the imposition of a particularly barbaric colonial regime on the peoples of the Belgian Congo (now the Republic of Congo). The son of Léopold I.

Albert I (1909–34). Easily the most popular of the dynasty, Albert's bravery in World War I, when the Germans occupied almost all of the country, made the king a national hero whose untimely death, in a climbing accident, traumatised the nation. The nephew of Léopold II and the father of Léopold III.

Léopold III (1934–51). In contrast to his father, Léopold III had the dubious honour of becoming one of Europe's least popular monarchs. His first wife died in a suspicious car crash; he nearly lost his kingdom by remarrying (anathema in a Roman Catholic country); and he was badly compromised during the

Royale, has been turned into **Musée de la Dynastie**, which tracks through the brief history of the Belgian royal family. It is all very professionally done, comprising a brisk chronological trawl juiced up by a wide range of personal artefacts – clothes, shoes, letters and the like – donated by the royals, with separate sections on each of the country's monarchs. There is a particularly detailed section on the recently

German occupation of World War II. During the war, Léopold remained in Belgium rather than face exile, fuelling rumours that he was a Nazi collaborator – though his supporters maintained that he prevented thousands of Belgians from being deported. After several years of heated postwar debate, during which the king remained in exile, the issue of his return was finally put to a referendum in 1950. Just over half the population voted in Léopold's favour, but there was a clear French/Flemish divide, with opposition to the king concentrated in French-speaking Wallonia. Fortunately for Belgium, Léopold abdicated in 1951 in favour of his son, Baudouin.

Baudouin I (1951–93). A softly spoken family man, Baudouin did much to restore the popularity of the monarchy, not least because he was generally thought to be even-handed in his treatment of the French- and Flemish-speaking communities. He also hit the headlines in April 1990 by standing down for a day so that an abortion bill (which he as a Catholic had refused to sign) could be passed. Childless, he was succeeded by his brother.

Albert II (post-1993). The present king will have his work cut out if he wants to become the national figurehead that his brother was. The Belgian royal family is one of the few unifying forces in a country divided by French-Flemish antagonisms; one slip off the linguistic tightrope could have untold consequences.

THE MUSÉE DE LA DYNASTIE AND PALAIS COUDENBERG

deceased King Baudouin, who seems to have been a kind and gentle soul, but the museum almost always dodges the controversies that have surrounded several of its kings. It is particularly shameless in its treatment of Léopold II: apparently, he loved to travel and was quite an adventurer, attributes which his Congolese victims (of whom there is scarcely a mention) would have been hard pressed to appreciate.

The museum also gives access to the labyrinth of caves that are all that remain of the **Coudenberg Palace**, which once occupied the top of the hill on what is now place Royale. A castle was built here in the eleventh century and enlarged on several subsequent occasions, but it was badly damaged by fire in 1731 and the site was cleared in 1775. The foundations were, however, left untouched and have recently been cleared of debris. Further restorative work is planned, but at the moment visitors can wander round these dusty foundations, a highlight of which is the Magna Aula, or great hall, built by Philip the Good in the 1450s. A map of the layout of the palace is provided at reception, but you still need a vivid imagination to get much out of a visit.

PARC DE BRUXELLES AND PLACE DU TRÔNE

Opposite the Palais Royal, the **Parc de Bruxelles** (Map 6, E3–I1) is the most central of the city's larger parks, along whose tree-shaded footpaths civil servants and office workers stroll at lunchtime, or race to catch the métro in the evenings. They might well wish the greenery was a bit more interesting. Laid out in the formal French style in 1780, the park undoubtedly suited the courtly – and courting – rituals of the times, but today the straight footpaths and long lines of trees merely seem tedious, though the classical statues dotted hither and thither do cheer things up.

Beside the park's southeast corner stands the **Palais des Académies** (Map 6, H4), a grand edifice that once served as a royal residence, but now accommodates the Francophone Academy of Language and Literature. Just beyond is the **place du Trône**, where the pompous equestrian statue of Léopold II was the work of Thomas Vinçotte, whose skills were much used by the king – look out for Vinçotte's chariot on top of the Parc du Cinquantenaire's triumphal arch (see p.104).

From place du Trône, it's a few minutes' stroll east to the EU Parliament building and the EU Quarter (covered in Chapter 6), or you can head north for the ten-minute walk along boulevard du Régent to the Musée Charlier.

MUSÉE CHARLIER

Map 3, H5. Mon 10am–5pm, Tues–Thurs 1.30–5pm, Fri 1.30–4.30pm; €2.50. Ⓦwww.musee-charlier-museum.be. Ⓜ Arts-Loi or Madou.

The enjoyable **Musée Charlier**, at avenue des Arts 16, just off the petit ring near place Madou, illustrates the artistic tastes of Belgium's upper middle class at the end of the nineteenth century. It holds the collection of Henri van Cutsem, a wealthy businessman who bought two adjacent properties here in 1890. Cutsem merged and modified the two buildings so that he could display his collection to best effect, even going to the trouble of having Victor Horta install glass roofs. He subsequently bequeathed the house and its contents to a sculptor he knew and admired, **Guillaume Charlier** (1854–1925). Charlier kept the collection pretty much intact and it includes a wide range of fine and applied arts, from Belgian tapestries and antique French furniture to Chinese porcelain and paintings by a number of lesser-known Belgian artists.

Each of the dozen or so rooms is crammed with artefacts, and it's this jumbled diversity which is the museum's principal charm. Nevertheless, in the Concert Room it's still worth tracking down James Ensor's *Flowers and Butterflies*, and Eugene Laermans' *The Promenade*, showing peasants out walking.

For more on James Ensor, see p.67.

PLACE DE LA LIBERTÉ AND PLACE DES BARRICADES

Map 3, H4–5.

From the Musée Charlier, it's a five-minute walk west to **place de la Liberté**, a leafy little square decorated with a statue of Charles Rogier (1800–85), a one-time member of the Provisional Government of 1830 and later a railway magnate. The square is at the heart of one of the more attractive parts of the city centre, a pocket-sized district where the mansions of the nineteenth-century bourgeoisie, built with dignified balconies and wrought-iron grilles, overlook wide, straight streets and fetching little piazzas. One of these squares, the somewhat dilapidated **place des Barricades**, is named after the impromptu barricades that were erected here against the Dutch in 1830. There's no plaque, but **no. 4** was once owned by Victor Hugo, who was exiled from France for supporting the revolution of 1848. It was a long exile – Hugo only returned to France after the fall of the Second Empire in 1870 – but one that he shared with other literary lights, notably Dumas and Baudelaire.

COLONNE DU CONGRÈS

Map 3, G5.

At the west end of rue du Congrès, the 47-metre-high **Colonne du Congrès**, on place du Congrès, was erected in 1850 to commemorate the country's first national parliament. The column sports a statue of Léopold I on top and four allegorical female figures down below, representing the freedoms enshrined in the Constitution: of worship, association, education and the press. The lions were added later, guarding the tomb of the unknown soldier, in front of which burns the eternal flame honouring Belgium's dead of the two World Wars. The column dominates a bleak belvedere, flanked by blank glass and concrete administration buildings and offering a singularly unflattering view of the city.

From the Colonne du Congrès, it's a ten-minute walk north along rue Royale to Le Botanique (see p.42), or five minutes' walk west down to the entertaining Centre Belge de la Bande Dessinée – the Belgian Comic Strip Centre (see p.40).

THE SABLON NEIGHBOURHOOD

The Sablon neighborhood anchors the southern end of the Upper Town and at its heart is **place du Petit Sablon** (Map 6, B7), a small rectangular area which was laid out as a public garden in 1890 after previous use as a horse market. The wrought-iron fence surrounding the garden is decorated with 48 statuettes representing the medieval guilds and inside, near the top of the slope, are ten more – slightly larger – statues honouring some of the country's leading sixteenth-century figures. The ten are hardly household names in Belgium never mind anywhere else, but one or two may ring a few bells: Mercator, the geographer and cartographer responsible for Mercator's projection of the earth's surface; William the Silent, the founder of the Netherlands; and the painter Bernard van Orley (see p.61). Here also, on top of the fountain, are the figures of the counts **Egmont and Hoorn**, clasping each other in brotherly fashion, as befits two men who were beheaded together on the Grand-Place for their opposition to the Habsburgs in 1568 (see p.293).

Count Egmont is further remembered by the **Palais d'Egmont** (Map 6, B7; no entry) at the back of the square. This elegant structure was originally built in 1534 for Françoise of Luxembourg, mother of the executed count. It was remodelled on several subsequent occasions and in 1972 it was here that Britain signed the treaty admitting it to the EEC.

Notre Dame du Sablon and the place du Grand Sablon

Opposite the foot of the park, the fifteenth-century church of **Notre Dame du Sablon** (Map 6, B7; Mon–Fri 9am–5pm, Sat 10am–5pm, Sun 1pm–5pm; free) began life as a chapel for the guild of archers in 1304. Its fortunes were, however, transformed when a statue of Mary, with healing powers, was brought here from Antwerp in 1348. The chapel became a centre of pilgrimage and a proper church – in high Gothic style – was built to accommodate its visitors. It's a handsome, honey-colour structure, though it did endure some inappropriate tinkering at the end of the nineteenth century, with arching buttresses, slender parapets, screeching gargoyles and delicate pinnacles, and it has greatly benefited from its recent refurbishment. The **interior** no longer holds the statue of Mary – the Protestants chopped it up in 1565 – but two carvings of the boat and its passengers recall the story, one in the nave, the other above the inside of the rue de la Régence entrance. The woman in the boat is one Béatrice Sodkens, the pious creature whose visions prompted her to procure the statue and bring it here. The occasion of its arrival in Brussels is still celebrated annually in July by the **Ommegang** procession (see p.278).

The church's **nave** is dark and gloomy, making it hard to pick out the Gothic detail, but there's no missing the lofty vaulted ceiling or the fancily carved stone tracery of the windows. Look out also for the grotesque **tombstone** of Claude and Jacqueline Bouton, members of Charles V's entourage, which, resting against the wall near the main entrance, displays two graphically realistic skeletons. More conspicuous is the black and white marble **funerary chapel** in the transept – a Baroque mausoleum for the earthly remains of the Tour and Taxis family, local worthies who founded the Belgian postal system.

Behind the church, the **place du Grand Sablon** (Map 6, A5–B6) is one of Brussels' most charming squares, a sloping wedge of cobblestones flanked by tall and slender town houses plus the occasional Art Nouveau facade. The square serves as the centre of one of the city's wealthiest districts, and is busiest at weekends, when an **antiques market** clusters below the church. Many of the shops on Sablon and the surrounding streets are devoted to antiques and art, and you could easily spend an hour or so window-browsing from one to another – or you can soak up the atmosphere eating or drinking in one of Sablon's cafés. The **Musée Postal et Musée des Télécommunications** (Map 6, A5; Tues–Sat 10am–4.30pm; free), at no. 40, holds a complete collection of Belgian stamps and oodles of old telecommunications equipment, though it is currently being revamped.

PALAIS DE JUSTICE AND PLACE LOUISE

From place du Grand Sablon, follow rue Ernest Allard up the hill to **place Poelaert**, named after the architect who designed the immense **Palais de Justice** (Map 3, D10 & Map 8, E1), a monstrous Greco-Roman wedding cake of a building, dwarfing the square and everything around it. It's possible to wander into the main hall of the building, a sepulchral affair with tiny audience tables where lawyers huddle with their clients, but really it's the size alone that is impressive – not that it pleased the several thousand towns-folk who were forcibly evicted so that the place could be built. Poelaert became one of the most hated men in the capital, and, when he went insane and died in 1879, it was widely believed a *steekes* (witch) from the Marolles had been sticking pins into an effigy of him. The square is also the site of two **war memorials**: the one on the corner, dating to 1923, pays tribute to the Anglo-Belgian alliance; the other in the middle of the square commemorates Belgian dead with Art Deco soldiers following an angel.

A stone's throw from the Palais de Justice, **place Louise**, part square, part traffic junction (Map 8, F2), heralds the start of the city's most exclusive shopping district. It's here and in the immediate vicinity that you'll find designer boutiques, jewellers and glossy shopping malls. The glitz spreads east along boulevard de Waterloo and south down the northernmost section of avenue Louise, which is described on pp.89–91.

St Gilles, Avenue Louise and Ixelles

Cobwebbed by tiny squares and twisting streets, home to a plethora of local bars and some of the capital's finest Art Nouveau houses, the neighbouring areas of St Gilles and Ixelles, just south of the petit ring, make a great escape from the hustle and bustle of the city centre. This is Brussels without the razzmatazz and tourists are few and far between, especially in **St Gilles**, the smaller of the two *communes*, which is often regarded as little more than an example of inner-city decay. Frankly, this is true enough of its most westerly section, comprising the depressing immigrant quarters of Gare du Midi and the downtrodden streets near Porte de Hal, but St Gilles gets more appealing the further east it spreads, its run-down streets left behind for refined avenues interspersed with dignified squares.

Ixelles, for its part, is one of the capital's most interesting and exciting outer areas, with a couple of enjoyable museums, and a diverse street-life and café scene. Historically, Ixelles has long drawn artists, writers and intellectuals – Karl Marx, Auguste Rodin and Alexandre Dumas all lived here – and even today it retains an arty, sometimes

Bohemian feel. A hallmark of Ixelles is its cheek-to-cheek diversity: the chic boutiques of the **Galerie Toison d'Or**, for instance, are just across the chaussée d'Ixelles from the rough-edged **Galerie d'Ixelles**, itself the focus of **Matongé**, the vibrant social centre of the district's Central African community, packed with late-night bars and cafés.

**The area covered by this chapter is shown
in detail on colour map 8.**

Ixelles is divided in two by **avenue Louise**, whose character is entirely different, as befits an administrative anomaly: the boulevard is counted as part of the city centre, and has been home to the haute bourgeoisie ever since Léopold II had the avenue laid out in the 1840s. It's here you'll find some of the city's most expensive shops and hotels, pricey jewellers, slick office blocks and the interesting **Musée Constantin Meunier**, sited in the sculptor's old house.

More than anything else, however, it's the dazzling array of **Art Nouveau** buildings clustering the streets of both St Gilles and Ixelles which really grab the attention. Many of the finest examples are concentrated on and around the boundary between the two *communes* – in between chaussée de Charleroi and avenue Louise. Here you'll find Horta's own house, now the glorious **Musée Horta**, as well as examples of the work of Paul Hankar and Armand van Waesberghe. Access to most of the city's Art Nouveau buildings is restricted, so you can either settle for the view from outside, or enrol on one of ARAU's specialist tours (see p.15).

ST GILLES

One of the smallest of the city's *communes*, **St Gilles** is also one of the most varied, stretching from the impoverished, sometimes threatening streets round the **Gare du Midi** and **Porte de Hal** to the affluent precincts of avenue Louise. In the poorer quarters, generations of political and economic refugees from the Mediterranean and North Africa have established themselves. The easterly sections of St Gilles are much more relaxed – and relaxing – and it's here you'll find the district's architectural highlight, the **Musée Victor Horta**.

Porte de Hal and the Hôtel Winssinger

The imposing **Porte de Hal** (Map 8, C3), standing on the edge of St Gilles at the southern tip of the petit ring, is the only one of the city's seven medieval gates to have survived – the rest were knocked down by Napoleon, but this one was left untouched because it was a prison. The gate is a massive, heavily fortified affair, with towers and turrets, battlements and machicolations, and – although it was clumsily remodelled in the 1870s – it gives a good idea of the strength of the city's former defences. The interior has a couple of good-looking rooms, where the medieval features of the original edifice have survived intact, and a parapet walkway provides extensive views over the city – or at least it will do when the Porte de Hal reopens after a seemingly interminable revamp.

Heading south from the gateway, down the **chaussée de Waterloo**, you're soon in the dishevelled heart of St Gilles, with the elaborate but distinctly dilapidated Art Nouveau houses of **rue Vanderschrick** (Map 8, C4) running off to the right. On the first corner of this side street is the Art Nouveau café *Porteuse d'Eau* (see "Drinking", p.211), but this is the only sign of gentrification around here, and, as an outsider, it's hard not to feel intrusive as you push on towards the soulless **place de Bethléem** (Map 8, B4), with its cheap and seedy restaurants. In fact, it's better to press on up the chaussée de Waterloo to the **parvis de St Gilles** (Map 8, C4), a chubby little square lined with handsome tenement houses that's the site of a lively fruit and vegetable **market** (Tues–Sun 6am–noon). From here, it's a short stroll east along rue de Jourdan to rue de l'Hôtel des Monnaies where, at no. 66, you'll find Victor Horta's **Hôtel Winssinger** (Map 8, D4). Dating from the 1890s, Horta's most creative period, the building sports a wide facade, with large ground-floor windows and a cluster of smaller windows. The front is relatively unscathed, but the interior has been badly mauled by subsequent alterations.

The Barrière de St Gilles to the Maison and Atelier Dubois

From the Hôtel Winssinger, push on south down rue de l'Hôtel des Monnaies until you reach the **Barrière de St Gilles** (Map 8, C6) – a seven-road junction that was, until the middle of the nineteenth century, the site of a toll gate. Close by, south again up avenue Paul Dejaer, is the *commune's* **Hôtel de Ville** (Map 8, C7), a heavy-duty, pseudo-Renaissance edifice, and behind that, at the top end of avenue Jef Lambeaux, rises the ersatz medieval castle which holds the **prison**.

Heading east from the prison, take the first right off avenue Ducpétiaux, turn left at the T-junction – down avenue de la Jonction – and at the end, at the corner of avenue Brugmann, you'll spot the **Hôtel Hannon** (Map 8, E8), a fine Art Nouveau extravagance designed by the architect Jules Brunfaut in 1903. The windows, equipped with Tiffany glass, are a special highlight – flowing, beautifully carved extravagances set against a facade whose brickwork is decorated with strips of stone. Next door, **Les Hiboux** – The Owls' House – is a more modest red-brick affair, but it does carry some attractive wrought iron grilles and stained glass, plus an sgraffiti decorative panel depicting two perky little owls.

Five minutes' walk away to the south, at avenue Brugmann 80, is Victor Horta's **Maison and Atelier Dubois** (Map 8, E9). Completed in 1906, towards the end of Horta's Art Nouveau period, the building is much simpler than some of his earlier works, though it still bears several of his familiar trademarks: a well-lit interior, exquisite carpentry in mahogany and oak, a mosaic floor, and a marble staircase. The building is not open to the public, but the exterior – a modest but subtle facade with curvaceous windows set off by the careful use of wrought iron – is mightily impressive.

Doubling back along avenue Brugmann, it's a short stroll to the **chaussée de Charleroi**, within easy striking distance of the Musée Victor Horta.

Musée Victor Horta

Map 8, F7. Tues–Sun 2–5.30pm; €4.95. Tram #91, #92.

The **Musée Victor Horta**, just off the chaussée de Charleroi at rue Américaine 23 & 25, occupies the two houses Horta designed as his home and studio at the end of the nineteenth century, and was where he lived until 1919. The only Horta house fully open to the public, the museum was opened in the late 1960s, part of a sustained campaign to stop the destruction of Brussels' architectural heritage and to publicise the charms of Art Nouveau. From the outside the building is quite modest, a dark, narrow terraced house with a fluid facade and almost casually knotted and twisted ironwork, but it is for his interiors that Horta is especially famous. Inside is a sunny, sensuous dwelling exhibiting all the architect's favourite flourishes – wide, bright rooms spiralling around a superbly worked staircase, wrought iron, stained glass, sculpture and ornate furniture, plus panelling made from several different types of wood.

MUSÉE VICTOR HORTA

VICTOR HORTA

The son of a shoemaker, Victor Horta (1861–1947) was born in Ghent, where he failed in his first career, being unceremoniously expelled from the city's music conservatory for indiscipline. He promptly moved to Paris to study architecture, returning to Belgium in 1880 to complete his internship in Brussels with Alphonse Balat, the architect to King Léopold II. Balat was a traditionalist, responsible for the classical facades of the Palais Royal – amongst many other prestigious projects – and Horta looked elsewhere for inspiration. He found it in the work of William Morris, the leading figure of the English Arts and Crafts movement, whose designs were key to the development of Art Nouveau. Taking its name from the Maison de l'Art Nouveau, a Parisian shop which sold items of modern design, Art Nouveau rejected the imitative architectures which were popular at the time – Neoclassical and neo-Gothic – in favour of an innovative style that was characterized by sinuous, flowing lines. In England, Morris and his colleagues had focused on book illustrations and furnishings, but in Belgium Horta extrapolated the new style into architecture, experimenting with new building materials – steel and concrete – as well as traditional stone, glass and wood.

In 1893, Horta completed the curvaceous Hôtel Tassel (see p.88), Brussels' first Art Nouveau building – "hôtel" meaning town house. Inevitably, there were howls of protest from the traditionalists, but no matter what his opponents said, Horta never lacked for work again. The following years – roughly

The **dining room** is superb, an inventive blend of white enamelled brickwork and exposed structural metal arches on a parquet floor. Lining the walls are six bas-reliefs carved by Pierre Braecke, five of which portray the arts depicted by the muses above the dresser: painting, music, sculpture,

1893 to 1905 – were Horta's most inventive and prolific. He designed over forty buildings, including the Hôtel Solvay (see p.88) and the Hôtel Winssinger (see p.82) as well as his own beautifully decorated house and studio, now the Musée Victor Horta (see p.83). The delight Horta took in his work is obvious, especially when employed on private houses, and his enthusiasm was all-encompassing – he almost always designed everything from the blueprints to the wallpaper and carpets. He never kept a straight line or sharp angle where he could deploy a curve, and his use of light was revolutionary, often filtering through from above, atrium-like, with skylights and as many windows as possible. Curiously, Horta also believed that originality was born of frustration, and so he deliberately created architectural difficulties, pushing himself to find harmonious solutions. Horta felt that the architect was as much an artist as the painter or sculptor, and so he insisted on complete stylistic freedom. It was part of a well-thought out value system that allied him with both Les XX (see p.93) and the Left; as he wrote, "My friends and I were reds, without however having thought about Marx or his theories."

Completed in 1906, the Maison and Atelier Dubois (see p.83) and the Grand Magasin Waucquez department store (p.40) were transitional buildings signalling the end of Horta's Art Nouveau period. His later works were more Modernist constructions, whose understated lines were a far cry from the ornateness of his earlier work. In Brussels, the best example of his later work is the Palais des Beaux-Arts of 1928 (see p.53).

literature, and architecture – with the sixth holding out a model of the Aubecq mansion, built by Horta in 1899 and demolished in 1950. The **staircase** is simply stunning too, a dainty spiralling affair which runs through the centre of the house up to the skylight, ensuring the house gets as

VICTOR HORTA

much light as possible. Decorated with painted motifs and surrounded by mirrors, it remains one of Horta's most ingenious creations. Also of interest is the modest but enjoyable selection of **paintings**, many of which were given to Horta by friends and colleagues, including works by Félicien Rops and Joseph Heymans.

WESTERN IXELLES

Wedged in between the chaussée de Charleroi and avenue Louise, **western Ixelles** is one of the most fashionable parts of the city, its more prosperous inhabitants occupying graceful late nineteenth- and early twentieth-century mansions. The district holds a fine sample of Art Nouveau houses, with the pick of them on or in the vicinity of **rue Defacqz** and **rue Faider**.

The church of Ste Trinité and place du Châtelain

Heading east from the Musée Victor Horta, take the first turning on the left – rue Africaine – for the parvis de la Trinité, the site of the sulky **church of Ste Trinité** (Map 8, G7), a run-down but imposing Baroque structure whose heavy-duty stonework fills out the square. The most interesting feature is the extravagant main facade, which was originally part of the church of St Augustin (1620), demolished to make way for the place de Brouckère in 1896. The facade was moved here block by block and although pollution and years of neglect have left their mark, it's still – with its swirling lines, pointed pediments and pilasters – an impressive structure. There are vague plans to restore the church, but at the moment it remains firmly closed – a shame because the stained-glass windows are allegedly quite stunning.

Just to the east of the church – along rue de l'Amazone – is **place du Châtelain**, a pleasant, tapering square lined with bars and cafés. Best known for its Wednesday afternoon food market (2–7pm) – where you can buy homemade wines, fine cheeses and a mouth-watering selection of cakes and pastries – it's also a relaxing place for a quiet drink or a spot of lunch. Incidentally, *Le Pain de Châtelain* serves what many locals regard as the best croissants in town.

Rue Defacqz: the Art Nouveau of Paul Hankar

Map 8, H5–F6.

From place du Châtelain, it's a short stroll northwest up rue Simonis to **rue Defacqz**, the site of several charming Art Nouveau houses. Three were designed by **Paul Hankar** (1859–1901), a classically trained architect and contemporary of Horta, who developed a real penchant for sgraffiti – akin to frescoes – and multicoloured brickwork. Hankar was regarded as one of the most distinguished exponents of Art Nouveau and his old home, at **no. 71**, is marked by its skeletal metalwork, handsome bay window and four sgraffiti beneath the cornice – one each for morning, afternoon, evening and night. Hankar designed his home in the early 1890s, making it one of the city's earliest Art Nouveau buildings. **Number 50** is a Hankar creation too, built for another painter, René Janssens, in 1898, and noteworthy for its fanciful brickwork. Next door, at **no. 48**, the house Hankar constructed for the Italian painter Albert Ciamberlani in 1897 sports a fine, flowing facade, decorated with sgraffiti representing the Ages of Man.

WESTERN IXELLES

Rue Faider and the Hôtel Tassel

Map 8, G6–H5.

There are more Art Nouveau treats in store on neighbouring **rue Faider**, where **no. 83** boasts a splendidly flamboyant facade with ironwork foliage round the windows and frescoes of languishing pre-Raphaelite women, all to a design by **Armand Van Waesberghe**. Directly opposite is rue Paul Émile Janson at the bottom of which, at no. 6, is the celebrated **Hôtel Tassel**, the building that made **Horta**'s reputation. The sinuous facade is appealing enough, with clawed columns, stained glass and spiralling ironwork, but it was with the interior that Horta really made a splash, an uncompromising fantasy featuring a fanciful wrought-iron staircase and walls covered with linear decoration. It's also a striking example of the way in which Horta tailor-made his houses to suit the particular needs of clients. In this case it was built for an amateur photographer and includes a studio and projection room.

Horta's Hôtel Solvay and Hôtel Max Hallet

At the end of rue Paul Émile Janson you hit avenue Louise, where a right turn will take you – in a couple of hundred metres – to the **Hôtel Solvay** at no. 224 (Map 8, I6), another Horta extravagance which, like the Musée Horta, contains most of the original furnishings and fittings. The 33-year-old Horta was given complete freedom and unlimited funds by the Solvay family (who made a fortune in soft drinks) to design this opulent town house, whose facade is graced by bow windows, delicate metalwork and contrasting types of stone. Inside, Horta commissioned an artist to paint a scene from the Solvay's summer cottage on the first staircase landing, but typically chose the dominant colours himself. Also on avenue Louise, five minutes' further along at no. 346, is Horta's **Hôtel Max Hallet** (Map 8, J8), a comparatively restrained structure of 1904, where the straight and slender facade is decorated with elegant doors and windows and an elongated stone balcony with a wrought iron balustrade. Just beyond, the modern **sculpture** stranded in the middle of the traffic island looks like a pair of elephant tusks, but is in fact a representation of the "V" for Victory sign of World War II. Named *Phénix 44*, it's the work of Olivier Strebelle.

From the Max Hallet residence, it's a quick tram ride north to the smart commercialism of place Louise or a ten-minute stroll south to the Musée Constantin Meunier (see below).

AVENUE LOUISE

Named after the eldest daughter of its creator, Léopold II, **avenue Louise** (Map 8, F2–J9) slices southeast from the petit ring, its beginnings lined with some of the city's most expensive shops and boutiques. Further along, shops give way to plush apartment blocks, the most visible part of the wealthy residential area which occupies the side streets around the avenue. It's here you'll find the diverting **Musée Constantin Meunier**, which displays a large sample of the work of the late nineteenth-century sculptor, and the **Abbaye de la Cambre**, whose pleasant gardens and old brick buildings are sited in the diplomatic zone at the end of the avenue.

The Musée Constantin Meunier

Map 8, I9. Tues–Fri & alternate weekends 10am–noon & 1–5pm; free; ℡02 508 32 11. Tram #93, #94.

The **Musée Constantin Meunier**, just off avenue Louise, about 500m beyond Victor Horta's Hôtel Max Hallet (see p.89), is at rue de l'Abbaye 59. It's housed in the unassuming home and studio of Brussels-born Constantin Meunier, who lived here from 1899 until his death at the age of 74 just six years later. Meunier began as a painter, but it's as a sculptor that he's best remembered, and the museum has an extensive collection of his dark and brooding bronzes.

The biggest and most important pieces are in the room at the back, where a series of muscular men with purposeful faces stand around looking heroic – *The Reaper* and *The Sower* are typical. There are oil paintings in this room, too: gritty industrial scenes like the coalfield of *Black Country Borinage* and the gloomy dockside of *The Port*, one of Meunier's most forceful works. In the other rooms, you'll find a few watercolours and drawings as well as more statues honouring the working class and its sufferings – there's *The Glass-blower*, *The Shrimp Fisherman* and the hunched figure of *Pain*. Meunier was angered by the dreadful living conditions of Belgium's workers, particularly (like van Gogh before him) the harsh life of the coal miners of the Borinage. This anger fuelled his art, which asserted the dignity of the working class in a style that was to be copied by the Social Realists of his and later generations. According to Hobsbawm's *Age of Empire*, "Meunier invented the international stereotype of the sculptured proletarian."

The Abbaye de la Cambre and Bois de la Cambre

In a lovely little wooded dell on the other side of avenue Louise from the Meunier Museum – and readily approached via rue de l'Aurore – lies the **Abbaye de la Cambre** (Map 8, K9; Mon–Fri 9am–noon & 3–6pm; free; tram #93, #94). Of medieval foundation, the abbey was suppressed by the French Revolutionary army and its attractive eighteenth-century brick buildings, which surround a pretty little courtyard, are now used by several government departments. On the courtyard is the main entrance to the lovely little abbey **church**, whose nave, with its barrel vaulting, is an exercise in simplicity. The church is an amalgamation of styles incorporating both Gothic and Classical features and it holds one marvellous painting, Albert Bouts' *The Mocking of Christ*, an early sixteenth-century work showing a mournful, blood-spattered Jesus. Behind the abbey's buildings are walled and terraced gardens, an oasis of peace away from the hubbub of avenue Louise.

Beyond the abbey, at the end of avenue Louise, the **Bois de la Cambre** is unpleasantly crisscrossed by the main commuter access roads in its upper reaches, but a good deal more agreeable around the lake that lies further to the south. It's Brussels' most popular park, bustling with joggers, dog-walkers, families and lovers at weekends, and is the northerly finger of the large **Forêt de Soignes** (see p.120), whose once mighty forests bear a clutch of dual carriageways, and, more promisingly, scores of quiet footpaths.

EASTERN IXELLES

Eastern Ixelles radiates out from the petit ring, its busy streets spined by the workaday **chaussée d'Ixelles**, whose long string of shops and stores meander down to **place Fernand Cocq** and ultimately **place Eugène Flagey**. It's the general flavour that appeals hereabouts rather than any specific sight, though there are a few exceptions, most notably the first-rate **Musée des Beaux-Arts d'Ixelles**, whose forte is modern Belgian art, the good-looking **church of St Boniface** and – less compellingly – the accumulated *objets d'art* of the **Musée Camille Lemonnier**.

South along the chaussée d'Ixelles and St Boniface

From the big and hectic square that is the **Porte de Namur** (Map 8, H1), it's a couple of minutes' walk down the **chaussée d'Ixelles** to two oddly contrasting shopping malls. On the right hand side are the slick boutiques of the **Galerie Toison d'Or**, and on the left, almost opposite, is the rough-and-ready **Galerie d'Ixelles**, the shopping centre of the city's Central and North African community. Walk through the Galerie d'Ixelles and you'll soon reach the **chaussée de Wavre**. Here, you can turn right and then take the second right to reach the pedestrianised **rue de Longue Vie** (Map 8, I12), the social – and sociable – heart of the African quarter, thronged with small cheerful bars and cafés playing African music and serving cheap beer and traditional food.

Close by, on rue de la Paix, is the imposing, Gothic pile of **St Boniface** (Map 8, I2). From the outside the church looks distressed and run down, but the cool interior boasts cathedral-like arches and immaculate stained-glass windows. Directly in front of the church lies the appealing **rue St Boniface**, home to a number of laid-back café-bars including the immensely popular *L'Ultime Atome* (see "Drinking", p.209).

Musée Camille Lemonnier

Map 8, J2. Admission by prior arrangement, Mon–Fri only; free; ⓣ02 512 29 68. Ⓜ Trône.

The **Musée Camille Lemonnier**, a short walk east of St Boniface at chaussée de Wavre 150, is dedicated to the eponymous Belgian intellectual, writer, dramatist and essayist, who was an influential member of the city's cultural elite for almost fifty years. A sharp-witted Francophone,

LES XX

Founded in 1883, Les XX was an influential group of twenty Belgian painters, designers and sculptors, who were keen to bring together all the different strands of their respective crafts. For ten years, they staged an annual exhibition showcasing both domestic and international talent and it was here that Cézanne, Manet and Gauguin were all exhibited at the very beginning of their careers. With members as diverse as Ensor and the architect-designer Henri van de Velde, Les XX never professed to be united by the same artistic principles, but several of its members, including Rysselberghe, were inordinately impressed by the Post-Impressionism of Seurat, whose pointillist *The Big Bowl* created a sensation when it was exhibited by Les XX in 1887.

Les XX – and the other literary-artistic groupings which succeeded it – were part of a general avant-garde movement which flourished in Brussels at the end of the nineteenth century. This avant-garde was deeply disenchanted with Brussels' traditional salon culture, not only for artistic reasons but also because of its indifference to the plight of the Belgian working class. Such political views nourished close links with the fledgling Socialist movement, and Les XX even ran the slogan "art and the people have the same enemy – the reactionary Bourgoisie". Indeed, the Belgian avant-garde came to see art (in all its forms) as a vehicle for liberating the Belgian worker, a project regularly proclaimed in *L'Art Moderne*, their most authoritative mouthpiece.

Lemonnier (1844–1913) started out writing for a literary review, the *Journal des Artistiques*, and subsequently turned his hand to novels, books of art criticism – including the *Histoire de Beaux-Arts en Belgique* (1887) – and political texts. There were also monographs on the artists of the day

– for instance Henri de Braekeleer, Alfred Stevens and Constantin Meunier – as well as oodles of stuff on the avant-garde Les XX (see p.93). Inevitably, Lemonnier's acid tongue created hostility and bitter arguments punctuated his career, most disagreeably with James Ensor.

Set up by Camille's daughter Louise in 1946, the **museum** is housed in an attractive late nineteenth-century building and holds an eclectic collection of *objets d'art*, everything from sculptures and paintings to gilded books. In the main room upstairs are paintings by Louise, hanging alongside portraits of her father by Emile Claus, Constantin Meunier and Isidore Verheyden. Other paintings of note include *The Fair* by Victor Gilsoul, and the bleak *Hunter in the Snow* by Emile Verheyden, Lemonnier's cousin. The finest of the sculptures are *The Foolish Song* by Jef Lambeaux and *Eternal Spring* by Auguste Rodin.

Place Fernand Cocq

From near the Musée Camille Lemonnier, rue de la Tulipe leads south back to the chaussée d'Ixelles and **place Fernand Cocq** (Map 8, I3), a small, refreshingly leafy square named after a one-time Ixelles burgomaster, and lined with a good selection of bars, including *Volle Gas* (see p.209) and *L'Amour Fou* (see p.208).

The square's centrepiece is the **Maison communale** (Map 8, I3), a sturdy Neoclassical building built by the Flemish architect Vanderstraeten for the opera singer **Maria Malibran**, née Garcia (1808–36), and her lover, the Belgian violinist Charles de Bériot. Malibran was one of the great stars of her day and her contralto voice created a sensation when she first appeared on the stage in London in 1825. Her father, one Manuel Garcia, trained her and organized her tours, but pushed his daughter into a most unfortunate marriage in New York. Mr Malibran turned out to be a bankrupt and Maria pluckily left husband and father behind, returning to Europe to pick up her career. She was fantastically successful and had this Ixelles mansion built for herself and Bériot in 1833. After her death, the house lay uninhabited until it was bought by the Ixelles *commune* in 1849; the gardens in which Maria once practised have been reduced to the small park which now edges the house.

Musée des Beaux-Arts d'Ixelles

Map 8, K4. Tues–Fri 1–6.30pm, Sat & Sun 10am–5pm; permanent collection free, admission charged for temporary exhibitions. Tram #81 or #82.

The excellent **Musée des Beaux-Arts d'Ixelles**, rue Jean van Volsem 71, is located about ten minutes' walk southeast of place Fernand Cocq, via rue du Collège. Established in an old slaughterhouse in 1892, the museum was enlarged and refurbished a few years back and since then it has built up an excellent reputation for the quality of its temporary exhibitions, ranging from Belgian surrealism through to Russian modernism. The permanent collection is mainly nineteenth- and early twentieth-century French and Belgian material, but there's a small sample of earlier paintings in the first wing, including *Tobie and the Angel* by Rembrandt and a sketch, *The Stork*, by Albrecht Dürer. In the same wing, Jacques-Louis David, one-time revolutionary and the leading light among France's Neoclassical painters, is well represented by *The Man at the Gallows*. There's also a wonderful collection of haunting works by Charles Herman, one of a group of Belgian realists who struggled to get their work exhibited in the capital's salons: until the late 1870s the salons would contemplate only Romantic and Neoclassical works. Also, look out for the large collection of posters featuring the work of Toulouse-Lautrec – thirty of his total output of thirty-two are displayed here.

MUSÉE DES BEAUX-ARTS D'IXELLES

95

The museum's two other wings hold an enjoyable sample of the work of the country's leading modern artists, from well-known figures such as the surrealists Magritte, Paul Delvaux and Marcel Broodthaers (*Casserole of Mussels*) to less familiar artists such as Edgar Tytgat, Rik Wouters and Constant Permeke. There's a smattering of sculptures, too, with the main event being Rodin's *La Lorraine* and *J.B. Willems*. Rodin used to have a studio nearby at rue Sans Souci 111, in the heart of Ixelles, and this was where he designed his first major work, *The Age of Bronze*. When it was exhibited in 1878, there was outrage: Rodin's naturalistic treatment of the naked body broke with convention and created something of a scandal – he was even accused of casting his sculptures round live models.

South to the étangs d'Ixelles

From the Musée des Beaux-Arts d'Ixelles – and place Fernand Cocq – it's an uneventful ten minutes' walk south to **place Eugène Flagey** (Map 8, K5), a bare, dispiriting expanse whose fringes are occupied by several matching structures built in the modernist style popular in Belgium during the 1930s. The largest – on the southeast side of the square – is the former National Broadcasting Institute, a sweeping structure of yellow brick and acres of glass that was completed in 1937. Long disused – though there are ambitious plans to revamp it – the building was and is (for reasons that are hard to fathom) fondly regarded by the locals, who call it **le paquebot** (Map 8, K6) for its resemblance to a luxury liner.

To the southwest of place Eugène Flagey lie the **étangs d'Ixelles** (Map 8, K6–8), two little lakes – really large ponds – that are flanked by several handsome Art Nouveau villas. **Avenue des Éperons d'Or**, running alongside the first lake, has the pick with **nos. 5 and 8–12** all designed

by the Delune brothers in the florid, busy style – with balconies, layered stonework, turrets and high gables – which
was their architectural hallmark. Across the lake, **avenue
Général de Gaulle 38 & 39** illustrate the work of another
Art Nouveau architect, Ernest Blérot, who specialized in
wrought ironwork and demonstrated his virtuosity by
building houses in pairs to heighten the effect. Close by, at
rue du Lac 6, stands another Delune creation, a narrow
house with exquisite stained-glass windows and decorated
with aqua-floral designs inspired by Japanese woodcuts.

SOUTH TO THE ÉTANGS D'IXELLES

The EU Quarter and Le Cinquantenaire

n the middle of the nineteenth century, Léopold II extended the boundaries of Brussels east of the petit ring to incorporate the grandiloquent monuments and grassy parks he had constructed. Smart residential areas followed along with a series of museums whose large collections reflected, so the king believed, Belgium's proper position amongst the leading industrial nations. Much of Léopold's grand design has survived – and provides the district's key attractions – but today it's overlaid with the uncompromising office blocks of the EU. These high-rises coalesce hereabouts to form the loosely defined EU Quarter – properly the **Quartier des Institutions Européennes**, home to the European Commission, whose civil servants support and advise the EU's ultimate decision-making body, the Brussels-based Council of Ministers, and various committees of the European Parliament (which sits in Strasbourg).

The area covered by this chapter is
shown in detail on colour map 2.

To enjoy a visit to this part of the city, you'll need to follow a clear itinerary, one which avoids the worst of the EU area, where the streets groan with traffic and a vast building programme has turned whole blocks into dusty construction sites. Essentially, this means dodging – as far as possible – rues de la Loi and Belliard, the two wide boulevards that serve as the area's main thoroughfares. The best place to start is in the vicinity of **Parc Léopold**, where, just a few minutes' stroll from the petit ring, you'll find the intriguing **Musée Wiertz**, exhibiting the huge and eccentric paintings of the eponymous artist, and the gleaming **European Parliament building**. From here, it's a ten-minute walk to **Le Cinquantenaire**, one of Léopold's most excessive extravagances, a triumphal arch built to celebrate the golden jubilee of Belgian independence and containing three museums, the pick of which is the wide-ranging **Musées royaux d'Art et d'Histoire**.

FROM PLACE DU TRÔNE TO THE EUROPEAN PARLIAMENT BUILDING

Part of the petit ring and on the métro line, **place du Trône** (Map 2, F7) is distinguished by its double lion gates and a sooty, life-size statue of Léopold II, perched on his horse. From here, **rue du Luxembourg** heads east to bisect a small park whose northern half contains a modest memorial to Julien Dillens, a popular nineteenth-century sculptor responsible for the effigy of Everard 't Serclaes on the Grand-Place (see p.23). Just along the street, the **place du Luxembourg** has had varying fortunes, but now it's on the up, with fashionable cafés moving in as its three-storey, stone-trimmed houses are refurbished. In the middle of the square is a statue of **John Cockerill** (1790–1840), a British entrepreneur who built a steel-making empire in southern

THE EU IN BRUSSELS

The European Union is operated by three main institutions, each of which does most of its work in Brussels:

The European Parliament sits in Strasbourg, but meets in Brussels for around six, two-day plenary sessions per year. It's the only EU institution to meet and debate in public. During sessions, MEPs – of whom there are currently just over 600 – sit in political blocks and not in national delegations. The Parliament has a President and 14 Vice-Presidents, each of whom is elected for two and a half years by Parliament itself. The President (or a Vice-President) meets with the leaders of the political groups to plan future parliamentary business. Supporting and advising this political edifice is a complex network of committees and these are mostly based in Brussels.

The Council of Ministers consists of the heads of government of each of the member states and the President of the European Commission (see below). They meet regularly in the much-publicized "European Summits". Most Council meetings are not, however, attended by the heads of government, but by a delegated minister. There are complex rules regarding decision-making: some subjects require only a simple majority, others need unanimous support. This political structure is underpinned by scores of committees and working parties made up of both civil servants and political appointees. These committees and working parties are based in Brussels.

The European Commission acts as the EU's executive arm and board of control, managing funds and monitoring all manner of agreements. The 20 Commissioners are political appointees, nominated by their home country, but once they're in office they are responsible to the European Parliament. The president of the Commission is elected for a three-year period of office. Over 10,000 civil servants work for the Commission, whose headquarters are in Brussels.

Belgium. His pioneering efforts certainly transformed the local economy – and his company still exists today – but the loyal workers at his feet stretch the point and so does the statue's inscription – *Au père des ouvriers* ("To the father of the workers").

On the far side of the square, behind the tatty Gare du Quartier Léopold railway station, rises a veritable cliff-face of EU office-block glass. To behold this behemoth at close quarters, follow the signs (to rue Wiertz) through the station. Fortunately, there's a breach in the office block dead ahead, and just beyond it – through the passageway and down the steps – is the **European Union Parliament building** (Map 2, H7), another glass, stone and steel whopper equipped with a curved glass roof that rises to a height of 70m. Completed in 1997, the building contains a large, semicircular assembly room as well as the offices of the President of the Parliament and their General Secretariat. The structure has its admirers, but is known locally as the "*caprice des dieux*". Although it depends on what's happening in the Parliament, you can usually take a free, thirty-minute audio-guided **tour** of the building (Mon–Thurs 10am–3pm, Fri 10am, Sat 10am, 11.30am & 2.30pm) – check opening times at the information centre in the passageway.

MUSÉE WIERTZ

Map 2, H7. Tues–Fri 10am–noon & 1–5pm; alternate weekends 10am–noon & 1–5pm; free. Ⓣ02 648 17 18. Ⓜ Trône.

Behind the European Parliament building at rue Vautier 62 – head right from the entrance, then swing left up the slope – the **Musée Wiertz** is devoted to the works of one of the city's most distinctive, if disagreeable, nineteenth-century artists. Once immensely popular – so much so that Thomas Hardy in *Tess of the d'Urbervilles* could write of "the staring and ghastly attitudes of a Wiertz museum" – Antoine-Joseph Wiertz (1806–65) painted religious and mythological canvases, featuring gory hells and strapping nudes, as well as fearsome scenes of human madness and suffering. The core of the museum is housed in his **studio**, a large, airy space that was built for him by the Belgian state on the understanding that he bequeathed his oeuvre to the nation. Pictures include *The Burnt Child*, *The Thoughts and Visions of a Severed Head* and a small but especially gruesome *Suicide* – not for the squeamish. There are also a number of smaller, quite elegantly painted quasi-erotic pieces featuring coy nudes, and a colossal *Triumph of Christ*, a melodramatic painting of which Wiertz was inordinately proud. Three adjoining **rooms** contain further macabre works, such as *Premature Burial* and (the most appalling of them all) his *Hunger, Folly, Crime*, in which a madwoman is pictured shortly after hacking off her child's leg and throwing it into the cooking pot. Mercifully, there is some more restrained stuff here too, including several portraits and more saucy girls in various states of undress. Wiertz eventually came to believe that he was a better painter than his artistic forebears, Rubens and Michelangelo. Judge for yourself.

MUSÉUM DES SCIENCES NATURELLES

Map 2, H8. Tues–Fri 9.30am–4.45pm, Sat & Sun 10am–6pm; €3.70. Ⓦwww.natural.sciences.net. Ⓜ Trône.

The **Muséum des Sciences Naturelles**, just along the street from the Musée Wiertz, at rue Vautier 29, holds the city's natural history collection. It's a large, sprawling museum divided into fifteen clearly signed areas, each of which focuses on a particular aspect of the natural world, and several of which try to be child-friendly – robotic dinosaurs and suchlike. The dinosaur section is, indeed, the most impressive, featuring **iguanodons** whose skeletons parade across the ground floor. Iguanodons were two-legged herbivores who grazed in herds and a whole group of them was discovered in the coal mines of Hainaut in the late nineteenth century. Other museum highlights include a first-rate collection of tropical shells, an insect room, a section comparing the Arctic and Antarctic, and a whale gallery featuring eighteen skeletons, including the enormous remains of a blue whale.

PARC LÉOPOLD

Map 2, I7.

On rue Vautier, almost opposite the Musée Wiertz, a scruffy back entrance leads into the rear of **Parc Léopold**, a hilly, leafy enclave landscaped around a lake. The park is pleasant enough, but its open spaces were encroached upon years ago when the industrialist Ernest Solvay began constructing the educational and research facilities of a prototype science centre here. The end result is a string of big, old buildings that spreads along the park's western periphery. The most interesting is the first you'll come to, the newly refurbished **Bibliothèque Solvay** (no set opening times), a splendid barrel-vaulted structure with magnificent mahogany panelling. Down below the library and the other buildings, at the bottom of the slope, is the main entrance to Parc Léopold, where a set of stumpy stone gates bear the legend "Jardin royal de zoologie". Léopold wanted the park to be a zoo, but for once his plans went awry.

From the front entrance to the park, it takes a little less than ten minutes to walk east along traffic-choked rue Belliard to the Parc du Cinquantenaire.

PARC LÉOPOLD

LE CINQUANTENAIRE

Map 2, K7.

The wide and largely featureless lawns of the **Parc du Cinquantenaire** slope up towards a gargantuan **triumphal arch** surmounted by a huge and bombastic bronze entitled *Brabant Raising the National Flag*. The arch, along with the two heavyweight stone buildings it connects, comprise **Le Cinquantenaire**, which was placed here by Léopold II for an exhibition to mark the golden jubilee of the Belgian state in 1880. By all accounts the exhibition of all things made in Belgium and its colonies was a great success, and the park continues to host shows and trade fairs of various kinds, while the buildings themselves – which are a brief walk from Métro Merode – contain extensive collections of art and applied art, weapons and cars, displayed in three separate museums.

Musées royaux d'Art et d'Histoire

Tues–Fri 9.30am–5pm, Sat & Sun 10am–5pm; €3.70.

The **Musées royaux d'Art et d'Histoire**, on the south side of the south wing of the complex, is made up of a maddening (and badly labelled) maze of pottery, carvings, furniture, tapestries, glassware and lacework from all over the world. There is almost too much to absorb in even a couple of visits, and your best bet is to pick up the plan and index at reception and select the areas which interest you most. There are enormous galleries of mostly run-of-the-mill Greek, Egyptian and Roman artefacts, complete with mummies of a jackal, crocodile and falcon. Elsewhere, another part of the collection has an assortment of Near and Far Eastern gods, porcelain, jewellery and textiles, and there are pre-Columbian Native American carvings and effigies too.

The **European decorative arts** sections have the most immediacy and these are located on Level 1 (Rooms 45–75) and Level 2 (Rooms 89–105). They are divided into over twenty distinct collections, featuring everything from Delft ceramics, altarpieces, porcelain and silverware through to tapestries, Art Deco and Art Nouveau furnishings. It's all a little bewildering, with little to link one set of artefacts to another, but the sub-section entitled **The Middle Ages to Baroque** (Level 1, Rooms 53–70) is outstanding and comparatively easy to absorb. This sub-section makes a cracking start in **Room 53** with *The Triumph of the Virtues*, a set of eight Brussels' tapestries dating from the middle of the sixteenth century, the heyday of the city's tapestry industry. **Room 56** also contains some fine tapestries, earlier works manufactured in Tournai, in southern Belgium, during the fifteenth century. These are much less languid, depicting scenes of tense and often violent drama as in the *Battle of Roncesvalles*, in which Christians and Moors slug it out in a fearsome, seething battle scene. The museum prides itself on its collection of medieval altarpieces and **Room 57** contains one of the best, the *Passion Altarpiece*, which is animated with a mass of finely detailed wooden reliefs. This altarpiece was carved in Brussels in the 1470s whereas the *Passion Altarpiece* in **Room 61** was made in Antwerp some fifty years later and is, in consequence, even more extravagant, sporting a veritable doll's house of figures.

Room 62 holds several more sixteenth-century Brussels' tapestries, including one depicting *The Legend of Notre Dame of Sablon* (see p.76); **Room 66** has some fine alabasters from Mechelen, just north of Brussels; and **Room 68** boasts a delightful double bed, a fancy, canopied affair produced for a Swiss burgher in the 1680s. Finally, don't leave without poking your nose round the **Art Nouveau** sections, especially **Room 50**,

MUSÉE ROYAUX D'ART ET D'HISTOIRE

where the display cases were designed by Victor Horta for a firm of jewellers, and now accommodate the celebrated *Mysterious Sphinx*, a ceramic bust of archetypal Art Nouveau design. It was the work of Charles van der Stappen in 1897.

Autoworld

Daily: April–Sept 10am–6pm; Oct–March 10am–5pm; €4.95.

Housed in a vast hangar-like building in the south wing of Le Cinquantenaire, **Autoworld** is a chronological stroll through the short history of the automobile, with a huge display of vintage vehicles, beginning with early turn-of-the-century motorized cycles and Model Ts. Perhaps inevitably, European varieties predominate: there are lots of vehicles from Peugeot, Renault and Benz, and homegrown examples, too, including a Minerva from 1925 which once belonged to the Belgian monarch. American makes include early Cadillacs, a Lincoln from 1965 that was also owned by the Belgian royals, and some great gangster-style Oldsmobiles; among the British brands, there's a practically new Rolls-Royce Silver Ghost from 1921, one of the first Austins, and, from the modern era, the short-lived De Lorean sports car. Upstairs is a collection of assorted vehicles that don't fit into the main exhibition. It's a bit of a mishmash, but worth a brief look for some early Porsches and Volvos, classic 1960s Jags and even a tuk-tuk from Thailand. The museum's major drawback is its lack of recent vehicles – few cars date from after the mid-1970s. That said, there's good English labelling, at least on the downstairs exhibits, and a decent museum shop, with lots of automobile-related gear, including a great selection of model cars.

AUTOWORLD

Musée royal de l'Armée et d'Histoire militaire

Tues–Sun 9am–noon & 1–4.30pm; free.

In the north wing of Le Cinquantenaire, on the other side of the triumphal arch from the other two museums, the **Musée Royal de l'Armée et d'Histoire militaire** displays collections tracing the history of the Belgian army from independence to the present day by means of weapons, uniforms and paintings. There are also modest sections dealing with "Belgian" regiments in the Austrian and Napoleonic armies, and, more interestingly, the volunteers who formed the nucleus of the 1830 revolution. Most spectacular are the galleries devoted to armoured cars, artillery and military aircraft, though it's far from required viewing. One surprise is that from the top floor you can get out onto the triumphal arch and enjoy extensive views over the city.

RUE DE LA LOI AND AROUND

The office blocks of the EU are concentrated along and between the two wide boulevards – **rues de la Loi and Belliard** (Map 2, G5–6 to I6–7) – which Léopold II built to connect his Parc du Cinquantenaire with the city centre. It's not an interesting area to visit as the EU remains committed to modernistic, state-of-the-art high-rises – surprising given the difficulties it has had with its best-known construction, the **Centre Berlaymont** (Map 2, I6), a huge office building on rue de la Loi beside Métro Schuman. When it was opened in 1967, the Berlaymont was widely praised for its ground-breaking design, but in 1991 it was abandoned for health and safety reasons – the building was riddled with asbestos and work still continues on its refurbishment.

Although EU buildings dominate this segment of the city, a small stretch of late nineteenth-century urban planning has survived, a ten-minute walk **north of the Centre Berlaymont** past the shops and cafés of rue Archimède. Here, two pleasant and leafy plazas – squares Ambiorix and Marie-Louise – were laid out in the 1870s on what had previously been marshland. By the end of the century, they had formed, along with the short avenue Palmerston which linked them, one of the city's most fashionable suburbs, where the residences of the bourgeoisie included several splendid examples of Art Nouveau. Nowadays, **square Ambiorix** (Map 2, I5) is largely overshadowed by modern apartments, but you shouldn't miss the superb wrought-iron and swirling stone facade of no. 11, one of the city's most ornate Art Nouveau buildings and the one-time home of a painter by the name of Georges de Saint-Cyr. Nearby, on **avenue Palmerston**, the Villa Germaine, at no. 24, exhibits striking patterned tiles and multicoloured bricks and down at the foot of the street are three wonderfully subtle buildings by Victor Horta: there's the austere facade of no. 3, whose white and blue stone trimmings lead round to an exuberant side-entrance; no. 2 is a charming corner house with a delicately carved, fluted stone facade; and no. 4 has a rigorous design softened by arched lintels and mosaics.

For more on Victor Horta, see p.84.

The south side of **square Marie-Louise** is occupied by a series of big old houses whose stone trimmings, balconies, dormer windows and high gables jostle each other. Leading off from the square is **rue du Taciturne** (Map 2, I5–6), whose most interesting building is no. 34, a lavish structure with an elegant facade of intricate window grilles and tiny black columns. It was designed by Paul Saintenoy, who was also responsible for the Old England building (see p.55).

Rue du Taciturne leads back to rue de la Loi, from where it's a couple of minutes' walk west to Métro Maalbeek.

The Outlying Districts

Brussels pushes out in all directions from the city centre and the inner suburbs, its present-day perimeter enclosing no fewer than nineteen *communes* and marked by the ring road, the RO. Within this circle, the city's **outlying districts** are little known by tourists but they do hold a handful of first-rate attractions as well as some lesser sights. All of the places mentioned are within easy reach of the centre by public transport.

The gritty *commune* of **Anderlecht**, to the immediate west of the petit ring, comes top in the order of places to visit, not only because it is home to one of Europe's most famous football teams – Anderlecht (see p.252) – but also as the location of the fascinating Maison d'Erasme, where Erasmus holed up for a few months in 1521, and the Musée Bruxellois de la Gueuze, devoted to the production of the eponymous brew. **Koekelberg**, just to the north, is less well-endowed – it has only the colossal Basilique du Sacré Coeur to offer – while the adjacent *commune* of **Jette** boasts the enjoyable Musée René Magritte, sited in the artist's old home and studio.

Continuing in a clockwise direction, the next *commune* is **Heysel**, where you'll find the Atomium, a hugely enlarged model of a molecule, and the infamous Heysel stadium, scene of the 1985 football crowd disaster. Next door is leafy **Laeken**, whose sprawling parkland is dotted with the accoutrements of the Belgian royals – their greenhouse, statues and monuments, as well as the main palace and a couple of regal follies, a Japanese tower and a Chinese pavilion.

The *communes* lying east and south of the city centre are of only modest appeal. Beyond the ring road to the east is the small town of **Tervuren**, site of the Musée Royal de l'Afrique Centrale, whose assorted African artefacts were first brought together by Léopold II. To the south of the city lies the **Forêt de Soignes**, a great chunk of forest criss-crossed by footpaths and scattered with picnic sites. West of the forest there's the greenery of prosperous **Uccle**, too, not to mention the fine art collection of the Musée David et Alice van Buuren.

The area covered by this chapter is shown on colour maps 1, 2 and 7.

ANDERLECHT

No one could say **Anderlecht** was beautiful, but it has its attractive nooks and crannies, particularly in the vicinity of **Métro St Guidon** on line #1B. Come out of the station, turn left and it's a few metres down the slope to place de la Vaillance, a pleasant triangular plaza flanked by little cafés and the whitestone tower and facade of the church of **Sts Pierre et Guidon** (Map 2, I3; Mon–Fri 9am–noon & 2.30–6pm; free). The facade, which mostly dates from the fifteenth century, is unusually long and slender, its stonework graced by delicate flourishes and a fine set of gargoyles. Inside, the church has a surprisingly low and poorly lit nave, in a corner of which is a vaulted chapel dedicated to **St Guido**, otherwise known as St Guy, a local eleventh-century figure. Of peasant origins, Guido entered the priesthood but he invested all of his church's money in an enterprise that went bust. He was sacked and spent the next seven years as a pilgrim, a sackcloth-and-ashes extravaganza that ultimately earned him a sainthood – as the patron saint of peasants and horses. The chapel contains a breezy Miracle of St Guido by Gaspard de Crayer, a local seventeenth-century artist who made a tidy income from religious paintings in the style of Rubens.

Elsewhere in the church, several of the walls are decorated with late medieval **murals** and although these are incomplete and difficult to make out in the prevailing gloom one or two make interesting viewing. On the north wall of the nave, look out for the brutal martyrdom of St Erasmus – who is having his guts ripped out – and opposite, in the Chapelle de Notre Dame de Grâce, the recently restored scenes from the life of St Guido. The **chancel** is of interest too – it was designed by Jan van Ruysbroeck, who was also responsible for the tower of the Hôtel de Ville (see p.18), and it contains two contrasting tombs. The earlier effigy, a recumbent knight wearing his armour, is conservative and formal, whereas the kneeling figure opposite is dressed in lavish, early Renaissance attire, his helmet placed in front of him as decoration.

Maison d'Erasme

Map 2, J3. Mon, Wed & Thurs, Sat & Sun 10am–noon & 2–5pm; €1.25. Ⓜ St Guidon.
From Sts Pierre et Guidon, it's just a couple of minutes' walk to the **Maison d'Erasme**, at rue du Chapitre 31 –

walk east along the front of the church onto rue d'Aumale and it's on the right behind the distinctive red brick wall. Dating from 1468, the house, with its pretty dormer windows and sturdy symmetrical lines, was built to accommodate important visitors to the church. Easily the most celebrated of these guests was **Desiderius Erasmus** (1466–1536), who lodged here in 1521. By any measure, Erasmus was a remarkable man. Born in Rotterdam, the illegitimate son of a priest, Erasmus was orphaned at the age of thirteen and was then defrauded of his inheritance by his guardians, who forced him to become a monk. He hated monastic life and seized the first opportunity to leave, becoming a student at the University of Paris in 1491. Throughout the rest of his life, Erasmus kept on the move – travelling between the Low Countries, England, Italy and Switzerland – and everywhere he went, his rigorous scholarship, sharp humour and strong moral sense made a tremendous impact. He attacked the abuses and corruptions of the Church, publishing scores of polemical and satirical essays which were read all over Western Europe. He argued that most monks had "no other calling than stupidity, ignorance . . . and the hope of being fed."

These attacks reflected Erasmus' determination to reform the Church from within, both by rationalising its doctrine and rooting out hypocrisy, ignorance and superstition. He employed other methods too, producing translations of the New Testament to make the Scriptures more widely accessible, and co-ordinating the efforts of like-minded Christian humanists. The Church authorities periodically harassed Erasmus, but generally he was tolerated not least for his insistence on the importance of Christian unity. **Luther** was less indulgent, bitterly denouncing Erasmus for "making fun of the faults and miseries of the Church of Christ instead of bewailing them before God." The quarrel between the two reflected a growing schism

MAISON D'ERASME

amongst the reformers that eventually led to the Reformation.

The **house** contains none of Erasmus' actual belongings, but a host of contemporary artefacts, all squeezed into half a dozen, clearly signed rooms. To get the most from a visit you should borrow the (English-language) catalogue from reception. The Cabinet de travail (study) holds original portraits of Erasmus by Holbein, Dürer and others, as well as a mould of his skull, but the best paintings are concentrated in the Salle du Chapitre (chapterhouse), which boasts a charmingly inquisitive *Adoration of the Magi* by Hieronymus Bosch, a gentle *Nativity* from Gerard David, and an hallucinatory *Temptation of St Anthony* by Pieter Huys. Huys was one of many artists to copy Bosch's more frantic work, though it's hard not to feel that the freakish beasts populating his painting are as much to titillate as terrify – and certainly the woman, as a symbol of temptation, is a good deal more voluptuous than anything Bosch would have painted.

Moving on, the Salle Blanche (white room) contains a good sample of first editions of Erasmus' work alongside an intriguing cabinet of altered and amended texts: some show scrawled comments made by irate readers, others are the work of the Inquisition and assorted clerical censors.

Musée Bruxellois de la Gueuze

Mon–Fri 9am–5pm, Sat & Sun 10am–5pm; €3. Ⓜ Gare du Midi.

The **Musée Bruxellois de la Gueuze**, rue Gheude 56, is located ten minutes' walk north of the Métro Gare du Midi via avenue Paul Henri Spaak and rue Limnander; to get there direct from Maison d'Erasme, take tram #56 from Métro St Guidon to Gare du Midi. Founded in 1879, the museum is home to the Cantillon Brewery, the last surviving Gueuze brewery in Brussels. Gueuze is still brewed here according to traditional methods: the beer, made only of wheat, malted barley, hops and water, is allowed to ferment naturally, reacting with natural yeasts peculiar to the Brussels air, and is bottled for two years before it is ready to drink. The museum gives a fairly dry explanation of the brewing process, while in the mustily evocative brewery itself you can see the huge vats the ingredients are boiled in before being placed in large oak barrels where the fermentation process begins. The results can be sampled at the tasting session at the end of your visit.

KOEKELBERG — SACRÉ COEUR

Map 1, C2. Church daily: Easter to Oct 8am–6pm; Nov to Easter 8am–5pm; free. Dome daily: Easter to Oct 9am–5pm; Nov to Easter 10am–4pm; €2.50.

From Métro Simonis – two short subway rides from Métro Gare du Midi – take tram #19 which rattles west round the edge of the lawns leading up to the ugliest church in the capital, the **Basilique du Sacré Coeur**, a huge structure – 140m long with a 90-metre-tall dome – which dominates the *commune* of **Koekelberg**. Begun in 1905 on the orders of Léopold II and still unfinished, the basilica was conceived as a neo-Gothic extravagance in imitation of the basilica to the Sacré Coeur in Montmartre, Paris – a structure which had made the Belgian king green with envy. But the construction costs proved colossal and the plans had to be modified. The result is a vaguely ludicrous amalgamation of the original neo-Gothic design with Art Deco features added in the 1920s. While you're here, it's worth climbing up to the top of the dome for a panoramic view of the city.

JETTE – MUSÉE RENÉ MAGRITTE

Map 1, C1. Wed–Sun 10am–6pm; €6 adults, € 5 under-23s. Garden open daily 10am–6pm, included in price of ticket. Ⓜ Pannenhuis.

To the north, Koekelberg fades into the prosperous suburb of **Jette**, home to the renowned **Musée René Magritte**, rue Esseghem 135, which contains a plethora of the surrealist's paraphernalia, as well as a modest collection of his early paintings and sketches.

Magritte lived with his wife Georgette on the ground floor of this house for 24 years, from 1930 to the mid-1950s, building a studio – which he named Dongo – in the garden. It was here he produced his bread-and-butter work, such as graphics and posters, though he was usually unhappy when working on such mundane projects. His real passions were painted in the dining-room studio, where the only work of art by another artist he possessed – a photo by Man Ray – is still displayed. The house also served as the headquarters for a group of Belgian Surrealists, most of whom were writers like Paul Noge, who met here every Saturday to concoct a number of shocking and subversive books, magazines and images.

The **ground floor** of the museum has been faithfully restored to recreate the artist's studio and living quarters, using mostly original ornaments and furniture, with the remainder carefully replicated from photographs. Hung behind a glass display near the indoor studio is the famous bowler hat which crops up in several of Magritte's paintings. Many features of the house itself also appear in a number of his works: the sash window, for instance, framed the painting entitled *The Human Condition*, while the glass doors to the sitting room and bedroom appeared in *The Invisible World*. Other parts of the interior, including the fireplace and staircase, as well as the lamppost in front of the house, also featured prominently in the painter's works.

The **first and second floors** of the museum are taken

RENÉ MAGRITTE

René Magritte (1898–1967) is easily the most famous of
Belgium's modern artists, his disconcerting, strangely haunting
images a familiar part of popular culture. He was born in a
small town just outside Charleroi, in southern Belgium. In 1915
he entered the Royal Academy of Fine Arts in Brussels and
was a student there until 1920. His appearances were few and
far between at the Academy as he preferred the company of a
group of artists and friends fascinated with the Surrealist
movement of the 1920s. Their antics were supposed to incorporate a serious intent – the undermining of bourgeois convention – but the surviving home movies of Magritte and his
chums fooling around don't appear very revolutionary today.

Initially, Magritte worked in a broadly Cubist manner, but in
1925, influenced by Giorgio de Chirico, he switched over to
Surrealism and almost immediately stumbled upon the themes
and images that would preoccupy him for decades to come.
The hallmarks of his work were striking, incorporating startling
comparisons between the ordinary and the extraordinary, with
the occasional erotic element. Favourite images included men
in bowler hats, metamorphic figures, enormous rocks floating

up by letters, telegrams, telegrams, lithographs, posters and
sketches, all displayed in chronological order. Among them
are two fine posters announcing the world film and fine arts
festivals which took place in Brussels in 1947 and 1949, as
well as Magritte's first painting, a naive landscape which he
produced at the tender age of 12. A number of Magritte's
personal objects are displayed in the **attic**, including the
easel used at the end of his life.

Magritte's mature work can be seen at the
Musées Royaux des Beaux Arts (see p.57)

RENÉ MAGRITTE

in the sky, tubas, fishes with human legs, bilboquets (the cup and ball game), and juxtapositions of night and day – one part of the canvas lit by artificial light, the other basking in full sunlight. He also dabbled in word paintings, mislabelling familiar forms to illustrate (or expose) the arbitrariness of linguistic signs. His canvases were devoid of emotion, deadpan images that were easy to recognise but perplexing because of their setting – perhaps most famously, the man in the suit with a bowler hat and an apple for a face.

He broke with this characteristic style on two occasions, once during the War – in despair over the Nazi occupation – and again in 1948, to revenge long years of neglect by the French artistic establishment. Hundreds had turned up to see Magritte's first Paris exhibition, but they were confronted with crass and crude paintings of childlike simplicity. These so-called Vache paintings created a furore, and Magritte beat a hasty artistic retreat behind a smokescreen of self-justification. These two experiments alienated Magritte from most of the other Surrealists but in the event this was of little consequence as Magritte was picked up and popularised by an American art dealer, Alexander Iolas, who made him very rich and very famous.

HEYSEL

Lying northwest of the city, **Heysel**, a 500-acre estate bequeathed to the authorities by Léopold II in 1909, is best described as a theme park without a theme. Its most famous attraction is the **Atomium** (daily: April–Aug 9am–8pm; Sept–March 10am–6pm; €5.45; Map 7, C2), a curious model of a molecule expanded 165 billion times, which was built for the 1958 World Fair in Brussels. The structure has become something of a symbol of the city. Unfortunately what it contains in its dilapidated interior is an unremarkable science museum, and the main interest is the feeling of disorientation when travelling from sphere to sphere by the escalator.

The Atomium borders a large trade fair area – the **Parc des Expositions**, where they held the World Fairs of 1935 and 1958 – and the **Stade du Roi Baudouin** (Map 7, A2–B2), formerly the infamous Heysel football stadium (see p.253) in which 39 (mainly Italian) supporters were crushed to death when a sector wall collapsed in 1985. International fixtures are held here, and it was the main Belgian venue for Euro 2000, which Belgium hosted jointly with Holland. The **Bruparck** (Map 7, C2–3) leisure complex is also close by, and although its commercial nature is not to everybody's taste, it's a handy place to take the kids. The child-oriented attractions include Océade, a water funpark, a gigantic cinema complex called Kinepolis, and Mini-Europe, where you can see scaled-down models of selected European buildings.

LAEKEN

Bordering Heysel on the east, around 3km north of the city, leafy **Laeken** is home to the royal family, who occupy a large out-of-bounds estate and have colonized the surrounding parkland with their monuments and memorials. From the south, Laeken is best approached on tram #52 or #92. Get off at the Araucaria tram stop, which is just behind the **Pavillon Chinois** (Map 7, H3) and just off avenue des Croix. This elegant and attractive replica of a Chinese pavilion was built here by Léopold II after he had seen one at the World Fair in Paris in 1900. The king intended his creation to be a fancy restaurant, but this never materialised and the pavilion now houses a first-rate collection of Chinese and Japanese porcelain (Tues–Sun 10am–4.30pm; €3, joint ticket with Tour Japonaise

€3.60). Across the road, and reached by a tunnel from beside the pavilion, is the matching **Tour Japonaise** (same times as Pavillon Chinois; €2.25, joint ticket with Pavillon Chinois €3.60), another of Léopold's follies, this time a copy of a Buddhist pagoda with parts made in Paris, Brussels and Yokohama, and now in use as a venue for temporary exhibitions – usually items from the Far East in the Musées Royaux d'Art et d'Histoire (admission extra, see p.57).

Around the corner behind the railings, along the congested avenue du Parc Royal, is the sedate **Château Royal** (no entry; Map 7, H6–I6), the main royal palace. Built in 1790, its most famous occupant was Napoleon, who stayed here on a number of occasions and signed the declaration of war on Russia here in 1812. Before the château is the **Serres Royales**, enormous greenhouses built for Léopold II, covering almost four acres and sheltering a mind-boggling variety of tropical and Mediterranean flora. The only problem is the restricted opening hours – the greenhouses are open to the public only during April and May (times from the tourist office, see p.9) and the queues to see them can be daunting.

Opposite the front of the royal palace, a wide footpath leads up to the fanciful neo-Gothic monument erected in honour of Léopold I, the focal point of the pretty **Parc de Laeken** (Map 7, F5–G5). The park is also home to the Stuyvenbergh Castle, once the residence of Emperor Charles V's architect, Louis Van Bodeghem, although now used to accommodate high-ranking foreign dignitaries.

One kilometre further south along avenue du Parc Royal is **Laeken cemetery**, the last resting place of many influential Belgians including the architect Joseph Poelaert (who designed the Palais de Justice), and artist Jef Dillen, whose tomb is marked by a copy of Rodin's *The Thinker*. Also buried here is Maria Felicia Garcia, the famous Spanish

LAEKEN

soprano better known as Maria Malibran (see p.94).

At the cemetery's entrance stands the neo-Gothic style church of **Notre Dame de Laeken**, which was designed by Joseph Poelaert and built in memory of Belgium's first Queen, Louise-Marie. Many of the country's royals are buried here within the Royal Crypt.

FORÊT DE SOIGNES

Some 5km southeast of the city, the leafy suburbs are left behind for the dense beech woodland of the **Forêt de Soignes**, one of Belgium's most beautiful national parks. Originally a royal domain used for hunting, it once covered over 27,000 acres; sadly, more than a century and a half of development has taken its toll. In the 1820s the king of the Netherlands gave the forest to the "General Society for promoting National Industry" and large parts of the forest were subsequently sold off, before it was turned over to the government in 1843. Further depletion followed when sections of the forest were cleared to make way for country estates, agricultural complexes and country houses, and in 1861 a huge slice was carved off to create a large urban park, now known as Bois de la Cambre (see p.91). Today just over one-third of the original forest remains.

What is left stretches from Bois de la Cambe in its most northerly reaches, 10km southeast to La Hulpe, and from Uccle in the west, some 9km east to the Arboretum Géographique which lies less than a kilometre south of Parc de Tervuren. Despite the piecemeal development, it still remains one of the region's most attractive spaces, and is a popular escape for walkers and cyclists, as well as horse riders, golfers and anglers.

To get there, take tram #44 from Métro Montgomery, a lovely trip, which takes you down the chestnut tree-lined avenue de Tervuren and into the forest, before reaching the terminus at Tervuren town. The forest is also accessible from Bois de la Cambe, although you have to cross the unpleasant chaussée de la Hulpe before you reach the forest's peaceful, winding footpaths.

TERVUREN

Six kilometres southeast of the city, the small town of **Tervuren** (Map 1, G3) is one of the prettiest (and greenest) places in the Brussels region. Bordered in the south by the beautiful Forêt de Soignes, dotted with grand old houses, and surrounded by lush woodland, it is no surprise the area is a popular place to live, particularly with British and Irish Eurocrats, although strangely enough it remains firmly off the tourist track.

Connected to the city by the ten-kilometre-long avenue de Tervuren, a route most easily covered by tram #44 from Métro Montgomery, its centrepiece is the impressive **Musée Royal de l'Afrique Centrale** situated in the Parc de Tervuren – an attractive park of ancient trees, manicured lawns, lakes and flower-beds. Once here, a few other sights also merit a visit, particularly the church of St Jean l'Évangéliste, on Tervuren's main square, and the Arboretum, which lies half a kilometre to the south.

Musée Royal de l'Afrique Centrale

Tues–Fri 10am–5pm, Sat & Sun 10am–6pm; €2.

Without a doubt Tervuren's main attraction is the **Musée Royal de l'Afrique Centrale**. Only a short walk along Leuvensesteeweg from the Tervuren tram terminal, it is housed in a pompous, custom-built pile constructed on the orders of King Léopold II around 1900. Personally presented with the vast Congo River basin by a conference of the European powers in 1885, Léopold became one of the

TERVUREN

country's richest men as a result. His initial attempts to secure control of the area were abetted by the explorer and ex-Confederate soldier Henry Stanley, who went to the Congo on a five-year fact-finding mission in 1879, just a few years after he had famously found the missionary David Livingstone. Even by the standards of the colonial powers, Léopold's regime was too chaotic and too extraordinarily cruel to stomach, and in 1908, one year before the museum opened, the Belgian government took over the territory, installing a marginally more liberal state bureaucracy. The country gained independence as Zaire in 1960, and its subsequent history has been one of the most bloodstained in Africa.

The museum was Léopold's own idea, a blatantly colonialist and racist enterprise which treats the Africans as a naive and primitive people, and the Belgians as their paternalistic benefactors. Nevertheless, the collection is undeniably rich if a little old-fashioned, and sometimes positively eccentric: one room is entirely devoted to examples of different sorts of timber. Unsurprisingly there is little about Léopold's administration or its savagery.

The most interesting displays cover many aspects of Congolese life, from masks, idols and musical instruments to weapons and an impressive array of dope pipes, and there's a superb 22-metre-long dugout canoe. The museum's grounds are also well worth a stroll, with the formal gardens set around a series of geometric lakes, flanked by wanderable woods.

The Town

From the museum, backtrack for a few minutes along Leuvensestweg until you reach Kerkstraat, where you'll find the prettily cobbled town square and a few sights worth investigating. The square itself is dominated by the imposing church of **St Jean l'Évangéliste**, a thirteenth-century Gothic church which contains the tomb of the Duke of Brabant, Antoine of Burgundy, who was killed at Agincourt in 1415. Close by, at Kerkstraat 33, the **Schaakbord art gallery** (Sat & Sun 2pm–5pm; free) exhibits a modest but palatable collection of paintings (mainly landscapes) from the nineteenth-century Tervuren school. The square is also home to *Glacerie Mont Blanc*, where you can pause for one of the delicious home-made ice creams.

From here, continue on Kerkstraat which turns into Pardenmaktstraat, after which take the first left down Pauwstraat, which runs into Arboretumlaan; this will bring you to Tervuren's **Arboretum Géographique**. Originally part of the Forêt de Soignes, this was converted into an arboretum in 1905 on the instructions of Léopold II, and was used to train European officers for the African and Asian colonies. Today it's home to hundreds of different species of trees – redwoods, maples, Scots pines and larches, to name but a few – and is a great place for an afternoon stroll.

UCCLE

South of the city, **Uccle** (Map 1, D3), is connected to Ixelles by avenue Brugmann and is best reached by tram #92, which can be taken at either place Stéphanie, which is a few hundred metres from Métro Louise, or, if you're coming from the centre, rue de la Régence. Originally a string of hamlets, Uccle only became a suburb in the mid-nineteenth century when the aristocracy, attracted by the lush greenery, took up residence here.

Chapelle Notre Dame des Afflingés at rue de Stalle 50, just off avenue Brugmann, is a lovely little church which dates back to the fifteenth century. Its centrepiece is

UCCLE

the beautiful stucco ceiling which was added in the seventeenth century. From here, a ten-minute walk along avenue Vanderaey will bring you to the tranquil **Cimetière Dieweg**, unused for burials since 1958, though a waiver was granted allowing Hergé, the creator of Tintin, to be interred here in 1983.

From the cemetery continue east up Diewag, crossing avenue de Wolvendael, and on the left you'll find the entrance to **Parc de Wolvendael**, a historic 45-acre estate, which is mentioned in documents dating back to 1209. It makes a lovely place for a picnic and afterwards you can view (from outside only) the small white stone castle built in 1753. Close by is the beautiful Louis XV summerhouse, a lovely building which, sadly, has been converted into an unimpressive restaurant.

From the park, head north to avenue de Fré, where on the corner of chemin du Crabbegat you'll find **Le Cornet**, a one-time tavern much-frequented by artists and writers throughout the nineteenth and early twentieth centuries. It is here that famous Belgian writer Charles de Coster sets a delightful scene in his epic novel *Till Ulenspiegel* (1867), where the hero, Till, meets women archers from Uccle.

Musée David et Alice van Buuren

Museum: Mon 2–6pm & Sun 1–6pm; €7.50. Garden: daily 2–6.30pm; €2.50.

Continue heading east along avenue de Fré, taking the first left after square de Fré up rue Roberts Jones until you reach avenue Léo Errera. Here, at no. 41, is the **Musée David et Alice van Buuren**, a superb little gallery housed in a glorious Art Deco building.

The museum was once the home of Dutch banker David van Buuren and his wife Alice, who bought the property in 1928 and between them created a house that would serve as a live-in museum for their collection of furniture, carpets and art. From 1928 to 1970, their home became a global salon of sorts, with great names like Satie, Magritte, Chanel, Ben Gurion and Lalique passing through. During World War II, David (who was Jewish) and Alice were forced to leave their home for five long years, but on their return – much to their surprise – the house and the works of art within it remained totally intact. The house became a museum in 1975, on the death of Alice van Buuren.

The fantastic Art Deco interior was created by a team of Dutch, Belgian and French master craftsmen, with the Cubist carpets the work of Gildding and the majority of the woodwork done by Dominique. The collection of art itself is incredibly diverse, spanning five centuries and including Flemish and Italian masters, as well as twentieth-century artists such as Signac, Van Dongen, Foujita, M. Ernst and G. Desmet. Works by van de Woestyne and James Ensor, still lifes by Fantin-Latour, several landscapes by the six-teenth-century painter Joachim Patenier, and sketches by van Gogh also decorate the walls. One of the highlights is a version of *The Fall of Icarus* by Bruegel the Elder on wood, a work David acquired shortly before his death in 1955.

The picturesque, maze-like **garden** outside, designed by Belgian landscape architect René Pechère, contains many rare species of rose, as well as 300 yew trees.

MUSÉE DAVID ET ALICE VAN BUUREN

Day-trips from Brussels

Almost all of Belgium is within easy striking distance of Brussels, making the list of possible excursions nearly endless. In this chapter we've picked out five of the most appealing destinations, all within an hour's travelling time by bus or train from the capital. To the south of Brussels lies **Waterloo**, site of Napoleon's final defeat at the hands of the Duke of Wellington in 1815. The battlefield has long been a popular tourist attraction and was once part of the "grand tour". Also to the south of Brussels, deep in the wilds of French-speaking Brabant, lies the Cistercian abbey of **Villers-la-Ville**, perhaps the most beautiful medieval ruins in the country and a popular "romantic" spot with newlyweds, who go there to have their photo snapped. The big city and port of **Antwerp**, to the north of the capital, is alluring too: it possesses a flourishing nightlife, medieval churches and first-rate museums, as well as an unrivalled collection of the work of its most celebrated son, Peter Paul Rubens.

Flanders stretches west of Brussels as far as the North Sea. In medieval times, this was the most prosperous and

ACCOMMODATION PRICE CODES

All the hotels detailed in this chapter have been graded according to the following price categories. All the codes are based on the rate for the least expensive double room during high season and do not take into account weekend discounts.

1 €50 and under   2 €50–65   3 €65–80
4 €80–110   5 €110–140   6 €140–170
7 €170 and over

urbanized part of Europe and its merchants grew rich from the profits of the cloth industry. Those heady days are recalled by **Bruges**, one of the most perfectly preserved medieval cities in Europe. It's easily the most popular tourist destination in Belgium, and in summertime the crowds can be oppressive, which makes neighbouring **Ghent**, another fine old Flemish cloth town with superb architecture and excellent art museums, doubly appealing.

WATERLOO

Map 1, F9.

Waterloo, now a run-of-the-mill suburb about 18km south of the centre of Brussels, has a resonance far beyond its size. On June 18, 1815, at this small crossroads town on what was once the main route into Brussels from France, Wellington masterminded the battle which put an end to the imperial ambitions of Napoleon. The battle turned out to have far more significance than even its generals realized, for not only was this the last throw of the dice for the formidable army born of the French Revolution, but it also marked the end of France's prolonged attempts to dominate Europe militarily. Subsequently, however, popular memory refused to villify Napoleon as the aggressor – and not just

WATERLOO

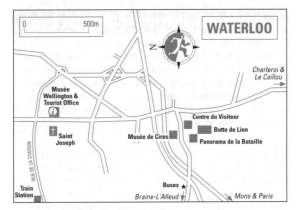

in France, but right across Europe, where the Emperor's bust was a common feature of the nineteenth-century drawing room. In part, this was to do with Napoleon's obvious all-round brilliance, but more crucially, he soon became a symbol of opportunity: in him the emergent middle classes of western Europe saw a common man becoming greater than the crowned heads of Europe, an almost unique event at the time.

The historic importance of Waterloo has not, however, saved the **battlefield** from interference – a motorway cuts right across it – and if you do visit you'll need a lively imagination to picture what happened and where, unless, that is, you're around to see the large-scale re-enactment which takes place every five years in June; the next one is scheduled for 2005. Scattered round the battlefield are several monuments and memorials, the most satisfying of which is the **Butte de Lion**, a huge earth mound that's part viewpoint and part commemoration. The battlefield is 3km north of the centre of Waterloo, where the **Musée Wellington** is the pick of the district's museums.

Arrival and information

There are several ways of getting to Waterloo and its scattering of sights, but the most effective is to make a circular loop by train, bus and train. Trains take you **direct to Waterloo** from any of Brussels' three main stations (Mon–Fri 3 hourly, Sat & Sun 1 hourly; 25min). From Waterloo train station, it's an easy fifteen minutes' **walk** – turn right outside the station building and then first left along rue de la Station – to Waterloo tourist office and the Musée Wellington (see below). After you've finished at the museum, you can take bus #W (every 30min) from across the street – the chaussée de Bruxelles – to the Butte de Lion (see below). The bus stops about 600m from the Butte de Lion – which you can't miss. After visiting the Butte, return to the same bus stop and catch bus #W onto **Braine-l'Alleud train station**, from where there is a fast and frequent service back to Brussels' three main train stations (Mon–Fri every 15min, Sat & Sun every 30min; 15min).

Waterloo **tourist office**, the Syndicat d'Initiative et de Tourisme, is handily located in the centre of town, next door to the Musée Wellington at chaussée de Bruxelles 149 (daily: April–Sept 9.30am–6.30pm; Oct–March 10.30am–5pm; ☏02 354 99 10, ✉tourisme.waterloo @advalvas.be). They provide free town maps and have several booklets recounting the story of the battle. The most competent of them is titled *The Battlefield of Waterloo Step by Step* (€4.40). The tourist office also sells (at €9.50) a combined ticket for all the battle-related attractions, though if you're at all selective (and you'll probably want to be) this won't work out as a saving at all.

WATERLOO

Accommodation and eating

There's no real reason to stay the night, but Waterloo tourist office does have the details of several **hotels**, amongst which the comfortable *Hotel Le 1815* (T02 387 00 60, F02 387 12 92; ❹) has the advantage of being near the Butte de Lion at route du Lion 367. For **food**, *La Brioche* is a pleasant café serving up a good line in sandwiches and cakes; it's located just up from the tourist office at chaussée de Bruxelles 161.

The Musée Wellington

Daily: April–Sept 9.30am–6.30pm; Oct–March 10.30am–5pm; €3.10.
Next door to the tourist office, at chaussée de Bruxelles 147, is the old inn where Wellington slept the night before the battle. The inn has been turned into the enjoyable **Musée Wellington**, whose displays detail the events of the battle with plans and models, alongside the assorted personal effects of Wellington, Alexander Gordon (his aide-de-camp) and Napoleon. In Wellington's bedroom, there are copies of the messages Wellington sent to his commanders during the course of the battle, curiously formal epistles laced with phrases like "Could you be so kind as..." and "We ought to...". There is also the artificial leg of Lord Uxbridge: Uxbridge is reported to have said during the battle, "I say, I've lost my leg," to which Wellington replied, "By God, sir, so you have!". After the battle, Uxbridge's leg was buried here in Waterloo, but it was returned to London when he died to join the rest of his body; in exchange, his artificial leg was donated to the museum. Neither were the bits and pieces of dead soldiers considered sacrosanct: tooth dealers roamed the battlefields of the Napoleonic Wars pulling out teeth which were then stuck on two pieces of board with a spring at the back – primitive dentures known in England as "Waterloos".

The church of Saint Joseph

Across the street from the museum, the church of **Saint Joseph** is a curious affair, its domed, circular **portico** of 1689 built as part of larger chapel on the orders of the Habsburg governor in the hope that it would encourage God to grant King Charles II of Spain an heir (see p.20). It didn't, but the plea to God survives in the Latin inscription on the pediment. The chapel behind the portico was demolished in the nineteenth century and its clumsy replacement is only noteworthy for its assorted **memorial plaques** to the British soldiers who died at Waterloo.

The battlefield – the Butte de Lion

From outside the church of Saint Joseph, pick up bus #W for the quick (4km) journey to the **battlefield** – a landscape of rolling farmland, punctuated by the odd copse and the occasional farmstead with whitewashed walls. A motley assortment of attractions is clustered on the ridge where Wellington once marshalled his army. Among them, the **Centre du Visiteur** (daily: April–Sept 9.30am–6.30pm; Oct 9.30am–5.30pm; Nov–Feb 10.30am–4pm; March 10am–5pm; €4.95) features a dire audiovisual display on the battle. You'd do better to walk up the adjacent hundred-metre-high **Butte de Lion** (same hours; €1). Built by local women with soil from the battlefield, the Butte marks the spot where Holland's Prince William of Orange – one of Wellington's commanders and later King William II of the Netherlands – was wounded. It was only a nick, so goodness knows how high they would have built the mound if William had been seriously wounded, but even as it is, it's a commanding monument, topped by a regal 28-ton lion atop a stout column. From the viewing platform, there's a panoramic view over the battlefield, and a plan identifies which army was where.

WATERLOO

THE BATTLE OF WATERLOO

Napoleon escaped from imprisonment on the island of Elba on February 26, 1815. He landed in Cannes three days later and moved swiftly north, entering Paris on March 20 just as his unpopular replacement – the slothful King Louis XVIII – high-tailed it to Ghent. Thousands of Frenchmen rushed to Napoleon's colours and, with little delay, Napoleon marched northeast to fight the two armies that threatened his future. Both were in Belgium. One, an assortment of British, Dutch and German soldiers, was commanded by the Duke of Wellington, the other was a Prussian army led by Marshal Blücher. At the start of the campaign, Napoleon's army was about 130,000 strong, larger than each of the opposing armies but not big enough to fight them both at the same time. Napoleon's strategy was, therefore, quite straightfor-ward – he had to stop Wellington and Blücher from joining together – and to this end he crossed the Belgian frontier near Charleroi to launch a quick attack. On June 16, the French hit the Prussians hard, forcing them to retreat and giv-ing Napoleon the opportunity he was looking for. Napoleon detached a force of 30,000 soldiers to harry the retreating Prussians, while he concentrated his main army against Wellington, hoping to deliver a knock-out blow. Meanwhile, Wellington had assembled his troops at Waterloo, on the main road to Brussels.

At dawn on Sunday June 18, the two armies faced each other. Wellington had some 68,000 men, about one third of whom were British, and Napoleon around 5,000 more. The armies were deployed just 1500 metres apart with Wellington on the ridge north of – and uphill from – the enemy. It had rained heavily during the night, so Napoleon delayed his first attack to give the ground a chance to dry. At 11.30am, the battle began when the French assaulted the fortified farm of Hougoumont, which was crucial for the defence of Wellington's right. The assault failed and at approximately 1pm there was more bad news for Napoleon when he heard that the Prussians had eluded their pursuers and were closing fast. To gain time he sent 14,000 troops off to impede their progress and at 2pm he tried to regain the initiative by launching a large-scale infantry attack against Wellington's left. This second French attack also proved inconclusive and so at 4pm Napoleon's cavalry charged Wellington's centre, where the British infantry formed into squares and just managed to keep the French at bay – a desperate engagement that cost hundreds of lives. By 5.30pm, the Prussians had begun to reach the battlefield in numbers to the right of the French lines and, at 7.30pm, with the odds getting longer and longer, Napoleon made a final bid to break Wellington's centre, sending in his Imperial Guard. These were the best soldiers Napoleon had, but, slowed down by the mud churned up by their own cavalry, the veterans proved easy targets for the British infantry, and they were beaten back with great loss of life. At 8.15pm, Wellington, who knew victory was within his grasp, rode down the ranks to encourage his soldiers before ordering the large-scale counterattack that proved decisive. The French were vanquished and Napoleon subsequently abdicated, ending his days in exile on St Helena. He died there in 1821.

THE BATTLE OF WATERLOO

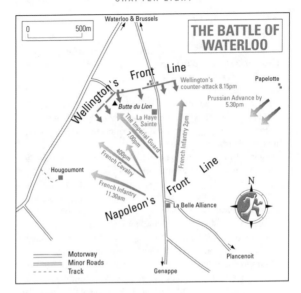

The battlefield's other museums

There are two more modest attractions at the base of the Butte, beginning with an uninspiring wax museum, the **Musée de Cires** (April–Sept daily 9.30am–7pm, till 6pm in October; Nov–March Sat & Sun 10am–5pm; €1.50), which has models of the soldiers of the various regiments along with their commanders. The second is the **Panorama de la Bataille** (daily: April–Sept 9.30am–6.30pm; Oct 9.30am–5.30pm; Nov–Feb 10.30am–4pm; March 10am–5pm; €2.70 or €7.45 with Centre du Visiteur & Butte), where a circular naturalistic painting (1912–13) of the battle, a canvas no less than 110m in circumference, is displayed in a purpose-built, rotunda-like gallery.

Le Caillou

Daily: April–Oct 10am–6.30pm; Nov–March 1–5pm; €1.50.

Napoleon spent the eve of the battle at **Le Caillou**, a two-storey brick farmhouse about 4km south from the Butte de Lion on the chaussée de Bruxelles, and you can visit this, too, though getting there without your own transport is a pain: you're reliant on bus #365A from opposite the Musée Wellington (every two hours). The museum, which includes Napoleon's army cot and death mask, is a memorial to the emperor and his army, but it's hardly riveting stuff.

VILLERS-LA-VILLE

Map 1, F9.

The ruined Cistercian abbey of **Villers-la-Ville** nestles in a lovely wooded dell about 35km south of Brussels, and is altogether one of the most haunting and evocative sights in the whole of Belgium. The first monastic community settled here in 1146, consisting of just one abbot and twelve monks. Subsequently the abbey became a wealthy local landowner, managing a domain of several thousand acres, with numbers that rose to about a hundred monks and three hundred lay brothers. A healthy annual income funded the construction of an extensive monastic complex, most of which was erected in the thirteenth century, though the less austere structures, such as the Abbot's Palace, went up in a second spurt of activity some four hundred years later. In 1794 the monastery was ransacked by French revolutionaries, and later on a railway was ploughed through the grounds. Today the site is wild and overgrown and the buildings are all in varying states of decay, but more than enough survives to pick out Romanesque, Gothic and Renaissance features and to make some kind of mental reconstruction possible.

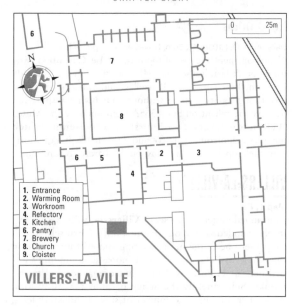

1. Entrance
2. Warming Room
3. Workroom
4. Refectory
5. Kitchen
6. Pantry
7. Brewery
8. Church
9. Cloister

VILLERS-LA-VILLE

Arrival and information

To get to Villers-la-Ville from Brussels, catch a Namur
train and change at Ottignies; the journey takes about an
hour. The abbey is 1.6km from Villers-la-Ville train station,
which consists of just two platforms. Near the platforms –
back towards Ottignies – you'll spot a small, faded sign to
Monticelli; follow the sign and you'll head up and over a
little slope until, after about 100m, you'll reach a T-junction; turn right and follow the road round.

There's nowhere to stay in Villers-la-Ville and there isn't
a tourist office as such, but the abbey sells both an in-depth

English guide to the ruins and (in French) a booklet detailing local walks.

The ruins

From the entrance a path crosses the courtyard in front of the Abbot's Palace to reach the **warming room** (*chauffoir*), the only place in the monastery where a fire would have been kept going all winter, and which still has its original chimney. The fire provided a little heat to the adjacent rooms: on one side the monks' **workroom** (*salle des moines*), used for reading and studying; on the other the large Romanesque-Gothic **refectory** (*réfectoire*), lit by ribbed twin windows topped with chunky rose windows. Next door is the **kitchen** (*cuisine*), which contains a few remnants of the drainage system, which once piped waste to the river, and of a central hearth, whose chimney helped air the room. Just behind this lies the **pantry** (*salle des convers*), where a segment of the original vaulting has survived, supported by a single column, and beyond, on the northwestern edge of the complex, is the **brewery** (*brasserie*), one of the biggest and oldest buildings in the abbey.

Abbey opening times: April–Oct daily 10am–6pm;
Nov–March daily except Tues 10am–5pm; €3.70.
For details of special events and to confirm opening
times, which sometimes change, call ☎071/87 95 55.

The most spectacular building, however, is the **church** (*église*), which fills out the north corner of the complex. It has the dimensions of a cathedral, with pure lines and elegant proportions, and displays the change from Romanesque to Gothic – the transept and choir are the first known examples of Gothic in the Brabantine area. It's 90m long and 40m wide with a majestic nave whose roof was

VILLERS-LA-VILLE

supported on strong cylindrical columns. An unusual feature is the series of bull's-eye windows which light the transepts. Of the original twelfth-century **cloister** (*cloître*) adjoining the church, a pair of twin windows is pretty much all that remains, though it is flanked by a two-storey section of the old monks' quarters. Around the edge of the cloister are tombstones and the solitary sarcophagus of the Crusader Gobert d'Aspremont.

ANTWERP

Map 1, F7.

Belgium's second city, **Antwerp**, fans out from the east bank of the Scheldt about 50km north of Brussels. It's not an especially handsome city – the terrain is too flat and industry too prevalent for that – but it does possess a vibrant and intriguing centre sprinkled with some lovely old churches and distinguished museums, reminders of its auspicious past as the centre of a large trading empire. In particular, there is the enormous legacy of **Rubens**, whose works adorn Antwerp's galleries and churches. The French laid the foundations of the city's present economic success during the Napoleonic occupation and Antwerp is now one of Europe's premier ports. It has also become the focus of the international diamond industry and, in the last few years, of the more nationalistic amongst the Flemish, who regard the city as their capital in preference to Brussels. It also lays claim to the title of fashion capital of Belgium, with many a young talent designing here.

Arrival and information

Most international and domestic trains stop at **Centraal Station**, on the edge of the city centre about 2km east of the main square – the Grote Markt (Map p.139, C2) – and con-

ANTWERP

A B C D E F G

① ② ③ ④ ⑤ ⑥ ⑦ ⑧ ⑨

Nationaal Scheepvaartmuseum

Vleehuis

Sint Pauluskerk

N

Stadhuis

Rockoxhuis Museum

St Carolus Borromeus

OLV Kathedraal

St Jacobskerk

Groenplaats

Beurs

Museum Plantin-Moretus

SCHOENMARKT

Meir MEIR Centraal Station

Rubenshuis

Wapper

Bourla

Mayer van den Bergh Museum

Maagdenhuis

Museum voor Schone Kunsten

M Tram/Metro Stations

0   200m

nected with the centre by **tram** (#2 or #15 to Groenplaats) from the adjacent underground station. A standard single fare **ticket** on any part of the city's transport system costs €1, a ten-strip *Rittenkaart* €7.45, a 24-hour unlimited travel tourist card €2.85. Tickets are available at underground stations, authorized newsagents, and from bus and tram drivers.

Antwerp's **tourist office** is at Grote Markt 15 (Map p.139, C2; Mon–Sat 9am–6pm, Sun 9am–5pm; ☏03 232 01 03, ⊕www.visitantwerpen.be). They have a comprehensive range of information on the city and its sights, including maps and a number of specialist leaflets – principally those detailing where to see the works of Rubens and his contemporary, Jacob Jordaens. They will also make **hotel reservations** on your behalf at no charge: the modest deposit you pay is subtracted from your final hotel bill.

The City

The centre of Antwerp is **Grote Markt**, at the heart of which stands the **Brabo fountain**, a haphazard pile of rocks surmounted by a bronze of Silvius Brabo, the city's first hero, depicted flinging the hand of the giant Antigonus – who terrorized passing ships – into the Scheldt. The north side of Grote Markt is lined with daintily restored sixteenth-century **guildhouses**, though also overshadowed by the **Stadhuis** (tours Mon, Tues, Thurs & Fri 11am, 2pm & 3pm, Sat 2pm & 3pm; €0.75) completed in 1566, and one of the most important buildings of the Northern Renaissance. Among rooms you can visit are the Leys Room, named after Baron Hendrik Leys, who painted the frescoes in the 1860s, and the Wedding Room, which has a chimneypiece decorated with two caryatids carved by Cornelius Floris, architect of the building.

Southeast of Grote Markt, the **Onze Lieve Vrouwe Cathedral** (Map p.139, D3; Mon–Fri 10am–5pm, Sat

●

10am–3pm, Sun 1–4pm; €2) is one of the finest Gothic churches in Belgium, mostly the work of Jan and Pieter Appelmans in the middle of the fifteenth century. Inside, the seven-aisled nave is breathtaking, if only because of its sense of space, an impression that's reinforced by the bright, light stonework revealed by a recent refurbishment. Four early paintings by **Rubens** are displayed here, the most beautiful of which is the *Descent from the Cross*, a triptych painted after the artist's return from Italy that displays an uncharacteristically restrained realism, derived from Caravaggio.

It takes about five minutes to walk southwest from the cathedral to the **Plantin-Moretus Museum**, on Vrijdagmarkt (Map p.139, D4; Tues–Sun 10am–5pm; €3.70), which occupies the grand old mansion of Rubens' father-in-law, the printer Christopher Plantin. One of Antwerp's most interesting museums, it provides a marvellous insight into how Plantin and his family conducted their business.

From here it's a brief stroll to the riverfront **Nationaal Scheepvaartmuseum** (Map p.139, B2; National Maritime Museum; Tues–Sun 10am–5pm; €3.70), which is located at the end of Suikerrui and inhabits the Steen, the remaining gatehouse of what was once an impressive medieval fortress. Inside, the cramped rooms feature exhibits on inland navigation, shipbuilding and waterfront life, while the open-air section has a long line of tugs and barges under a rickety corrugated roof. Crossing Jordaenskaai, it's a short walk east to the impressively gabled **Vleeshuis** (Map p.139, C2; Tues–Sun 10am–5pm; €2.50), built for the guild of butchers in 1503 and now used to display a substantial but incoherent collection of applied arts – everything from antique musical instruments to medieval woodcarvings.

Just north of here, along Vleeshouwersstraat, **St Pauluskerk** (Map p.139, D1; May–Sept daily 2–5pm; free)

ANTWERP

is a dignified late Gothic church built for the Dominicans in the early sixteenth century. Inside, the airy and elegant nave is decorated by a series of paintings depicting the "Fifteen Mysteries of the Rosary", including Rubens' exquisite *Scourging at the Pillar* of 1617.

East to the Rubenshuis and St Jacobskerk

It's a ten-minute walk east from the cathedral to the **Rubenshuis** at Wapper 9 (Map p.139, G4; Tues–Sun 10am–5pm; €4.95), the former home and studio of the artist, now restored as a (very popular) museum. Unfortunately, there are only one or two of his less distinguished paintings here, but the restoration of the rooms is convincing. Rubens died in 1640 and was buried in **St Jacobskerk**, north of here at Lange Nieuwstraat 73 (Map p.139, G3; April–Oct Mon–Sat 2–5pm; €1.75). Rubens and his immediate family are buried in the chapel behind the high altar, where in one of his last works, *Our Lady Surrounded by Saints*, he painted himself as St George, his two wives as Martha and Mary, and his father as St Jerome.

South of the centre

About ten minutes' walk southeast of Groenplaats, the **Mayer van den Bergh Museum**, at Lange Gasthuisstraat 19 (Map p.139, E5; Tues–Sun 10am–5pm; €3.70), contains delightful examples of the applied arts, from tapestries to ceramics, silverware, illuminated manuscripts and furniture, in a crowded reconstruction of a sixteenth-century town house. There are also some excellent paintings, including works by Quentin Matsys and Jan Mostaert, but the museum's most celebrated work is **Bruegel's** *Dulle Griet* or "Mad Meg", a misogynistic allegory in which a woman, loaded down with possessions, stalks the gates of Hell.

ANTWERP

Further south still (tram #8 from Groenplaats), the **Museum voor Schone Kunsten** (Fine Art Museum; Map p.139, A9; Tues–Sun 10am–5pm; €3.70) has one of the country's better fine art collections. Its early Flemish section features paintings by Jan van Eyck, Memling, Rogier van der Weyden and Quentin Matsys. Rubens has two large rooms to himself, in which one very large canvas stands out: the *Adoration of the Magi*, a beautifully human work apparently completed in a fortnight. The museum also displays a comprehensive collection of modern Belgian art with Paul Delvaux and James Ensor being particularly well represented.

Accommodation

Cammerpoorte
Map p.139, C5.
Nationalestraat 38 ⓣ03 231 97 36, ⓕ03 226 29 68.
A budget, two-star hotel with forty, plain modern rooms, but it is – and this is something of a rarity in Antwerp – close to the Grote Markt. ❹

Rubens Grote Markt
Map p.139, D2. Oude Beurs 29 ⓣ03 226 95 82, ⓕ03 225 19 40, ⓔhotel.rubens@glo.be.
One of the best hotels in town, the Rubens is a lovely little place with tastefully furnished, modern rooms in an old building just a couple

of minutes' walk north of the Grote Markt. ❺

Scoutel Jeugdverblifcentrum
Stoomstraat 3 ⓣ03 226 46 06, ⓕ03 232 63 92, ⓦwww.vvksm.be.
A spick and span hostel-cum-hotel offering frugal but perfectly adequate doubles and triples with breakfast. It's situated about 5min walk from Centraal Station. There's no curfew (guests have their own keys), but be sure to check in before 6pm when reception closes. Reservations are advised, €23.30 for a single room. €35 for a double.

ANTWERP

Eating

Hippodroom

Map p.139, A8. Léopold de Waelplaats 10 ☏03 248 52 52.

Smooth and polished restaurant offering a wide range of Flemish dishes from around €18 per main course.

De Matelote

Map p.139, B3. Haarstraat 9 ☏03 231 3207.

Modish, pastel-painted fish restaurant off Grote Pieter Potstraat, near the Grote Markt. Serves delicious – if expensive – food.

Pizzeria Antonio

Map p.139, C2. Grote Markt 6. Tasty and swiftly served pasta and pizza.

De Stoemppot

Map p.139, B3. Vlasmarkt 12 ☏03 231 36 86.

Stoemp is a traditional Flemish dish consisting of puréed meat and vegetables – and this is the best place to eat it. Closed Wed.

Drinking

Café 't Katshuis

Map p.139, B3. Grote Pieter Potstraat 18.

Handily situated off Suikerrui, this small and darkly lit bar is an enjoyable and popular place for a drink. One of several fashionable bars on this street.

Café de Muze

Map p.139, D3. Melkmarkt 15. With its bare brick walls and retro film posters, this laid-back and central little place is a busy spot. Occasional live music – mainly jazz and blues.

Het Elfde Gebod

Map p.139, D3. Torfbrug 10. On one of the tiny squares fronting the north side of the cathedral, this bar is something of a tourist trap, but it's still worth visiting for the kitsch religious statues which cram the interior; avoid the food.

ANTWERP

De Vagant

Map p.139, C3–4.
Reyndersstraat 21.
A specialist gin bar serving an extravagant range of Belgian and Dutch jenevers in spruce, modern surroundings.

De Volle Maan

Map p.139, C3. Oude Koornmarkt 7.
Lively, likeable and offbeat bar close to the Grote Markt.

GHENT

Map 1, D8.

Just 56km from Brussels, the Flemish city of **Ghent** has a long and illustrious history. It was the seat of the counts of Flanders and the largest town in western Europe during the thirteenth and fourteenth centuries, its prosperity built upon the cloth trade. It's now Belgium's third largest city, a thriving, busy place with an amiable atmosphere and an outstanding assortment of medieval buildings, the pick of which is St Baafskathedraal, home to a remarkable painting, the *Adoration of the Mystic Lamb* by Jan van Eyck. Ghent is less immediately picturesque than Bruges, but this is much to its advantage in so far as it's never overrun by tourists.

Arrival and information

Trains from Brussels pull in at **Ghent St Pieters station**, some 2km south of the city centre; **trams** #1, #10 and #13 run to the central square, Korenmarkt (Map p.147, E4). A couple of minutes' walk east of the Korenmarkt, the **tourist office** (Map p.147, E4; daily: April–Oct 9.30am–6.30pm; Nov–March 9.30am–4.30pm; ℡09 266 52 32, ⓦwww.gent.be) is located in the old Cloth Hall, the Lakenhalle, on the Botermarkt. They provide a comprehensive range of information, including a full list of **accommodation**, which they will book on your behalf

GHENT

for a refundable deposit. The best way to see the sights is on foot, but Ghent is a large city and you may find you have to use a **tram or bus** at some point. A day pass (*dagpas*), valid for one day's unlimited travel on the public transport system, costs just €2.85; a standard single fare costs €1. Tickets can be bought direct from the driver.

The City

The best place to start an exploration of Ghent's city centre is the mainly Gothic **St Baafskathedraal**, squeezed into the eastern corner of St Baafsplein (Map p.147, F5; daily: April–Oct 8.30am–6pm, Nov–March 8.30am–5pm; free). St Baaf's mighty nave, begun in the fifteenth century, is supported by tall, slender columns that give the whole interior a cheerful sense of lightness, though the seventeenth-century marble screens spoil the effect by darkening the choir. In a small side chapel (April–Oct Mon–Sat 9.30am–5pm, Sun 1–5pm; Nov–March Mon–Sat 10.30am–4pm, Sun 2–5pm; €2.50) to the left of the entrance is Ghent's greatest treasure, **Jan van Eyck**'s *Adoration of the Mystic Lamb*. The altarpiece's cover screens display a beautiful Annunciation scene with the archangel Gabriel's wings reaching up to the timbered ceiling of a Flemish house, while below, the donor and his wife kneel piously alongside statues of the saints. The restrained exterior painting, however, is merely a foretaste of what's within – a striking, visionary work of art that would have been revealed only when the shutters were opened on Sundays and feast days. On the upper level sit God the Father, the Virgin and John the Baptist in gleaming clarity; to the right are musician-angels and a nude, pregnant Eve; and on the left is Adam plus a group of singing angels who strain to read their music. In the lower panel the Lamb, the symbol of Christ's sacrifice, is approached by bishops, saintly virgins

GHENT

0 — 150 m

N

Dampoort Train Station (100 m)

St Baafsabdij

Leie

Museum voor Volkskunde

Mad Meg

Toreken

Stadhuis

Lakenhalle & belfry

Schouwburg

St-Baafskathedraal

St Niklaaskerk

Geldmunt

Gravensteen

Vismarkt

Museum voor Sierkunst

City Boat Trips

St Michielsbrug

Leie

Museum A.V. Haeghen

Ketelbrug

St Pieters Train Station

Bus Station & Museum voor Schone Kunsten

Rabotstraat

Holstraat

Oudehoutlei

Coupure Rechts

Coupure

Coupure Links

Wispelbergstraat

and Old and New Testament figures in a heavenly paradise seen as a sort of idealized Low Countries. It's a fabulous painting, after which the rest of the cathedral is a something of an anticlimax, though you could drop by the **crypt** (same hours and ticket), which preserves features of the earlier Romanesque church. Full of religious bric-à-brac, the crypt displays several fine reliquaries and a superb medieval triptych, Justus van Gent's *Crucifixion of Christ*.

Just west of St Baaf's, the fifteenth-century **Lakenhalle** (Cloth Hall) is little more than an empty shell, whose first-floor entrance leads to the adjoining **Belfry** (tours daily; €2.50), a much-amended edifice from the fourteenth century. A glass-sided lift climbs up to the roof and affords excellent views over the centre. The facade niches of the **Stadhuis** across the street (Map p.147, E4; tours May–Oct Mon–Thurs; €2.50) were intended to hold a set of statues, but the money didn't last. The present carvings, representing the powerful and famous in characteristic poses – including the architect Rombout Keldermans rubbing his chin and studying his plans for the building – were inserted only at the end of the nineteenth century. The interior is hardly riveting, but the tour does include a visit to the handsome Pacificatiezaal hall. The last of this central cluster of buildings is **St Niklaaskerk** (Map p.147, E4; Tues–Sun 10am–5pm, Mon 2–5pm; free), an architectural hybrid dating from the thirteenth century. Inside, the giant-sized Baroque high altar is no mean piece, with its mammoth representation of God the Father glowering down its back surrounded by a flock of cherubic angels.

Dodging the trams of the **Korenmarkt** and heading west, you pass the main post office building, close to which the **St Michielsbrug** bridge (Map p.147, D4) offers fine views of the towers and turrets that pierce the skyline. The bridge also overlooks the city's oldest harbour, the **Tussen**

Bruggen (Between the Bridges), from whose quays **boats** leave for trips around the neighbouring canals from March to early November (daily every 15 minutes; 10am–7pm; €4.20). The **Korenlei**, the western side of the harbour, is home to a series of solid, high-gabled merchants' houses dating from the eighteenth century, while the **Graslei**, opposite, accommodates the charming, late medieval guild-houses of the town's boatmen and grainweighers.

A couple of minutes' walk north of Graslei, **Het Gravensteen** (Map p.147, D2; daily: April–Sept 9am–6pm; Oct–March 9am–5pm; €4.95), the Castle of the Counts of Flanders, looks sinister enough to have been lifted from a Bosch painting. Cold and cruel, its dark walls and unyielding turrets were first raised in 1180 as much to intimidate the town's unruly citizens as to protect them. Beside the main courtyard stand the castle's two main buildings, the **keep** on the right and to the left the **count's residence**, riddled with narrow, interconnected staircases set within the thickness of the walls. A self-guided tour takes you through the labyrinth.

East of the castle are the part-gentrified, medieval cobbled lanes and alleys of the **Patershol** (Map p.147, E1–2), home to the most fashionable of the city's restaurants and the **Museum voor Volkskunde**, Kraanlei 65 (Tues–Sun 10am–12.30pm & 1.30–5pm; €2.50), a series of restored almshouses where a chain of period rooms depicts local life and work in the eighteenth and nineteenth centuries.

South of the city centre, Ghent's main shopping street, **Veldstraat** (Map p.147, E5–D7), heads off towards the **Museum voor Schone Kunsten**, Nicolaas de Liemaeckereplein 3 (Tues–Sun 9.30am–5pm; €2.50), which holds the city's most extensive fine art collection. On display is a first-rate sample of Flemish painting including works by Bosch, Pieter Bruegel the Younger, Jordaens, van Dyck and Frans Hals.

GHENT

Accommodation

Erasmus

Map p.147, C4. Poel 25 ⓣ09 224 21 95, ⒻO9 233 42 41, ⒺHotel.erasmus@proximedia.be. Ghent's most distinctive hotel, located in an old and commodious townhouse a few yards away from the Korenlei. A small, family-run hotel, with excellent breakfasts. ❹

Gravensteen

Map p.147, D3. Jan Breydelstraat 35 ⓣ09 225 11 50, ⒻO9 225 18 50, ⓌWww.gravensteen.be.

A small hotel in an attractively restored nineteenth-century mansion. Some of the rooms are small, but they're snug enough and several overlook the castle. ❸

Youth Hostel,

Map p.147, D2. Jeugdherberg De Draecke, St Widostraat 11 ⓣ09 233 70 50, ⒻO9 233 80 01, ⒺYouthhostel.gent@skynet.be. Excellent, well-equipped and smart youth hostel in the city centre, 5min north of the Korenmarkt. Breakfast is included. €13 per person.

Eating

Patisserie Bloch

Map p.147, E5. Veldstraat 60, on the corner with Volderstraat. One of the best and busiest tearooms in town, serving delicious cakes, coffee and snacks. Open Mon–Sat 10am–5pm, closed Sun.

Malatesta

Map p.147, D3. Hooiaard 2. A fashionable and inexpensive café-restaurant

offering tasty pizza and pasta dishes. Open Mon–Fri 11am–11pm.

't Marmietje

Map p.147, D3. Drabstraat 30. On a side street off the Korenmarkt, an intimate restaurant serving excellent traditional Flemish cuisine at reasonable prices. Closed Sun & Mon.

Pascalino

Map p.147, F4. Botermarkt 11. A straightforward, inexpensive café offering snacks and filling meals of sound quality until 9.30pm every night. Handy location, opposite the Stadhuis.

Drinking

't Dreupelkot

Map p.147, E3. Groentenmarkt 10. A cosy bar specializing in jenever, of which it stocks over 100 brands, all kept at icy temperatures.

De Tap en de Tepel

Map p.147, D2. Gewad 7. A dark bar with an open fire and a clutter of antique furnishings. Wine is the main deal, served with a wide selection of cheeses. Closed Sun–Tues & most of Aug.

Het Waterhuis aan de Bierkant

Map p.147, E3. Groentenmarkt 9. Over 100 types of beer in a pleasant bar near the castle. An informative beer menu makes choosing easy.

BRUGES

Map 1, B7.

Bruges is one of the most beautifully preserved medieval cities in western Europe and it draws visitors in their thousands. Inevitably, the crowds tend to overwhelm the town's charms, but as a day-trip destination from Brussels – it's just an hour away by train – Bruges is hard to resist: its museums hold some of the country's finest collections of Flemish art and its intimate streets, woven around a pattern of narrow canals, live up to even the most inflated tourist hype.

Bruges came to prominence in the thirteenth century when it shared effective control of the **cloth trade** with its great rival, Ghent, turning high-quality English wool into

BRUGES

clothing that was exported all over the known world. It was an immensely profitable business, and it made the city a centre of international trade. By the end of the fifteenth century, however, Bruges was in decline, principally because the Zwin River – the city's vital link to the North Sea – was silting up. By the 1530s, the town's sea trade had collapsed completely, and Bruges simply withered away. Frozen in time, Bruges escaped damage in both World Wars to emerge the perfect tourist attraction.

Arrival and information

Bruges **train station** adjoins the **bus station**, about 2km southwest of the town centre. Beside the station, there's an **information and hotel booking office** (Mon–Sat 10.30am–6pm; no phone), which will make reservations in return for a deposit which is deducted from your final hotel bill.

If the twenty-minute walk into the centre doesn't appeal, you could get a local bus from outside the train station: most head off either to the Biekorf or the neighbouring Markt, bang in the centre of town; the single fare costs €1. The **tourist office** (April–Sept Mon–Fri 9.30am–6.30pm, Sat & Sun 10am–noon & 2–6.30pm; Oct–March Mon–Fri 9.30am–5pm, Sat & Sun 9.30am–1pm & 2–5.30pm; ☎050 44 86 86, ℻050 44 86 00, ⓦwww.brugge.be) is situated just footsteps away from the Markt, at Burg 11 (Map p.154, E5). They also operate an accommodation booking service, issue free maps and display bus and train timetables.

Half-hour boat trips around the central canals leave every few minutes from a number of jetties south of the Burg; March–Nov daily 10am–6pm; €4.70. For the rest of the year there's a sporadic service on the weekend only.

BRUGES

A B C D E F G

1 2 3 4 5 6 7 8 9

BIDDERSTRAAT LANGE RAAMSTRAAT · BALIE · LANGEREI · POTTERIEREI · BLIJKE INDERSTR · E ZORGHESTRAAT

H LOSSCHAERT · ST JORISSTRAAT · JAN MIRAELSTRAAT · SCHRIJVERSSTR · HOEDENMAKERSSTRAAT · W OSTELO · OSTERSTRAAT

JAN BONINSTRAAT · AUGUSTIJNENREI · SPANJAARDSTRAAT · GOUDEN-HANDSTRAAT · CARMERSSTRAAT · JERUZALEMSTR

E Z E L S T R A A T · ZAKSKE · GRAUW · WERKERSSTRAAT · AGTERSTRAAT · GOUDEN HANDREI · OOSTERL.-PLEIN · WOENSDAG-MARKT · GENTHOF · BLEKERSSTR · ST ANNAREI

ST JAKOBS PLEIN · ST JAKOBSSTRAAT · ACADEMIESTR · JAN VAN EYCKPLEIN · SPIEGELREI · ENGELSE STR · SPINOLARE · KONINGSTR · KONINGSTR · V TEYE STR · DA · MINNEW PLEIN

LEEUWSTRAAT · ST JAKOBSTRAAT · KUIPERSSTRAAT · VLAMINGSTRAAT · KRAAN PLEIN · ST JAN PLEIN · ST JANSSTRAAT · GROOT BOUDEWIJNSTR · ST ANNAREI

MOERSTRAAT · EIER-MARKT · KRIOC · LANIERSTR · ST WALLBURGASTR · TWIJNSTRAAT · HOOGSTRAAT · ROUMERSDK · PREDIKHERENSTR · GROENEREI

MUNT PLEIN · GELDMUNTSTRAAT · PHILIPSTOCKSTRAAT · BURGSTRAAT · MARKT · **Hallen and Belfry** · BREIDELSTRAAT · **Stadhuis** · BURG · STENDMEMERSDK · BRAAMBERGSTR · WAALSE

ONTVANGERSSTRAAT · ST AMANDSSTRAAT · GARRE · **Heilig Bloed Basiliek** · HUIDENVET · TERSPLEIN · ROZENHOEDK · WALSE · KON · PARK · Astridpark

HELMSTRAAT · KORTSTRAAT · STEENSTRAAT · HALLESTRAAT · WOLLESTRAAT · OUDE BURG · DIJVER · EEKHOUTSTRAAT · GROENINGE · STATIONSTRAAT

VELD STRAAT · NOORDZANDSTRAAT · KEMEL STRAAT · SIMON STEVIN PLEIN · NIEUWSTRAAT · **Arentshuis Museum** · **Groeninge Museum**

MATHIASSTRAAT · ZILVERSTRAAT · **St Salvators-kathedraal** · ST STEENSTRAAT · MARIASTRAAT · GUIDO GEZELLE-PLEIN · **Gruuthuse Museum** · EEKHOUTSTRAAT

Train & Bus Stations · ZUIDZANDSTRAAT · ST SALVATORS · GOEZEPUTSTR · **Onze Lieve Vrouwekerk** · GROENINGE

KTE VULDERSSTRAAT · KL.H. GEESTSTRAAT · ST JAN IN DE MEERS · **St Jans Hospitaal** · **Memling Museum** · ASTANJEBOOMSTR · GENTWEG

ABDIJBEKE DIENSTSTR · ST OBRECHTSSTR · WESTMEERS · BAKKERSSTR · NIEUWE WERKHUISSTR

ZONNEKEMEERS · WAL PLEIN · *Begijnhof & Minnewater* · OUDE GENTWEG · GENTWEG

N

0 — 100 m

The City

The older sections of Bruges fan out from two central squares, Markt and Burg. **Markt** (Map p.154, C5), edged on three sides by nineteenth-century gabled buildings, is the larger of the two, an impressive open space, on the south side of which rises the octagonal **Belfry** (Map p.154, D5; daily 9.30am–5pm; €2.50), which was built in the thirteenth century when the town was at its richest. Inside, the staircase passes the room where the town charters were locked for safekeeping, and an eighteenth-century carillon, before emerging onto the roof. At the foot of the belfry, the quadrangular **Hallen** is a much-restored edifice dating from the thirteenth century, its arcaded galleries built to facilitate the cloth trade.

The Burg
Map p.154, E5.

From the Markt, Breidelstraat leads through to the **Burg**, whose southern half is fringed by the city's finest group of buildings. One of the best of these is the **Heilig Bloed Basiliek** (Basilica of the Holy Blood; daily: April–Sept 9.30am–noon & 2–6pm; Oct–March Mon, Tues & Thurs–Sun 10am–noon & 2–4pm, Wed 10am–noon; free) on the right, named after the holy relic that found its way here in 1150. The basilica divides into two parts. Tucked away in the corner, the **lower chapel** is a shadowy, crypt-like affair, originally built at the beginning of the twelfth century to shelter another relic, that of St Basil, one of the great figures of the early Greek Church. Next door, approached up a wide staircase, the **upper chapel** was built at the same time, but it's impossible to make out the original structure behind the excessive nineteenth-century decoration. The building may be disappointing, but the rock crystal phial that contains the Holy Blood is stored within a magnificent silver **tabernacle**, the gift of Albert and Isabella of Spain in 1611. One of the holiest relics in medieval Europe, the phial supposedly contains a few drops of blood and water washed from the body of Christ by Joseph of Arimathea. The Holy Blood is still venerated in the upper chapel on Fridays at 6pm, and reverence for it remains strong, not least on Ascension Day when it is carried through the town in a colourful but solemn procession.

To the left of the basilica, the **Stadhuis** has a beautiful, turreted sandstone facade from 1376, though its statues of the counts and countesses of Flanders are much more recent. Inside, the magnificent Gothic Hall (daily 9.30am–5pm; €3.75) boasts fancy vault-keys depicting New Testament scenes and romantic paintings commissioned in 1895 to illustrate the history of the town.

The Groeninge Museum
Map p.154, E7.

Heading south from the Burg, through the archway next to the Stadhuis, you come to Blinde Ezelstraat ("Blind Donkey Street"), which leads south across the canal to the huddle of picturesque houses crimping the **Huidenvettersplein**, the old tanners' quarter that now holds some of the busiest drinking and eating places in town. Nearby, the Dijver follows the canal to the **Groeninge Museum**, Dijver 12 (April–Sept daily 9.30am–5pm, Oct–March Wed–Mon 9.30am–5pm; €6.20), which boasts an outstanding collection of early Flemish paintings. Among them are several works by Jan van Eyck, who lived and worked in Bruges from 1430 until his death eleven years later. Featured also are works by Rogier van der Weyden, Hans Memling, Gerard David and Hieronymus Bosch, whose paintings are crammed with mysterious beasts, microscopic mutants and scenes of awful cruelty. The museum's selection of late sixteenth- and

BRUGES

seventeenth-century paintings is far more modest, though highlights here include canvases by Pieter Bruegel the Younger and Pieter Pourbus. The modern paintings are distinguished by the spooky surrealism of Paul Delvaux and by Constant Permeke, noted for his dark and earthy representations of Belgian peasant life.

The rest of the city centre

Also on the Dijver, in a big old mansion just west of the Groeninge Museum, is the **Arentshuis Museum** (Map p.154, D7; April–Sept daily 9.30am–5pm, Oct–March Wed–Mon 9.30am–5pm; €2), which contains two separate collections. The ground-floor **Kant Museum** displays an excellent sample of Belgian lace, while upstairs is the **Brangwyn Museum**, which exhibits the moody naturalistic paintings of the artist Sir Frank Brangwyn, who was born in Bruges of Welsh parents in 1867.

Close by, at Dijver 17, the **Gruuthuse Museum** (Map p.154, D7; April–Sept daily 9.30am–5pm, Oct–March Wed–Mon 9.30am–5pm; €3.20) is sited in a rambling fifteenth-century mansion and holds a varied collection of fine and applied art, including intricately carved altarpieces, musical instruments, magnificent tapestries and many different types of furniture. Beyond the Gruuthuse rises the **Onze Lieve Vrouwekerk** (Map p.154, C8; Mon–Fri 10–noon & 2–5pm, Sat 10–noon & 2–4pm, Sun 2–4pm; €1.75), a massive shambles of a church among whose treasures are a delicate marble *Madonna and Child* by Michelangelo and the striking Renaissance **mausoleums** of Charles the Bold and his daughter Mary of Burgundy.

Opposite the church, the **St Jans Hospitaal** complex contains a well-preserved fifteenth-century dispensary and the small **Memling Museum** (Map p.154, C8; April–Sept daily 9.30am–5pm; Oct–March Thurs–Tues 9.30am–5pm; €1.75). This holds six exquisite works by Hans Memling, a

German-born, fifteenth-century artist who spent most of his working life in Bruges. From here, it's a short walk northwest to the **Sint Salvators-kathedraal** (Map p.154, B7; Mon 2–5.45pm, Tues–Fri 8.30–11.45am & 2–5.45pm, Sat 8.30–11.45am & 2–5pm & Sun 9–10.15am & 3–5.45pm; free), a replacement for the cathedral destroyed by the French army in the eighteenth century. Emerging from a long-term restoration, the soaring columns and arches are quite splendid, but it's the wonderful, flowing tapestries hanging in the choir which really catch the eye.

Accommodation

Adornes

Map p.154, G3. St Annarei 26 Ⓣ050 34 13 36, Ⓕ050 34 20 85, Ⓔhotel.adornes@proximedia.be. A tastefully converted old Flemish town house with antique charm. Great location, too, at the junction of two canals near the east end of Spiegelrei. ❸.

Egmond

Minnewater 15 Ⓣ050 34 14 45, Ⓕ050 34 29 40, Ⓦwww.egmond.be. A rambling old house on the southern edge of the city centre. Attractive rooms in a quiet location at surprisingly affordable prices. ❹.

Passage Budget Hotel

Map p.154, A7. Dweerstraat 28 Ⓣ050 34 02 32, Ⓕ050 34 01 40. Simple but well-maintained rooms a ten-minute stroll west of the Markt. Next door to and run by the same owner as the *Passage Hostel*. ❶

Passage Hostel

Map p.154, A7. Dweerstraat 26 Ⓣ050 34 02 32, Ⓕ050 34 01 40. The most agreeable hostel in Bruges, accommodating fifty people in ten comparatively comfortable dormitories at €11 per person.

BRUGES

Walburg

Map p.154, F4.
Boomgaardstraat 13 ⓣ050 34
94 14, ⓕ050 33 68 84.
A charming, family-run,
four-star hotel with thirteen
spacious if slightly spartan
rooms. In a quiet location
two minutes' east of the
Burg. ❺.

Eating

Den Dyver

Map p.154, E7. Dijver 5 ⓣ050
33 60 69.
First-rate restaurant
specializing in traditional
Flemish dishes cooked in
beer – the quail and rabbit
are magnificent. Expensive;
reservations advised. Closed
Wed, also Tues in winter.

Erasmus

Map p.154, D6. Wollestraat 35.
A straightforward, brightly lit
café with reasonably priced,
mostly Flemish dishes, plus a
wide range of Belgian brews.
A couple of hundred metres
south of the Markt. Closed
Mon except July & Aug.

Het Dagelijks Brood

Map p.154, E5.
Philipstockstraat 21.
An excellent bread shop
which doubles as a
wholefood café with one,
long wooden table. The
mouth-watering homemade
soup and bread makes a meal
in itself. In a central location,
just footsteps away from the
Burg. Open 7am to 6pm;
closed Tues.

Taverne Curiosa

Map p.154, D4. Vlamingstraat
22.
A lively bar-restaurant in an
old vaulted cellar, a couple of
minutes' walk north of the
Markt. Specialities are grilled
meats, smoked fish and
regional dishes, with a wide-
ranging beer menu to wash it
down. Closed Mon and one
week in July.

Drinking

't Brugs Beertje
Map p.154, B6. Kemelstraat 5.
A small and friendly speciality beer bar that claims a stock of two hundred ales. Five minutes' walk southwest of the Markt, off Steenstraat. Closed Wed in winter.

't Dreupelhuisje,
Map p.154, B6. Kemelstraat 9.
A tiny bar specializing in jenevers and advocaats, of which it has an excellent range. Closed Tues.

De Garre
Map p.154, D5. De Garre 1.

Down an alley off Breidelstraat between the Markt and the Burg, this cramped but cosy café-bar has a good range of Belgian beers and tasty snacks. Closed Wed.

Oude Vlissinghe
Map p.154, F2. Blekerstraat 2.
With its wood panelling, old paintings and long wooden tables, this is one of the oldest and most distinctive bars in Bruges. A couple of minutes' walk from Jan van Eyckplein: follow Spinolarei and it's a turning on the right.

BRUGES

LISTINGS

Accommodation

Brussels has no shortage of places to stay. Some of the most opulent – as well as some of the most basic – are scattered around the charming, cobbled lanes near the **Grand-Place** – an attractive option which puts you at the centre of the action. If you want something a little quieter and cheaper, **Ste Catherine**, a ten-minute walk west of the Grand-Place in the Lower Town, is the place to make for. Here you'll find a good selection of low- to mid-range hotels and you're not too far away from the nightlife of trendy place St Géry. Another cluster of hotels can be found just beyond the southern edge of the centre in one of the older and more prosperous residential areas around **avenue Louise**, with fairly easy access to the centre by métro.

Despite the number of hotels in Brussels, finding accommodation can still prove difficult, particularly in the **spring** and **autumn** when the capital enjoys its **high seasons**. However, as many of the capital's hotels cater for a European business clientele, the low season is generally considered to be July and August. This is mainly because the institutions of the European Union close down for the summer – and when the EU goes on holiday, so do the Eurocrats. The upshot is, in stark contrast to many other European cities, prices in some of the capital's larger hotels actually go down during the summer. Another bonus is that

ACCOMMODATION PRICE CODES

All the hotels detailed in this chapter have been graded according to the following price categories. All the codes are based on the rate for the least expensive double room during high season and do not take into account weekend discounts.

① €50 and under **②** €50–65 **③** €65–80 **④** €80–110
⑤ €110–140 **⑥** €140–170 **⑦** €170 and over

substantial discounts are offered on **weekends**, again when the suits have gone home.

Unless you fancy trudging halfway across the city only to find there's no room, book in advance. Hotel and youth hostel **reservations** can be made from outside Belgium through the central tourist office (℡02 513 89 40, ⓦwww.tib.be). If you do find yourself in the unfortunate position of being bedless, the tourist office on the Grand-Place can give you a list of hotels and make bookings on the spot or, alternatively, contact one of the Bed and Breakfast agencies (see p.172).

Our hotel listings are divided into the following areas: the Grand-Place and around (p.165); the Lower Town (see p.168); the Upper Town (see p.170); Ixelles and Avenue Louise (see p.171).

HOTELS

Prices in the capital's hotels vary hugely, but a little negotiation can sometimes get you a better price than the one on display, and remember too that many hotels offer group reductions. In most places breakfast is included in the price of the room, but this is not always the case so it's a good idea to check first. Generally speaking, standards in Belgian

HOTELS

hotels are fairly high and you can usually be sure that a wide range of facilities and services – bar, restaurant, TV, air conditioning – is available. An increasing number of hotels will accommodate children for free if they stay in their parents' room; others require that you pay the cost of an extra bed. The imaginatively titled brochure **Hôtels**, available free from the Belgian tourist office, usually up-to-date, tells you exactly what's on offer, and ranks the capital's hotels according to a five-star system devised by the tourist office.

THE GRAND-PLACE AND AROUND

Amigo
Map 4, C4. Rue de l'Amigo 1-3 ⓣ 02 547 47 47, ⓕ 02 513 52 77, ⓦ www.rfhotels.com. Ⓜ Bourse.
Don't let the fact this was formerly a jail put you off. This charming hotel is one of Brussels' oldest, and boasts impeccable service, a central location just around the corner from the Grand-Place, and elegant furnishings including Flemish tapestries, paintings and Oriental rugs. The country-style bedrooms have huge bathrooms, and a few look out on the Town Hall's impressive spire. ❼

Aris
Map 4, D3. Rue du Marché-aux-Herbes 78–80 ⓣ 02 514 43 00, ⓕ 02 514 01 19, ⓦ www.arishotel.be. Ⓜ Bourse.
Aesthetically not the most pleasing of buildings, despite the nineteenth-century stone facade – but the 55 modern rooms are clean and functional and you're just 20m from the Grand-Place. Prices are slightly inflated during the week. Facilities include TV, air conditioning and wheelchair access. ❺

Auberge Saint-Michel
Map 4, D4. Grand-Place 15 ⓣ 02 511 09 56, ⓕ 02 511 46 00. Ⓜ Gare Centrale.
The only place to look out over the Grand-Place, this impressive hotel occupies the Duke of Brabant's old

mansion and is an ideal location for exploring the centre. The rooms range from the small and basic at the back of the building, to the more elegant period rooms at the front (advance booking required). Think twice if you're a light sleeper – poor noise insulation and Grand-Place revellers may make you a grouch in the morning. ❹

Des Eperonniers
Map 4, D5. Rue des Eperonniers 1 ⓣ02 513 53 66, ⓕ02 511 32 30. Ⓜ Gare Centrale.
Family-owned hotel whose primary attraction is its location just off the Grand Place. The surrounding area can get loud at night so aim for rooms at the back of the hotel. For the price and the location, it's unbeatable. ❶

Le Dix-Septième
Map 4, F6. Rue de la Madeleine 25 ⓣ02 502 57 44, ⓕ02 504 64 24, Ⓦwww.ledix septieme.be. Ⓜ Gare Centrale.
Just a 2min walk from the Grand-Place, this renovated seventeenth-century mansion

is simply gorgeous. Rooms are decorated in either Louis XVI or French Renaissance style, and parquet flooring, crystal chandeliers and pastel-painted woodwork add to the flavour. Most rooms feature fully fitted kitchens, and facilities include a sauna and vaulted-ceiling bar. ❼

La Légende
Map 4, B5. Rue du Lombard 35 ⓣ02 512 82 90, ⓕ02 512 34 93, Ⓦwww.hotel-la-legende.com. Ⓜ Bourse.
Simple, no-frills accommodation in an old building set around a courtyard in the heart of the city. Although there are forty en-suite rooms available, you'll need to book in advance – the cheap prices and a central location make it very popular. ❸

La Madeleine
Map 4, F3. Rue de la Motagne 22 ⓣ02 513 29 73, ⓕ02 502 13 50, Ⓦwww.hotel-la-madeleine.be. Ⓜ Gare Centrale.
A terrific budget hotel right near the Grand-Place. Its squeaky-clean, airy rooms

and welcoming staff make it very popular, so you'll need to book early. ❹

Le Meridien

Map 4, F5. Carrefour de l'Europe 3 ⓣ 02 548 42 11, ⓕ 02 548 40 80, ⓦ www.lemeridien-brussels .com. Ⓜ Gare Centrale. Modern and expansive 224–room five-star in a convenient location next to Gare Centrale. Although it doesn't have as much character as some of the hotels in the area, it's worth noting that on weekends there's a fifty percent reduction on all rooms, which means you can pick up a double for €173 – a bargain, though breakfast isn't included. ❼

Hotel Mirabeau

Map 3, B7. Place Fontainas 18–20 ⓣ 02 511 19 72, ⓕ 02 511 00 36, ⓦ www.users.skynet .be/hotelmirabeau. Ⓜ Bourse. Located just before the seedy Midi quarter begins, this six-story hotel provides basic comforts for a very reasonable price. Rooms on the terraced second and third floors are recommended. Good for

those on a very tight budget, and you can bargain with the management for reduced rates for longer stays. ❸

Mozart

Map 4, D5. Rue Marché aux Fromages 23 ⓣ 02 502 66 61, ⓕ 02 502 77 58, ⓦ www.hotel-mozart.be. Ⓜ Gare Centrale. Relatively cheap rooms and a friendly atmosphere make it worthy of consideration, but if you want to get any sleep make sure you avoid the rooms overlooking "Pitta street", where hordes of restless locals noisily consume falafel until the early hours. ❹

Radisson SAS

Map 3, E5. Rue Fosse-aux-Loups 47 ⓣ 02 219 28 28, ⓕ 02 219 62 62, ⓦ www.radissonsas .com. Ⓜ Gare Centrale. Hidden down a dark side street near the Grand-Place, the palatial *Radisson* is centred around an enormous glass-roofed atrium and is filled with all the amenities you could ever need. The hotel's *Sea Grill* restaurant serves up some of the finest – and most expensive – seafood in the capital. ❼

THE GRAND-PLACE AND AROUND

La Vieille Lanterne

Map 4, A6. Rue des Grands Carmes 29 ⓣ 02 512 74 94, ⓕ 02 512 13 97. Ⓜ Gare Centrale.

Small but friendly family-oriented pension close to the Manneken Pis and only a short stroll from the Grand-Place. Each room has a shower and, at €62 for a double, it's good value for money. There are only six rooms, so make sure you reserve well in advance. Breakfast not included. ➋

THE LOWER TOWN

- - - - - - - - - - - - - - - -

Arlequin

Map 4, A6. Rue de la Fourche 17–19 ⓣ 02 514 16 15, ⓕ 02 514 22 02, ⓦ www.arlequin.be. Ⓜ de Brouckère.

The decor won't exactly set you on fire and rooms are modest, but staff are very courteous, reservations are not always necessary and you're at the centre of the downtown action. ➎

Astrid

Map 3, D4. Pl du Samedi 11 ⓣ 02 219 31 19, ⓕ 02 219 31 70, ⓦ www.astridhotel.be. Ⓜ Ste Catherine.

Built in 1994, the *Astrid* isn't as atmospheric as some of the other hotels in Ste Catherine – but it's clean, modern and each of its 100 rooms comes equipped with bathroom, TV and individual safe. At weekends and during the low season a standard double costs as little as €74. Group reductions offered and wheelchair access. ➎

Atlas

Map 3, C5. Rue du Vieux Marché-aux-Grains 30 ⓣ 02 502 60 06, ⓕ 02 502 69 35, ⓦ www.atlas-hotel.be. Ⓜ Bourse.

Quiet and comfortable four-star hotel situated only a 10min walk from the Grand-Place in the gentrified Ste Catherine district. The rooms, though blandly decorated, are well equipped – bathroom, TV, mini-bar – and wheelchair accessible. ➏

La Bourse

Map 3, C5. Rue Antoine Dansaert 11 ⓣ 02 512 60 10,

Ⓕ 02 512 61 39. Ⓜ Bourse.
Though a tad frayed around
the edges, this hotel is
popular with young budget
tourists and it's easy to see
why – it's within spitting
distance of the fashionable
place St Géry and only a
stroll from the Grand-Place.
A standard double with
shower, toilet, and TV costs
€55, breakfast included. ❷

George V

Map 4, B5. Rue 't Kint 23 Ⓣ 02
513 50 93, Ⓕ 02 513 44 93,
Ⓦ www.george5.com. Ⓜ Bourse.
Comfortable Georgian hotel
offering clean rooms just
5min from the Bourse. Good
value, especially on weekends
when the price drops by ten
percent. Breakfast is thrown
in, but it's not much to write
home about. ❸

Métropole

Map 3, D4. Pl de Brouckère 31
Ⓣ 02 217 23 00, Ⓕ 02 218 02
20, Ⓦ www.metropolehotel.com.
Ⓜ de Brouckère.
Arguably Brussels' finest
hotel, the *Métropole* dates
back to 1895 and boasts some
of the most exquisite Empire

and Art Nouveau decor to be
found in the capital. Rooms
are spacious and combine
period touches with the usual
modern amenities. There's a
good restaurant and lively
piano bar too. ❼

New Hotel Siru

Map 3, F3. Pl Rogier 1 Ⓣ 02
203 35 80, Ⓕ 02 203 33 03,
Ⓦ www.conforthotelsiru.com.
Ⓜ Rogier.
No two rooms are alike in
this 101-room recently refurbished Art Deco hotel. In the
late 1980s, a team of 130
Belgian artists – painter
Roger Somerville and sculptors César Bailleux and
Hanneke Beaumont included
– were given carte blanche to
decorate the corridors, paint
the walls, and put works of
art in every bedroom. It's
worth staying here at least
one night for the novelty
value, although the compact
rooms aren't cheap (€108 for
the cheapest double in the
high season and €79 in July
& August), and the area,
though safe, is hardly attractive or at the centre of the
action. ❹.

Hotel Noga

Map 5, D2. Rue du Beguinage 38 ⓣ 02 218 67 63, ⓕ 02 218 16 03, ⓔ info@nogahotel.com. Ⓜ de Brouckère.

This renovated hotel offers some of the best value-for-money accommodation in and around the place St Catherine. Cheerful en-suite rooms decked out in primary colours cost just €79 a night. ❸

THE UPPER TOWN

- - - - - - - - - - - - - - - - - - - -

Alfa Sablon

Map 3, E8. Rue de la Paille 2–4 ⓣ02 513 60 40, ⓕ 02 511 81 41, ⓔ jeanmarie.willems@alfasablon .gth.be. Tram #91, #92, #93, #94. Pleasant enough, if unexceptional, modern hotel situated right next to the atmospheric place du Grand Sablon, known principally for its antiques and collector's market. Slightly cheaper than other hotels in the vicinity. Wheelchair access. ❹

Astoria

Map 3, F7. Rue Royale 103 ⓣ 02 227 05 05, ⓕ 02 217 11 50, Ⓦ www.sofitel.com.

Ⓜ Gare Centrale.

Winston Churchill once stayed at this grand 120-room hotel, which is handily placed near the Parc de Bruxelles and the Palais Royal. Home to an Orient Express-style "Pullman Bar", and beautifully decorated with original turn-of-the-century fixtures and fittings, the *Astoria* has a real time-warp feel to it. However, time travel doesn't come cheap these days, so expect to pay an arm, leg and torso for the experience. ❼

Jolly Hotel du Grand Sablon

Map 3, E8. Rue Bodenbroeck 2–4 ⓣ 02 518 11 00, ⓕ 02 512 67 66, Ⓦ www.jollyhotels.it. Tram #91, #92, #93, #94.
Pretty expensive for what you get, but this plush, 200-room hotel does look over the lovely place du Grand Sablon with its terraced cafés and designer shops. The excellent restaurant and convivial bar rate as the other main attractions, but the cheapest double costs €248. Reservations not always necessary. Wheelchair access. ❼

La Tasse d'Argent

Map 3, H5. Rue du Congrès 48 Ⓣ 02 218 83 75, Ⓕ 02 218 83 75. Ⓜ Madou.

A pleasant, family-run hotel, popular with Belgians and only a stone's throw away from Métro Madou. The building is impressive and dates back to 1885, while the more ordinary interior comes with all mod cons. With just eight rooms available, you'll need to reserve in advance. ❷

IXELLES AND AVENUE LOUISE

Argus

Map 8, G2. Rue Capitaine Crespel 6 Ⓣ 02 514 07 70, Ⓕ 02 514 12 22, Ⓦ www.hotel-argus.be. Ⓜ Porte de Namur.

Not in the city centre, but a good location nonetheless, close to avenue Toison d'Or. The rooms are a bit on the small side, but they're cosy enough and the service is impeccable. A nice alternative to the gargantuan – and expensive – hotels that pepper the neighbourhood. ❹

Barsey Hotel Mayfair

Map 8, J9. Av Louise 381–383 Ⓣ 02 649 98 00, Ⓕ 02 640 17 64, Ⓔ reservations@mayfair.be. Tram #93, #94.

Close to the bustling Chatelain area, the former *Mayfair* hotel has been completely renovated. The interior is flamboyant and filled with warmth, rooms are huge and brilliantly designed and service is hushed and rapid. Popular with a business clientele. Doubles begin at €263, dropping as low as €136 at the weekend. ❼

Conrad International

Map 8, G3. Av Louise 71 Ⓣ 02 542 42 42, Ⓕ 02 542 42 00, Ⓦ www.brussels.conradinternational.com. Ⓜ Louise. Tram #93, #94.

One of the capital's top hotels, the overblown *Conrad International* was former U.S. president Clinton's top choice when in town, and boasts large rooms, comprehensive facilities and impeccable service. ❼

Four Points

Map 8, I5. Rue Paul Spaak 15 Ⓣ 02 645 61 11, Ⓕ 02 646 63 44, Ⓦ www.fourpoints.com.

Tram #93, #94.

Close to the Chatelain area and just 5min from Place Louise, this hotel boasts plain, ample-sized rooms, a charming garden and an excellent restaurant, *La Vacherie*, which serves up delicious Swiss specialities – the cow leitmotif decor is good for a giggle. **7**

Rembrandt

Map 8, H3. Rue de la Concorde 42 Ⓣ 02 512 71 39, Ⓕ 02 511 71 36. Tram #93, #94. Quiet, pension-style hotel with clean and comfortable rooms close to avenue Louise. It's well-placed, reasonably inexpensive and popular with an older clientele. While all rooms are equipped with showers, you'll have to pay slightly more to get an attached toilet. **2**–**3**

ST GILLES

Les Bluets

Map 8, G4. Rue Berckmans 124 Ⓣ 02 534 39 83, Ⓕ 02 534 39 83. Ⓜ Louise.
Charming pension-style hotel whose moderate prices – doubles start at €65 – and lovely garden keep its ten rooms permanently full. Situated in a bustling area full of bars and restaurants, just off chaussée de Charleroi and near the Métro Louise. **3**

B&BS

For those on a tight budget, staying at a B&B can prove a cheaper alternative to a hotel, and the standard of accommodation can be just as good. The tourist office on the Grand-Place can make reservations for free; alternatively, contact one of the budget accommodation agencies listed below. Rooms are often comfortable although location is sometimes a problem – don't expect to be in the centre of things.

Bed & Brussels

Map 8, J7. Rue Kindermans 5 Ⓣ 02 646 07 37, Ⓕ 02 644 01

14, Ⓦ www.BnB.Brussels.be.
Agency with a good reputation: the standards of

rooms are usually high and they can generally obtain a double for under €40.

Taxistop Bed & Breakfast

Map 3, E5. Rue du Fossé-aux-Loups 28 ⓣ 02 223 22 31, ⓕ 02 223 22 32. Closed Sat & Sun. One of the best-known B&B agencies, with a wide range of budget accommodation. You are charged a nominal reservation fee; if you book from outside Belgium it costs an extra €12 on the price of the room, whereas if you wait until you're in the country the tariff is reduced to €7.50.

YOUTH HOSTELS

If you don't like communal living or the idea of a complete stranger snoring in your ear all night, don't panic – Brussels has its fair share of **youth hostels** offering cheap, modern and private accommodation. Practically all the hostels in the capital have a majority of comfortable singles, doubles, and rooms for four. Prices vary slightly, but generally speaking a single costs around €20, a double €15 and a quad €12 per person. Most hostels are located either within the petit ring – Botanique in particular has three good hostels – or just outside it and close to a métro. If you don't have an IYHF membership card, rooms will cost an extra €2.50. You can buy a card from any youth hostel for €12 – worth it if you're staying for longer than five days.

Bruegel

Map 3, A3. Rue du Saint-Esprit 2 ⓣ 02 511 04 36, ⓕ 02 512 07 11, ⓦ www.vjh.be. ⓜ Gare Centrale. This official IYHF hostel, housed in a modern building, has 135 beds and a basic breakfast is included in the overnight fee: singles €20.50, doubles €15 and quads €12.25 per person. Dinner costs an extra €6.80 and sheets will set you back €3.25. You're paying a little extra for the central location, by the church of Notre Dame de la Chapelle close to the Upper Town, but you have to be back by 1am or you may find yourself wandering the streets. Check-in 7am–1pm.

Le Centre Vincent Van Gogh

Map 3, H3. Rue Traversière 8 ⓣ 02 217 01 58. Ⓜ Botanique. A rambling, spacious, 210-bed hostel with a good reputation and friendly staff, though it can seem a bit chaotic. Prices are fairly standard – singles €20.5, doubles €15 and quads €12 per person – but its main advantage is that there's no curfew. Breakfast is included and there are sinks in all rooms, but sheets will cost you an extra €3.25. Good-value, if a little bland, meals – pasta, salads etc – can be purchased from the hostel bar for around €5.

Jacques Brel

Map 3, H4. Rue de la Sablonnière 30 ⓣ 02 218 01 87, ⓕ 02 217 20 05, Ⓦ www.bruxelles.brel@laj.be. Ⓜ Botanique. An official IYHF hostel, modern, comfortable, and with a hotel-like atmosphere, close to Métro Madou and Métro Botanique. Breakfast is included in the price: €20.5 for singles, €15 for doubles and €12.25 for quads per person. There's no curfew (you get a key), and cheap meals can be bought on the premises. Very close in comfort to some of the capital's hotels.

Sleep Well

Map 3, E4. Rue du Damier 23 ⓣ 02 218 50 50, ⓕ 02 218 13 13, Ⓦ www.sleepwell.be. Ⓜ Botanique. Bright and breezy hostel close to the city centre, only a 5min walk from place Rogier. Hotel-style facilities include a bar-cum-restaurant which serves traditional Belgian beers and well-priced local culinary specialities. There's also an excellent information point for tourists and, unlike many of its rivals, the place has full disabled access. Prices are €23.75 for singles for the first night and €20.5 for every night after that, €18 (and then €14.8) for doubles, and €16.3 (€13) for quads.

CAMPSITES

Although there are around twelve **campsites** in the greater Brussels area, only a few make feasible bases for the city. They tend to be used by caravaners trying to escape the hustle and bustle of the capital, as opposed to backpackers trying to save a few pounds on their accommodation costs. The accepted wisdom seems to be that it's just not worth the effort of camping and commuting, especially as the métro, tram and bus services shut down around the same time as the capital's bars, clubs and music venues begin to warm up. However, if you're set on the idea, the following campsites have the best reputations.

Internationale Camping
Autostrade 100, Londerzeel
☎ 02 230 94 92.
Although outside the city, it has the advantage of being open all year round. Either take the train to Londerzeel and walk 2km, or get the bus – direction Boom – from the Gare du Nord and walk 200m.

Paul Rosmant
Warandeberg 52, Wezembeek-Oppem ☎ 02 782 10 09.
Only 10km east of the city, *Paul Rosmant* is the closest campsite to Brussels. To get there, either take the métro (#1B Stockel line) to Kraainem and then the #30 bus to St Pietersplein (last bus leaves at 8.21pm) or take the métro to Stockel and then the #39 tram to Marcelisstraat. Open April–Sept.

Veldkant
Veldkantstraat 64, Grimbergen ☎ 02 269 25 97.
One of the most popular campsites, the *Veldkant* is about 15km north of the city centre beyond Laeken. From the Bourse take tram #52, #55, #58 or #81 to Gare du Nord and then catch bus #G to the terminus, after which it's a 15min walk. Open Jan–Nov.

CAMPSITES

Eating

Thanks to its excellent food and diversity of cuisine, Brussels has moved into the European culinary limelight. While not the cheapest of cities to eat out in, its thousands of restaurants offer consistently high quality fare and spectacular value for money. The excellence exhibited by restaurants like *Comme Chez Soi* has trickled down to mainstream dining, and as a result, there really is no excuse for eating poorly. With the natives expecting this minimum level of quality, even the trendiest of restaurants are obliged to have a cuisine which matches the sleek decor. Apart from the excellence of the native Belgian fare, the city is among Europe's best for sampling a wide range of different cuisines – from the ubiquitous Italian places, through to Spanish, Vietnamese, Japanese and Russian restaurants.

Restaurants aside, it's worth remembering many **bars and cafés** serve food. Though this is often limited to pastas, soups and *croques monsieurs*, many have wider-ranging menus usually consisting of traditional Brussels fare (see Chapter Eleven). There are also plenty of *frites* stands and pitta places around the Grand-Place, notably on rue du Marché aux Fromages, known locally as "Greek Street", and on rue des Bouchers.

PRICE GUIDE

Restaurants in this chapter are graded into one of four categories, according to the price, serving a starter and a main course, without drinks or dessert.

Inexpensive: under €20
Moderate: €20–32
Expensive: €32–44
Very expensive: over €44

Unfortunately, Brussels is lacking when it comes to specifically catering for **vegetarians**, but many restaurants, particularly Middle Eastern ones, serve a good selection of vegetarian dishes.

The **Lower Town** is great for good-quality cuisine that doesn't cost the earth. The fashionable rue Antoine Dansaert is an excellent place to start, with several stylish restaurants. The Lower Town also holds the frenetic rue des Bouchers, a restaurant ghetto well worth checking out. There's another cluster of good restaurants around the lovely place du Grand Sablon in the **Upper Town**, although the food doesn't come cheap and you may find yourself paying extra for the pretty scenery. Out of the town centre, **Ixelles** is home to some of the capital's finest restaurants, particularly at the place Stéphanie end of chaussée de Charleroi, but also close by the attractive place du Châtelain. The **EU Quarter** holds a few spots that rise above the average business lunch gulp-down, while the *commune* of **Ganshoren** is home to two of the finest restaurants in the city.

Generally speaking, most places are **open** from noon to 3pm and from 7pm to 11pm. Sundays and Mondays tend to be the quietest days, and some restaurants close down altogether in July and August. It's not usually necessary to make

EATING

BELGIAN SPECIALITIES

anguilles au vert	eels in green sauce
faisan à la brabançonne	pheasant in butter, white wine and chicory
carbonnade flamande	beef braised with beer, onions, carrots and sometimes prunes
crevettes roses/grises	red/grey shrimps – used in salads
croque monsieur	toasted cheese and ham sandwich
dame blanche	ice cream with melted chocolate
gaufres au chocolat	chocolate waffles
kip-kap	jellied meat (often sold in bars)
lammekezoet	fresh herring croquettes
lapin à la kriek	rabbit in cherry beer
poulet à la Bruxelles	chicken stuffed with cheese and basted in beer
poulet à la framboise	chicken in raspberry beer
salade à l'ardennaise	salad with strips of Ardennes ham
steak américaine	raw minced steak
stoemp	mashed potatoes and mashed seasonal vegetables with sausages and/or bacon
waterzooi	stew with eels, fish, or chicken, cooked in a broth enriched with cream

a **reservation** midweek, but it's highly advisable on Friday and Saturday nights.

Restaurant **prices** vary, depending on where you eat and when. Lunch menus are considerably less expensive than evening menus, whereas the *plat du jour* – the main course meal of the day – is often great value for money and usually available all day.

Service charges are automatically included, and you need only leave a tip if service is above average.

THE GRAND-PLACE AND AROUND

Aux Armes de Bruxelles

Map 4, E2. Rue des Bouchers 13 Ⓣ 02 511 55 50.
Ⓜ Bourse.
Tues–Sun noon–11.15pm.
Closed June 19–July 16.
Moderate.

Right in the middle of the restaurant district near the Grand-Place, this polished spot divides into a formal restaurant popular with the pearls-and-blue-rinse brigade, and a simple bistro with wooden benches, both of which serve old-fashioned Belgian cuisine to a very high standard. Renowned for its *moules* and Flemish *carbonnades*.

Brasserie de la Roue d'Or

Map 4, C6. Rue de Chapeliers 26 Ⓣ 02 514 25 54.
Ⓜ Bourse.
Daily 12.30pm–12.30am.
Closed July 15–Aug 15.
Moderate.

This old brasserie, handily located close to the Grand-Place, serves generous portions of Belgian regional specialities, such as *poulet à la Bruxelles*, and a mouthwatering selection of seafood. Also recommended are the delicious lamb with mustard and the endive salad with salmon.

Chez Léon

Map 4, E2. Rue des Bouchers 18–22 Ⓣ 02 511 14 15.
Ⓜ Bourse.
Daily noon–11pm. Moderate.
This touristy Brussels institution has been serving Belgian specialities like *moules au vin blanc* and *poulet à la framboise* for over a century. It's not the classiest of eateries, however, and has a tendency to deliver ever blander versions of Belgian cuisines – gruff service too.

L'Idiot du Village

Map 2, C7. Rue Notre Seigneur 19 Ⓣ 02 502 55 82.
Tram #93, #94.
Mon–Fri noon–2pm & 7.15–11pm. Closed July 15–Aug 15. Moderate.

THE GRAND-PLACE AND AROUND

Behind the candle-lit, modest entrance on a narrow side street in the Marolles quarter lies a gastronomic wonderland. Intimate and dimly-lit, the simple wooden tables and low levels of noise mean that the dining experience is as discreet as it is delicious. The *escargots au confit* with herb ravioli are a must.

't Kelderke

Map 4, D4. Grand-Place 15 Ⓣ 02 513 73 44. Ⓜ Gare Centrale.
Daily noon–2am. Moderate.
You can't get more Belgian than this well-known restaurant, housed in a boisterous cellar on the Grand-Place. The impressive range of cuisine includes *moules, stoemp, carbonnade flamande à la bière*, and *waterzooi*. And while the waiters can be a little stuffy, the house beer – the 't Kelderke – will smooth things over nicely.

La Maison du Cygne

Map 4, D4. Rue Ch Buls Ⓣ 02 511 82 44. Ⓜ Gare Centrale.

Mon–Fri noon–2pm & 7–10pm, Sat 7–10.30pm. Very expensive.
The gorgeous location overlooking the Grand-Place is enough to make this restaurant a real hit, but add to that some awesome French and Belgian cuisine and you can see why it's regarded as one of the capital's top spots. The warm *langoustines* and mango curry is highly recommended. Admittedly a meal here costs the earth, so it's best reserved for a special treat.

Tapas Locas

Map 4, B4. Rue du Marché au Charbon, 74 Ⓣ 02 502 12 68. Ⓜ Bourse or de Brouckère.
Daily 7pm–1am. Inexpensive.
This light, informal Spanish restaurant in a trendy area attracts a mainly youthful clientele, and serves a wide range of excellent cheap tapas at €2 a portion. Standard tapas such as tortilla, calamares or chorizo are listed in the menu and there is a changing selection of more unusual dishes chalked up on the blackboards. Spanish wine and sangria are both €1.80 a glass.

Taverne du Passage

Map 4, E3. Galerie de la Reine 30 ⓣ 02 512 37 31. Ⓜ Gare Centrale.
Daily noon–midnight. Closed Wed & Thurs June & July. Moderate.
Popular with Belgian families, this traditional Art Deco place is well known for its excellent Sunday lunches (€37), and for serving delicious classic Belgian dishes such as *anguilles au vert*. There's also a number of vegetarian options including a tasty cheese fondue for only €7. Their Belgian beer menu is also worth perusing.

Vert de Gris

Map 3, D8. Rue des Alexiens 63 ⓣ 02 514 21 68.
Ⓜ Bourse.
Tues–Fri noon–2pm, 7–11pm, Sat & Sun 7pm–midnight. Moderate.
A varied crowd of young and old, couples and families gathers to dine at this large restaurant, which offers up fusion cuisine with heavy Belgian and French accents. The interior is a little dark, but there's a pleasant outdoor rear terrace, with views of the pretty Eglise de la Chapelle.

THE LOWER TOWN

L'Achepot

Map 5, C5. Pl Ste Catherine 1 ⓣ 02 511 62 21. Ⓜ Ste Catherine or de Brouckère.
Mon–Sat noon–3pm, 6–10.30pm. Moderate.
A welcoming, family-run restaurant in the trendy Ste Catherine district. Vegetarians would probably have a coronary if they saw the amount of hearty Belgian meat dishes on the menu, but carnivores will find *L'Achepot* the ideal place for consuming huge chunks of flesh, especially on cold winter evenings. The menu is traditional Belgian and French and includes *lapin à la kriek* as well as a variety of recipes involving tripe.

Ateliers de la Grande Île

Map 2, C5. Rue de la Grande Île 33 ⓣ 02 512 81 90.
Ⓜ Bourse.
Tues–Sun 8pm–1am. Closed Aug. Moderate.

Only a couple of minutes' walk from place St Géry, located in a converted nineteenth-century foundry, this winding, candlelit, Russian restaurant serves large and hearty meat dishes, and a delicious array of flavoured vodkas. You also get to eat, drink and be merry to the accompaniment of live gypsy violin music. It's worth paying a visit simply for the joyous, if a tad eccentric, atmosphere.

Bla Bla & Gallery

Map 3, C9. Rue des Capucins ⓣ 02 503 59 18. Ⓜ Louise. Daily 7pm–11pm. Brunch 10.30am–4pm Sat & Sun. Moderate.

Bla Bla is the latest Brussels restaurant to take a stab at the suave interior/*nouvelle cuisine* combo, with excellent results. Sit back in the leather bench seats and tuck into delicious mozzarella, artichoke and pancetta ravioli or duck carpaccio. While the brick walls and high ceilings keep the noise levels high, the ambience is buzzing and friendly, and there's live piano music during the week. Excellent service too.

Bonsoir Clara

Map 5, C6. Rue Antoine Dansaert 22 ⓣ 02 502 09 90. Ⓜ Bourse. Daily noon–2.30pm & 7–11.30pm, Sat & Sun 7–11.30pm. Moderate.

One of the capital's trendiest restaurants on arguably the hippest street in Brussels. Although part of a group which includes *Zebra* and *Kasbah*, *Bonsoir Clara* has its own identity – moody, atmospheric lighting, 1970s geometrically mirrored walls and zinc-topped tables. The wine list is particularly well chosen, and the food excellent. Expect to find a menu full of Mediterranean, French and Belgian classics and make sure you reserve.

Comme Chez Soi

Map 3, C7. Pl Rouppe 23 ⓣ 02 512 29 21. Ⓜ Anneessens. Tues–Sat noon–1.30pm & 7–9.30pm. Closed July & Christmas to Jan 1. Very expensive.

Tucked away in the corner of place Rouppe, near Brussels-Midi train station, *Comme Chez Soi* is a gastronomic legend. The restaurant's successful blending of new and more traditional French cuisine has cemented the loyalty of an extremely varied clientele, who come to have their taste buds massaged by dishes such as spring chicken with crayfish béarnaise sauce. The three fixed menus on offer are the most "cost-effective" ways to dine, with the four-course lunch costing €50. Exquisite and discreet service. Reservations are necessary weeks, if not months, in advance.

Domaine de Lintillac

Map 5, A3. Rue de Flandre 25 Ⓣ 02 511 51 23. Ⓜ Compte de Flandre.
Tues–Sat noon–2pm & 7.30–10.30pm. Inexpensive.
Delicious cuisine from the southwest of France at this warm, easy-going restaurant. The prices are ridiculously cheap for what could just be some of the best *foie d'oie* and *foie gras* in Brussels. Down to

earth and full of character, the relaxed ambience and clientele make it perfect for family outings.

Ecailler du Palais Royal

Map 2, D6. Rue Bodenbroeck Ⓣ 02 521 87 51. Tram #94.
Mon–Sat noon–2.30pm & 7–10.30pm. Closed Easter & Aug. Very expensive.
Arguably the finest seafood restaurant in Brussels, with refined service and classically elegant decor. A dressy older crowd rules the *salles*, and while prices are of the gulp-and-swallow variety, a mere mouthful is sure to convince. Solo travellers are well catered for at the English counter.

Le Gourmandin

Map 2, D7. Rue Haute 152 Ⓣ 02 512 98 92. Ⓜ Louise.
Noon–2.30pm & 7–10.30pm. Closed Sat noon, Sun & Mon night & July 15–31. Moderate.
Situated in a tiny townhouse just below the Palais de Justice, this very intimate restaurant, with only twenty places, serves up French cuisine you won't forget in a

hurry. Fine dishes such as succulent garlic-roasted breast of Bresse chicken are delicately prepared in the open kitchen as diners look on. Take a taxi and be sure to reserve.

Iberica

Map 3, C4. Rue de Flandre 8 Ⓣ 02 511 79 36. Ⓜ Ste Catherine.
Mon & Tues, Thurs–Sun 11.30am–3pm & 6.30–11pm. Closed Wed & Aug 5–24. Inexpensive.

A Spanish restaurant at the place Ste Catherine end of rue de Flandre, favoured by expat Spanish. The decor verges on the tacky – red velvet-like wallpaper and mock Tudor beams – but the paella is second to none. It's fairly good value for money, with most tapas costing around €6.

Kasbah

Map 5, C6. Rue Antoine Dansaert 20 Ⓣ 02 502 40 26. Ⓜ Bourse.
Daily noon–2.30pm & 7pm–12.30am. Moderate. Popular with a youthful,

groovy crowd, this Moroccan eatery is famous for its enormous portions of couscous and other North African specialities. It's run by the same people as *Bonsoir Clara* next door, and although equally hip, the lantern-lit decor makes it seem slightly less fashion-conscious and far more welcoming. Vibrant atmosphere and set menus from €18.

La Marée

Map 5, A3. Rue de Flandre 99 Ⓣ 02 511 00 40. Ⓜ Ste Catherine.
Mon–Sat noon–2.30pm & 6–10pm. Closed Sun & Tues night. Moderate.

There's another *La Marée* on rue au Beurre, so don't get confused – this one is a pocket-sized bistro specializing in fish and mussels in the Ste Catherine district. Although the decor is pretty basic, it has a cosy feel, and the food is creatively made and reasonably priced. The menu includes eight different types of mussels dishes from €10, and Burgundy snails and steaks from €11.

Pasta Basta

Map 5, C9. Rue de la Grande Île 34 ⓣ 0477/20 20 90. Ⓜ Bourse.
Daily 7pm–midnight.
Inexpensive.

Situated in the heart of the St Géry area, this pasta-lovers' delight is popular with a young crowd. It serves up a constantly changing menu, as well as staples such as cannelloni with spinach and ricotta. A DJ spins tunes every Friday and Saturday night; the cosy interior barely manages to contain the jumping crowd, zesty cuisine and slamming beats.

THE UPPER TOWN

Aux Bons Enfants

Map 3, E8. Pl du Grand Sablon 49 ⓣ 02 512 40 95.
Tram #92, #93, #94.
Daily except Wed noon–2.30pm & 6.30–10.30pm. Closed mid-July to end Aug. Moderate.
A well-established, cosy old Italian place, housed in a seventeenth-century building on the attractive place du Grand Sablon. Expect to find rustic-style decor, classical music and a menu of simple but tasty Italian dishes – steaks, pasta, hearty soups, pizza – at reasonable prices.

Au Chat Perché

Map 3, E8 Rue de la Samaritaine 20 ⓣ 02 513 52 13.
Tram #92, #93, #94.
Tues–Fri noon–2.30pm & 7–11pm, Sat 7–11pm. Closed mid-July to mid-Aug. Moderate.
Just west of place du Grand Sablon, an excellent French resto which serves up very tasty and copious salads, pastas and quiches in pleasant, if a tad chintzy, surroundings. It's a good spot for lunch, and ideal in the evenings for an intimate candlelit dinner. Impressive vegetarian selection, and cheaper than some neighbouring restaurants. Occasional live jazz.

La Grande Porte

Map 3, E8. Rue Notre Seigneur 9 ⓣ 02 512 89 98.
Ⓜ Anneessens.
Mon–Fri noon–3pm & 6pm–2am, Sat 6pm–2am.
Moderate.
On the northern edge of the

THE UPPER TOWN

Marolles near Notre Dame de la Chapelle, and some distance from the métro, this is a long, narrow and cosy old café, whose walls are plastered with ancient posters and photos. The food is good and hearty – *stoemp*, mussels, *carbonnade flamande* – and you're quite free to just go for a drink. Be warned, though, that it can get very crowded, and the food can be very slow to arrive.

The Lunch Company
Map 3, F9. Rue de Namur 16 ⓣ 02 502 09 76. Ⓜ Porte de Namur. Mon–Sat noon–5pm. Inexpensive.
Tucked away on a small street just off the blvd de Waterloo shopping area, *The Lunch Co.* serves up terrific sandwiches and salads and also does typical English high teas, with scones and delicate salmon and cucumber sandwiches. The decor is minimalist and there's also a superb little garden.

Lola
Map 3, E8. Pl du Grand Sablon 33 ⓣ 02 514 24 60.

Tram #92, #93, #94. Daily noon–3pm & 6.30–11.30pm. Moderate.
A very trendy restaurant, whose clean lines and dark leather seats reflect the modern and classic French cuisine on offer – including lobster cake with spinach. It's not cheap – main courses are around €15 – but the food is delicious and the service good. Reservations are a must.

Le Pain Quotidien
Map 3, E8. Rue des Sablons 11 ⓣ 02 513 51 54. Ⓜ Louise. Mon–Fri 7.30am–7pm, Sat & Sun 8am–7pm. Inexpensive.
One of an extremely successful chain of bakery cafés serving simple but delicious home-baked food such as croissants, quiches and pastries. Expect to find plain wooden decor, ochre colours and a whole range of goodies on sale – chocolate cookies, homemade jams and great coffee. Excellent food and a relaxing atmosphere.

Premier Comptoir Noi
Map 8, F4. Ch de Charleroi 39 ⓣ 02 537 44 47. Ⓜ Louise.

THE UPPER TOWN

Mon–Fri noon–2pm,
7–10.30pm, Sat 7–10.30pm.
Closed Sun. Inexpensive.

A recently opened branch of
the the excellent Thai
restaurant in Linkebeek, on
the outskirts of Brussels.
Don't be put off by the
bright-yellow facade: behind
it is a simple and welcoming
interior in which attentive
Thai waitresses swiftly serve
diners with incredibly spicy
raw scampis and red
pepper/bamboo chicken at
very modest prices.

Au Stekerlapatte

Map 3, C10. Rue des Prêtres
4 ⓣ 02 512 86 81. Ⓜ Hôtel des
Monnaies.
Tues–Sun 7pm–1am. Moderate.

A famous old brasserie near
the Palais de Justice,
frequented by a youngish
crowd who come for the
typical Belgian cuisine – beef
casseroles, grilled pork, *poulet
à la Bruxelles* – and friendly
atmosphere. Main meals are
in excess of €18, but the
food is delicious and the
original early twentieth-
century bistro decor is an
attractive bonus.

ST GILLES

Beni Znassen – Chez Mustapha

Map 8, C4. Rue de l'Eglise 81
ⓣ 02 534 11 94. Ⓜ Parvis de
St Gilles.
Wed–Sun 6.30pm–1am. Closed
July & Aug. Inexpensive.

This off-the-beaten-track
Moroccan restaurant, just
behind the Parvis de St
Gilles, attracts an eclectic
crowd united only by their
appreciation of tasty, well-
priced North African food.
The decor is a bit on the
dingy side, but somehow it
adds to its attraction. Great
couscous.

Chelsea

Map 8, F4. Ch de Charleroi 85
ⓣ 02 544 19 77. Ⓜ Louise.
Tues–Fri noon–2pm & 7–11pm,
Sat 7–11pm. Moderate.

A wine bar, restaurant and
cigar lounge all rolled into
one. The pretty garden and
sumptous interior, with
furniture from Rajastan,
oriental carpets and
contemporary art, are
guaranteed to lull you into a

state of contentment. The tasty food (for example, caviar of vegetables with olive oil) won't disappoint, either. Reservations recommended.

La Maison Berbere

Map 8, F8. Ave Brugmann 1 ⓣ02 539 48 56. Tram #91, #92. Daily noon–3pm, 6–10.30pm. Inexpensive.

Located in a former theatre and full of North African flavour, with dozens of overhead lanterns, ceramic-tile tables and earthen colours. Does excellent couscous, but anything from the reasonably priced menu will have you smacking your lips.

Les Salons de l'Atalaide

Map 8, F4. Ch de Charleroi 89 ⓣ02 537 21 54. Ⓜ Louise. Tram #91, #92. Daily 11.30am–3pm & 7pm–midnight, closed July 22–Aug 15. Moderate.

Voguish Belgian–French restaurant housed in an atmospheric and stunningly impressive 1900s building a few minutes' walk from place Stéphanie. The food – pasta, salads, steaks – is fair to moderate in quality and the service is a little gruff, but it's worth going just for the decor – high ceilings, arches, drapes, mirrors and candles. Reservations a must.

SiSiSi

Map 8, F5. Ch de Charleroi 174 ⓣ02 534 14 00. Tram #91, #92. Mon–Fri 10am–2am, Sat & Sun noon–1am. Inexpensive.

A late-opening café in the St Gilles neighbourhood, with large windows so you can watch the world drift by. It's a good spot for lunch – the delicious pittas and pizzas are particularly recommended – and enjoys a loyal following of hip, young things.

IXELLES AND AVENUE LOUISE

- -

L'Amadeus

Map 8, G5. Rue Veydt 13 ⓣ02 538 34 27. Ⓜ Louise. Tram #91, #92. Tues–Sun 6.30pm–midnight, Sun also 10am–2.30pm. Closed Jan 1–8, July 21–Aug 15. Moderate.

AVENUE LOUISE AND IXELLES

A restaurant and wine bar in the attractive one-time studio of Auguste Rodin, not far from place Stéphanie, just off chaussée de Charleroi. Modern and classic Belgian cuisine are on offer, including delicious guinea fowl with juniper berries and the house speciality *Burbot waterzooi*. There's also an excellent wine list, which is rotated once a month to highlight different regions, and an eat-all-you-want brunch on Sunday (10am–2pm) for €18.

Chez Marie

Map 8, K6. Rue Alphonse de Witte 40 ⊕ 02 644 30 31. Tram #81.
Mon–Fri noon–2pm & 7.30–10.30pm, Sat 7.30–10.30pm. Moderate.
This well-known and long-established Ixelles haunt serves impressive, mostly French, cuisine in lavish but not snobbish surroundings. There's also an extensive wine list. You can get a lovely two-course lunch for a very reasonable €14.75. You'll need to reserve in advance.

Le Doux Wazoo

Map 1, E3. Rue du Relais 21 ⊕ 02 649 58 52. Bus #95, #96. Tues–Fri noon–2.30pm & 7–11pm, Sat & Mon 7–11pm. Closed July 15–Aug 15. Inexpensive.
Long-established bistro with a friendly atmosphere, just west of the ULB University. The decor is 1930s style, with old posters and a collection of small clocks. The classic French cuisine – roast duck and *foie gras*, Burgundy ham – is both tasty and good value for money. Set menus from €25.

EAT

Map 8, G7. Rue de l'Aqueduc 103 ⊕ 02 537 22 90. Tram #93, #94.
Daily noon–2.30pm, also Wed 7pm–10.30pm. Inexpensive.
A straight-up, large and modern eatery open only for lunch – except Wednesday when Chatelain hosts its weekly market. You can pick and choose from a range of house dishes, most of them of the salad and pasta variety. The servings are generous and fresh, and the service is

quick to flash a smile. Healthy dining in a smart setting, and prices remain supremely modest.

Le Fils de Jules

Map 8, G7. Rue du Page 37 ℡ 02 534 00 57. Tram #81. Bus #54.
Mon–Thurs noon–2pm & 7–11pm, Fri & Sat 7–11pm. Moderate.

Basque chefs serve up first-class cuisine from southwestern France at this small Art Deco-inspired restaurant. The setting, in the swankiest part of Ixelles, is a perfect backdrop to the delightful food. Reservations usually necessary, particularly on weekends.

Gioconda' Store Convivio

Map 8, G7. Rue de l'Aqueduc 76 ℡ 02 539 32 99. Tram #81. Bus #54.
Mon–Sat noon–2.30pm & 6.30–10.30pm. Inexpensive.

This bright, wedge-shaped wine and pasta shop doubles up as a restaurant and is a great place for a spot of lunch or an evening meal. The

prices are fairly cheap, and the food – mainly Italian pasta dishes – is nice and tasty. There's usually an upbeat, chatty atmosphere, and the entertainment is provided by the amusingly manic Italian waiting staff. Good for vegetarians.

Le Macaron

Map 8, H7. Rue de Mail 1 ℡ 02 537 89 43. Tram #81. Bus #54.
Tues–Sun 6.30pm–1am. Inexpensive.

Charming French restaurant just off place du Châtelain on the corner of rue de Mail. The convivial ambience, homely surroundings and cheap fish, meat and pasta dishes – main meals under €9 – mean the place is often packed to bursting, even on weekdays. The spaghetti bolognese is superlative.

Le Mess

Map 1, D3. 1 Blvd Louis Schmidt ℡ 02 734 03 36. Tram #90, #23.
Daily except Sat midday noon–2.30pm & 7–11pm. Moderate.

Traces of *Le Mess*'s former incarnation as a military barracks live on in the efficient service, spotlessly white tablecloths and Starck decor of dark wood and mood lighting. Tasty sushi lunches, and rich flavoursome dishes such as salmon with bacon. The large first-floor terrace is as prim and proper as the main dining rooms, although a little noisy given its proximity to the six-lane boulevard.

Notos

Map 8, H6. Rue de Livourne 154 ⊤02 513 29 59. Tram #94. Bus #93.
Tues–Sun 7–11pm. Closed Aug 15–31. Moderate
Airy and well illuminated Greek restaurant near the Chatelain area. If you've come looking for traditional mezzes and sirtakis you'll be disappointed: *Notos* serves up a far more refined and flavourful cuisine. Reservations are firmly recommended.

Ô-Chinoise-Riz

Map 8, G7. Rue de l'Aqueduc 94 ⊤02 534 91 08. Tram #81.
Bus #54.
Mon–Fri noon–2.30pm & 6–11pm, Sat & Sun 6–11pm. Inexpensive.
This small restaurant, just round the corner from place du Châtelain, is where the Chinese come to eat Chinese food. The food is excellent and you get the spectacle of frantic cooks boiling and sizzling your meal in the open-plan kitchen, thereby ensuring you'll leave with smelly clothes. It's also remarkably cheap by Brussels standards. Sample the crispy chicken with vegetables and the won-ton soup.

Pablo's

Map 2, E7. Rue de Namur 51 ⊤02 502 41 35. Ⓜ Porte de Namur. Bus #71.
Mon–Sun noon–3pm & 6pm–midnight. Closed Sun midday. Moderate.
Tex-Mex joint just across the road from Métro Porte de Namur. Although there's always a good atmosphere, the food – spare ribs, steaks, tacos, and tasty burritos – is a tad pricey for what you get. A great place to go with a

AVENUE LOUISE AND IXELLES

bunch of loud and frolicking friends. On the plus side, the desserts, especially the cheesecakes, are delicious, and there's a long bar serving interesting and lethal cocktails. Reservations aren't accepted, so go early to avoid a long wait.

Le Passiflore

Map 8, G6. Rue du Bailli 97 ⓣ 02 538 42 10. Tram #81. Bus #54.
Mon–Fri 8am–7pm, Sat & Sun 9am–7pm. Inexpensive.
Overlooking the Baroque church of Ste Trinité, this trendy but relaxing café serves light lunches, including homemade salmon and spinach quiche, crêpes, and a variety of salads, all for under €8. It's usually packed on Sunday mornings, when hordes of pasty-faced late-twenty-something revellers attempt to cure their hangovers with one of the good-value continental breakfasts. The *croque monsieurs* are the finest in the capital.

Pizza Marseille

Map 8, G8. Ch de Waterloo 412 ⓣ 02 534 28 20. Bus W.
Daily noon–2.30pm & 7–10.30pm. Inexpensive.
A fascinating blend of 26 different kinds of *pastis* and delicious pizzas from Marseille. Brightly coloured tables create a childlike feel, but the thin-dough pizzas with toppings that vary from *pastis*-flavoured prawns to saffron chicken and fresh figs are very grown-up indeed. Don't leave without sampling the Rolls-Royce of *pastis*: the Versinthe.

La Quincaillerie

Map 8, G7. Rue du Page 45 ⓣ 02 538 25 53. Tram #81. Bus #54.
Mon–Fri noon–2pm & 7pm–midnight, Sat & Sun 7pm–midnight. Expensive.
The chic, stylish and downright loaded make their way to this delightful restaurant, occupying an old hardware shop, a couple of streets away from Musée Horta. Well known for its mouthwatering Belgian and French cuisine, specialities

include fish and fowl, often cooked up in imaginative ways. There's normally a reasonably priced *plat du jour* for €9, but the à la carte is very pricey.

Shanti

Map 1, D3. Ave Adolphe Buyl 68 ⓣ 02 649 40 96. Tram #93, #94.
Tues–Sat noon–2pm & 6.30pm–10pm. Closed July 15–Aug 15. Inexpensive.
First-class vegetarian restaurant – popular with meat-eaters too – set in a lovely neo-Baroque oriental interior filled with plants. Dishes include fish tandoori and tofu and crab combinations. A bio and natural products store occupies the ground floor.

Touch and Go

Map 8, I2. Rue St Boniface 12. Ⓜ Porte de Namur.
Mon–Sat noon–2.30pm & 6.30pm–12.30am, Sun 6.30pm–12.30am. Inexpensive.
A cheap and trendy pitta chain – ideal if you want to catch a tasty snack and you're in a hurry. Although more

upmarket than the average fast-food joint, the turnover is almost as rapid and the food – exotic pitta fillings and salads – is scrumptious. Other branches are at avenue Paul Héger 20, and rue de Livourne 131.

Tutto Pepe

Map 8, G6. Rue Faider 123 ⓣ 02 534 96 19. Tram #81.
Mon–Fri noon–2.30pm & 7–11pm, Sat 7–11pm. Moderate.
Located just off rue du Bailli, this intimate eight-table Italian is romantic without being clichéd. *Tutto Pepe* combines tasteful, rustic-style decor, a background soundtrack of Italian opera, and a simple menu of tasty Italian staples such as tagliatelle, spaghetti and bruschetta.

W-Double You

Map 8, J9. Ave Louise 519 ⓣ 02 644 97 77. Tram #93, #94.
Daily except Sat midday & Sun noon–11.30pm. Moderate.
Brussels' cool crowd flocks to this cosy, modern restaurant –

all soft colours, plush surroundings and smooth tunes. The food, including tasty pizzas and pasta with chicken, is as palatable as the decor, though the service is slightly haughty.

Yamato

Map 8, H2. Rue Francart 11 ⓣ 02 502 28 93. Ⓜ Porte de Namur.
Mon–Sat noon–2pm & 7–10pm. Inexpensive.
A tiny, busy Japanese restaurant with minimalist decor, just round the corner from place St Boniface. If you like authentic Japanese food this noodle bar is the place to come – it's fairly cheap (€8 for a main) and full of character.

Yamayu Santatsu

Map 8, I3. Ch d'Ixelles 141 ⓣ 02 513 53 12. Ⓜ Porte de Namur.
Daily except Sun midday & Mon noon–2pm & 7–10pm. Moderate.
This well-established sushi and sashimi restaurant is one of the finest in Brussels. With the interior organized around the sushi bar, the owner shouts orders to underlings as he presses strips of fresh fish, his wife works the minimalist room as best she can and the whole spectacle is worthy of its own write-up. Usually packed, you should be snappy with your orders and settle down with some cold sake for the considerable wait. Highly recommended, and reservations are essential.

EU QUARTER AND ST JOSSE

Bodeguilla

Map 2, J6. Rue Archimède 65–67 ⓣ 02 736 34 49. Ⓜ Schuman.
Mon–Sat 7–11pm. Inexpensive.
A simple Spanish tapas bar hidden away in the basement of the expensive *Le Jardin d'Espagne* restaurant. The place seems to be a second home to legions of Spanish expats, no doubt attracted by the home cooking and cheap prices. Great place for a quick snack before hitting the town.

EU QUARTER AND ST JOSSE

GANSHOREN RESTAURANTS

Two of the finest restaurants in the city can be found northwest of the city centre in the *commune* of Ganshoren. If you're making the trip by public transport, the nearest métro station is Ⓜ Simonis.

Claude Dupont Ave Vital Riethuisen 46 (Map 1, B1; Wed–Sun noon–2pm & 7–9.45pm, closed July; ☏ 02 426 00 00). Excellent townhouse restaurant renowned for its exquisite service, classic decor and superb gourmet French cuisine – try the sole and scallops with champagne sauce. Reserve in advance and take a taxi as it's a fair distance from the métro station. Very expensive.

Bruneau Ave Broustin 75 (Map 1, B1; noon–2pm & 7–10pm, closed Tues night, Aug & Feb 1–10; ☏ 02 427 69 78). A gastronome's delight with a well-deserved reputation. Superb modern decor – all minimalist styling and smooth lighting – and astounding French food from media darling Jean-Pierre Bruneau. Lovely garden when the weather permits. Is it worth it? Yes, and yes again... Very expensive.

Restaurant de la Bonne Humeur
Map 2, I4. Ch de Louvain 244 ☏ 02 230 71 69. Bus #29. Mon, Thurs–Sun noon–2pm, 6.30–9.30pm. Moderate.
If you want traditional *moules* and *frites* then forget the crass *Chez Léon* and come to this authentic, well-known, family-run restaurant with a great atmosphere.

Sahbaz
Map 2, G2. Ch de Haecht 102 ☏ 02 217 02 77. Tram #92, #93. Daily 11.30am–3pm & 6pm–midnight. Inexpensive.
This Turkish restaurant is the best in the capital. The food is cheap and delicious, the staff friendly and attentive, and there are usually cheerful crowds all week. Just beyond the northern boundary of St Josse in Schaerbeek, an area

EU QUARTER AND ST JOSSE

reputed for street crime, so it may be worth getting a taxi home.

Version Originale

Map 2, L7. Ave des Celtes 11 ⓣ 02 732 64 69. Ⓜ Merode. Mon–Fri noon–2.30pm & 6.30–11pm, Sat 6.30–11pm. Moderate.

Milking the movie theme, with black-and-white photographs of film stars and other cinema-related bits and bobs, the "Original Language" delivers when it comes to the food: zesty French cuisine, such as duck with caramelized pears, at slightly inflated prices. Perhaps its main draw, however, is the characterful rooftop terrace, with its vaulted arches and kitsch decoration.

Drinking

Drinking in Brussels, as in the rest of the country, is a joy. The city has an enormous variety of bars and cafés. Sumptuous Art Nouveau bars sit alongside swanky, Parisian-style, terraced cafés; traditional drinking dens with ceilings stained by a century's smoke nestle next to hi-tech cyber bars; and speciality beer bars offer hundreds of different types of ale.

The city's bars are concentrated mostly in the **centre**: around the Grand-Place, Bourse and the place St Géry. Recently, the area has seen a proliferation of trendy bars in which the fashion-conscious youth of Brussels drink beer, cocktails and flavoured vodkas until the wee small hours. When the weather allows, crowds spill on to the terraces and streets, making for an amazingly upbeat ambience.

Although the **Upper Town** doesn't have as much to offer, there is a number of smoky, velour-furnished bars near the Toison d'Or shopping area, on the chaussée de Charleroi. Venturing out of the petit ring can also be worthwhile, especially if you head to laid-back **Ixelles** or **St Gilles**, where you'll find a selection of fashionable bars and cafés and an almost inexhaustible supply of small local hangouts. The **EU quarter** around place Schuman also offers a decent selection of watering holes, the majority of them Irish or British pubs.

Belgians make little or no distinction between **bars** and **cafés**, and the two words tend to be used interchangeably; most bars serve food, and practically all cafés serve beer and other types of alcohol – cafés often have a terrace, but then again so do many bars.

As **opening hours** in Brussels are not officially restricted, bars and cafés can stay open as long as they want, usually until the last soaks slide out. In practice, most close around 2am, although at the weekend it's often much later.

Prices for drinks can vary hugely depending on where you are. As a general rule you pay over the odds for the privilege of drinking around the Grand-Place, though not necessarily in the streets around it. If you're paying more than €2.50 for a beer, you're paying too much. Spirits are relatively expensive, and a gin and tonic can cost you between €3.50 and €4, though the measures are often generous. There's a good selection of reasonably priced wines (especially white and red Burgundy) available by the bottle or glass. **Food** is served in most places, ranging from sandwiches and *croques monsieurs*, to more exotic fare.

THE GRAND-PLACE AND AROUND

Arteaspoon
Map 3, C5. Rue des Chartreux 11. Ⓜ de Brouckère.
Mon–Thurs 10am–midnight, Fri & Sat 11am–2am.
An art gallery and bar-restaurant rolled into one, this is a buzzing place with a vibrant crowd. The decor is minimalist, with oak furniture, and there's a lovely little mezzanine. It does a variety of cocktails and long drinks as well as delicious quiches and salads. The art on display is by local artists.

La Bécasse
Map 4, C2. Rue du Tabora 11. Ⓜ de Brouckère.
Mon–Thurs 10am–midnight, Fri–Sun 11am–2am.

This ancient bar, with long wooden benches and heavy Moorish architecture, has an excellent beer menu. It's one of the few places in Belgium, for instance, where you can drink Lambic (see p.308). It also serves house *gueuze* and "blanche de Bruxelles". Drinks are served in earthenware jugs. The food, however, is of rather poor quality.

Au Bon Vieux Temps
Map 4, D3. Rue du Marché-aux-Herbes 12. Ⓜ de Brouckère.
Daily 1pm–12.30am.
Tucked away down an alley and only a minute's walk from the Grand-Place, this is a cosy old place, with tile-inlaid tables and a seventeenth-century chimneypiece. The building dates back to 1695 and the stained-glass window depicting the Virgin Mary and St Michael was originally in the local St Guoliche parish church. Popular with British servicemen just after the end of World War II, the bar still has comforting old-fashioned signs advertising Mackenzie's Port and Bass pale ale. A great

place for a quiet, contemplative drink.

Le Cirio
Map 4, B2. Rue de la Bourse 18. Ⓜ Bourse.
Daily 10am–1am.
Established in 1886 and seriously threatening to usurp the *Falstaff* as king of the Brussels brasseries, this airy bar is lavishly decorated in fin-de-siècle style, with wood panelling and scattered aspidistras. It's said to have been frequented by Jacques Brel and is popular with an older clientele. The olde worlde decor and relaxed atmosphere make this a great place to rest your feet after a hard day's schlepp. Do try their "half-and-half", made up of champagne and white wine – a drink the house claims to have invented.

Le Cygne Café
Map 4, D4. Grand-Place 9. Ⓜ Bourse.
Mon–Fri 12.15–2pm, 6.30pm–1am, Sat 6.30pm–1am.
Believe it or not, this venerable establishment on the Grand-Place used to be

THE GRAND-PLACE AND AROUND

Karl Marx's local. In fact, historians insist Marx polished off the Communist Manifesto at meetings of exiled German socialists here. The only reminder today is a plaque on the wall commemorating the founding, in April 1885, of the Belgian Socialist Party. The café also serves capital food and is nice for a quiet drink, but is probably a bit too bourgeois now for Karl.

Le Falstaff

Map 4, B3. Rue Henri Maus 17–23. Ⓜ Bourse.
Sun–Thurs 11.30am–2am, Fri & Sat 11.30am–4am.

This hugely impressive Art Nouveau bar, close to the Bourse, attracts a mixed bag of tourists, Eurocrats and bourgeois Bruxellois, and is a great place to sit back and soak up some atmosphere. The *plat du jour* is good value at €8.70, though Belgian specialities, such as sumptuous beef stewed the Flemish way (with fried potatoes), is slightly pricey at €12. There's also a mouthwatering selection of Flemish cakes and tarts. The

entertainment is provided by the amusingly po-faced staff.

A L'Imaige Nostre Dame

Map 4, D3. Impasse de Cadeaux 3. Ⓜ Bourse.
Daily 11.30am–1am, Sun from 4pm.

Hidden down an alleyway just off the Grand-Place, this traditional drinking den is frequented by a mixed bag of Eurocrats, Bruxellois and stray tourists. While the building dates back to 1664, it has the look and feel of a traditional English steak-house. Bar food, like spaghetti bolognese, is available.

Le Roy d'Espagne

Map 4, C3. Grand-Place 1. Ⓜ Bourse.
Daily 10am–1am.

Housed in a seventeenth-century guildhouse (the bakers'), this popular tourist bar combines Baroque facades, wicker lampshades, pigs' bladders, hanging marionettes, and a bust of Charles II. A slightly macabre large stuffed horse also adds to the Bruegelian atmosphere. The fine views of the Grand-

Place from the rooms upstairs and the terrace, and the reasonable bar prices, mean it's often packed, especially in the summer. Overpriced sandwiches and a hot and cold buffet of meats, salads and soups are available.

Au Soleil
Map 4, A5. Rue de Marché au Charbon 86. Ⓜ Bourse. Daily 10am–2.30am.
Formerly a men's clothing shop, this trendy café on the laid-back rue de Marché quenches the thirst of young arty Brussels types, as well as stray tourists who've wandered down from the Grand-Place. Cheap bar snacks are on offer – soup of the day is only €2.25 – and there's a pleasant terrace where you can while away

the day over a coffee or something a little stronger. A good atmosphere, but it's often difficult to get a seat come nightfall.

Théâtre de Toone
Map 4, D3. Petite rue des Bouchers, Impasse de Schuddeveld 6. Ⓜ Bourse. Daily 10am–2.30am.
This congenial bar belonging to the Toone puppet theatre is just north of the Grand-Place but quite difficult to locate, hidden away as it is down an alleyway in the heart of the fish restaurant quarter. When you eventually get there you'll find two small rooms with old posters on rough plaster walls, a reasonably priced beer list, a modest selection of snacks, and a soundtrack of classical and jazz.

THE LOWER TOWN

Beursschouwburg
Map 3, C6. Rue Auguste Orts 20–28. Ⓜ Bourse. Thurs–Sat 7.30pm–4am.
Hip and happening, this large

industrial-space café-bar regularly serves up a mixture of bangra, drum 'n' bass, acid jazz, and funk, for the Love Parade generation. The clientele is mostly cool, artsy Flemish types that you don't see anywhere else. Get there before 11pm if you want a table at the weekend or the chance to catch a live band or DJ set. For listings check out their freebie *Beursschouwburg* available in most of the trendy bars and cafés in the area.

Café Métropole
Map 3, D4. Pl de Brouckère 31. Ⓜ de Brouckère.
Daily 9am–1am.
Sumptuously ritzy fin-de-siècle café, belonging to an equally opulent hotel with exquisite Renaissance decor, including stained-glass windows and ornate candelabras. This place seems to have instant stress-relieving properties and after five minutes of sipping coffee in utter luxury you feel like the world's a pretty civilized place after all. If you've cash to spare, you might indulge in a brunch of smoked salmon or caviar.

Coasters
Map 3, C6. Rue des Riches-Claires 28. Ⓜ Bourse.

Daily 8pm–8am.
This cosy, two-roomed bar around the corner from *Java* is where students come to play table football and take advantage of the very generous happy hour (8–11pm). However, in the early hours, especially on weekends, the place becomes a pulsating mass of nubile young bodies, when clubbers, not quite ready for their cocoa, pile in to dance to the latest tracks.

Le Corbeau
Map 3, E4. Rue St Michel 18. Ⓜ de Brouckère.
Sun–Thurs 9.30am–12.30am, Fri & Sat 9.30pm–2am.
During the day, this tavern, just off rue Neuve, is a little sleepy to say the least, but by the evening, especially on weekends, the place is taken over by students and drinking competitions. Table-dancing is not unheard of.

D.N.A.
Map 3, C6. Rue Plattesteen 18–20. Ⓜ de Brouckère.
Mon–Thurs & Sun 9.30am–12.30am, Fri & Sat

9.30pm–2am.

Has a reputation as an alternative bar, popular with the post-rock crowd, but also attracts a wider clientele, drawn by its great trip-hop music and occasional rock concerts. A place to let your hair down. Plenty of hearty Belgian beers, though nothing too exotic, while the food is the standard salad, pasta and sandwich fare.

Fin de Siècle

Map 3, C5. Rue des Chartreux 9. Ⓜ Bourse.
Daily 5pm–3am; kitchen open till 1am.

This charming and civilized café-bar is home to a young arty twenty- and thirty-something crowd who come for the vibrant atmosphere and top-class Italian, Greek, and Iranian food. The decor's pretty impressive as well, especially the original Art Nouveau facade and stained-glass windows. On the downside, you often have to wait for a place at one of the long stripped-wood tables.

La Fleur en Papier Doré

Map 3, D7. Rue Alexiens 55. Ⓜ Anneessens.
Sun–Thurs 11am–2am, Fri & Sat 11am–4am.

One of the capital's most eccentric bars, this mad temple of surrealism has walls covered with doodles and poems, deer antlers hanging from the ceiling, and enough bric-à-brac to start a junk shop. Legend has it Magritte and the Dadaists used to get tanked up here in the 1920s and apparently it was also the chosen venue for the novelist Hugo Claus's second wedding reception. The place is still frequented by artistic and literary types, as well as amiable local lunatics who seem to drink Leffe Triple from dusk till dawn. Just south of the Grand-Place near the bowling alley.

Goupil Le Fol

Map 3, D6. Rue de la Violette 22. Ⓜ Gare Centrale.
Daily 7.30pm–6am.

This unusual bar, between the Grand-Place and the Manneken Pis, should not be missed, especially if you are interested in traditional French singing of the likes of Edith Piaf or Belgium's very own Jacques Brel. Every surface is covered with *chanson française* memorabilia and it lives up to its reputation as a former brothel, with three floors of cosy corners, sink-into sofas, and dimmed red lights. It's worth a visit simply for the flea-market-style decor, if not for the delicious and extremely potent fruit wines which come in a variety of combinations at a slightly pricey €5.

Le Greenwich

Map 3, C5. Rue des Chartreux 7. Ⓜ Bourse.
Daily noon–1am.
An oasis of calm in a commercial storm, this smoky, traditional chess bar, next door to *Fin de Siècle*, has been patronized by generations of chess and backgammon enthusiasts, including, according to the locals, Magritte. Although a little down-at-heel, the cheap beer and get-away-from-it-all atmosphere easily make up

for it. The crowd varies from ancient pipe-smokers to suave twenty-somethings.

Le Java

Map 3, C6. Rue St Géry 31. Ⓜ Bourse.
Daily 3pm–3am.
Close to the attractive place St Géry, this small triangular bar seems perpetually thronged with city slickers and funksters living it large on schnapps and cocktails. If you like Gaudí-inspired decor, groovy music, and a kicking atmosphere, you're home.

Mappa Mundo

Map 3, C5. Rue du Pont de la Carpe 2. Ⓜ Bourse.
Mon–Fri 8am–4am, Sat & Sun 10am–5am.
The latest bar on the scene from the French entrepreneurs who have reinvigorated Brussel's nightlife with *Zebra*, *Bonsoir Clara* and *Kasbah*. This is an oak-lined pub where people come for some serious drinking. They serve a copious breakfast all morning and there is a brunch on

Sundays for which you have to reserve. The rest of the food consists of bagels, pittas, salads, soups and is served from 11am to 3pm and from 6pm to 1am.

Memesse

Map 3, C6. Rue St Christophe 20. Ⓜ Bourse.
Mon–Sat 9.30am–2am.
A quick saunter from place St Géry, *Memesse* has a welcoming atmosphere, partly created by the warm ochre colours of the decor. Delicious house wines sold by the glass are an unusual touch. Good salads and pasta dishes are available during lunch and dinner periods.

à la Mort Subite

Map 2, E4. Rue Montagne aux Herbes Potagères 7. Ⓜ Gare Centrale.
Daily 11am–1am.
Just northeast of the Grand-Place, a Twenties bar that borrowed its name from a widely available bottled beer. Expect to find a long, narrow room with nicotine-stained walls and mirrors, a thirty-somethingish clientele and an animated atmosphere, not forgetting the surliest bar staff in Brussels. Snacks are served, or just order a plate of cheese cubes to accompany your beer.

O'Reilly's

Map 3, C6. Pl de la Bourse 1. Ⓜ Bourse.
Sun–Thurs 11am–1am, Fri & Sat till 2am.
This large Irish theme bar directly opposite the Bourse is the unofficial venue for Irish supporters when there's an Irish rugby or football game on (see p.256). It's also the only bar in the centre which screens live English Premiership football. Although nothing to write home about, it's a handy enough meeting place, except on Friday and Saturday nights when the bar is mobbed with drunken revellers. Food (fries, baked potatoes, Irish stew, salmon, chicken) is available from 11am till 10pm.

Le Roi des Belges

Map 3, C5. Rue Jules van Praet 35–37. Ⓜ Bourse.

Sun–Thurs 11am–1am, Fri &
Sat till 2am.

Blending a brasserie with
neo-industrial design isn't an
easy one to pull off, but the
Roi des Belges does so regally.
It's a bit cramped inside, and
the upstairs is very smoky,
but the crowds never seem
to tire of squeezing in and
out of here. The
summertime terrace is the
choice location.

Le Velvet Café

Map 3, D6. Rue de la Tête
d'Or 1. Ⓜ Bourse.
Mon–Thurs noon–2am, Fri–Sun
till 3am.

Done out in orange and blue
velour with Alessi-designed
lights and chairs, this is a
comfortable place to relax in
and sip luscious cocktails. The
floor above becomes the
Velvet Room on Thursday
nights, when a blend of
groove and R n' B shakes
rumps.

Wilde

Map 3, C6. Blvd Anspach 77.
Ⓜ Bourse.
Mon–Thurs noon–2am, Fri–Sun
till 3am.

A cool London bar directly
transplanted into the heart of
Brussels, catering to the EU
crowd, especially the Irish
contingent. There's plenty of
Guinness on tap. Playing hip
or house music, this is a great
place to warm up before the
night really begins. An
upstairs floor opens on
weekends when the ground
floor gets too packed.

Zebra

Map 3, C5. Pl St Géry 33–35.
Ⓜ Bourse.
Mon–Thurs noon–2am, Fri–Sun
till 3am.

This small but trendy bar on
the corner of place St Géry
was the first venture of the
French crew who own *Kasbah*
and *Mappo Mundo*. It is still
the supreme location – anyone
who is anyone has been here
at some point – and attracts a
young chic crowd who come
for the upbeat atmosphere and
groovy music. It's also
terrifically popular in the
summer when people come
out to read their newspapers
on the large terrace.

THE LOWER TOWN

THE UPPER TOWN

Le Perroquet

Map 3, D8. Rue Watteau 31.
Ⓜ Gare Centrale.
Daily 10.30am–1.30am.
This small, semicircular café-bar, a two-minute walk from place du Grand Sablon, has stained-glass windows, Art Nouveau decor and a pleasant terrace out front. Young and old rub shoulders over cheap salads and pittas, whilst those of a more dipsomaniacal disposition work their way through the long list of speciality beers. Although it's often difficult to get a seat on a Friday or Saturday night, it's worth the hassle.

De Skievers Architeck

Map 3, C10. Pl du Jeu de Balle 50. Ⓜ Porte de Hal.
Daily 6am–1am.
The smartest place on the square, this high-ceilinged, airy café-bar has an impressive traditional beer menu, newspapers to browse, and serves a wide range of cheap but tasty

meals and snacks. "The Slanted Architect" is named after its designer, Joseph Poelaert, who also put up the Palais de Justice and cleared more than a hundred small working-class houses in the process. The locals gave him his disparaging nickname because when viewed from the Marolles quarter the Palais looks like it slopes to one side. It's often busy on Sunday afternoons after the market at Jeu de Balle.

De Ultieme Hallucinatie

Map 3, H3. Rue Royale 316.
Ⓜ Botanique.
Mon–Fri 11am–2am, Sat & Sun 5pm–3am.
On the outskirts of the city centre, this well-known and fancifully ornate Art Nouveau bar is done up like an old 1920s train car and is popular with a youngish crowd who come for the excellent choice of beers and reasonably priced food – omelettes, lasagne, etc. The

lavishly decorated restaurant in the front also comes highly recommended, although on the downside, the area has a bad reputation for street crime.

IXELLES

L'Amour Fou
Map 8, I3. Ch d'Ixelles 185. Bus #71.
Sun–Thurs 9am–2am, Fri & Sat till 3am.

An upbeat café off place Fernand Cocq, where you can drink a delicious selection of vodkas, mescal and tequila while checking your emails or taking in the latest works of obscure European artists which decorate the walls. The spacious central room with high ceilings has a wonderful air of elegance. There's also a rear room filled with immense blue Ikea couches and soft lighting. The food is quite good and includes such staples as *croques monsieurs*; the kitchen is open from 11am till 1am. It's often busy and service is highly erratic.

Bar Parallèle
Map 8, I3. Place Fernand Cocq 25. Bus #71.
Daily 11.30am–1am.

The third tip of the geographical triangle that includes Volle Gas and L'Amour Fou. A nifty outdoor terrace and large, spartan interior help create a relaxed atmosphere. Attracts a bouncy young crowd on the weekends.

Le Majestic Club
Map 8, I7. Rue du Magistrat 33. Tram #93, #94.
Mon–Thurs 6pm–2am, Fri & Sat until 3am.

A Baroque-meets-boudoir decor of chandeliers, leather, mirrors, wood and forged iron. Attracts fake tans, politicians and show-biz types: Brussels doesn't get more glam than this. It serves excellent food too, such as grilled salmon with pasta, and the service and selection of cocktails are impeccable. Strict door policy.

Le Tavernier

Map 1, D3. Ch de Boendael 445. Bus #71.
Sun–Thurs 10am–2am, Fri & Sat 10am–4am.

A cool, happening bar, filled with students and other bouncing bunnies, so who else could be behind it but Fred Nicolay, owner of the *Zebra* and *Mappa Mundo*. It's all here: there's a great outdoor terrace, exposed brick and slightly scruffy furnishings, DJs, concerts and movies projected on giant screens.

L'Ultime Atome

Map 8, I2. Rue St Boniface 14. Ⓜ Porte de Namur.
Sun–Thurs 8am–2am, Fri & Sat 10am–2am.

A large selection of beers and wines, simple but tasty cuisine (open till 12.30am), and late opening hours, make this funky café-bar a hit with the trendy Ixelles crowd weekdays and weekends alike. Its location, on the laid-back rue St Boniface, also makes it a great place to sit outside with a newspaper in the summer.

Volle Gas

Map 8, I3. Pl Fernand Cocq 21. Ⓜ Porte de Namur.
Daily 11am–2am.

On place Fernand Cocq, this traditional bar-brasserie serves classic Belgian cuisine in a friendly, family atmosphere. The Brussels specialities on offer include the delicious *carbonnades de boeuf à la Gueuze* – beef in beer. There's also occasional live jazz, although when there is a band playing the bar prices tend to go through the roof.

AVENUE LOUISE AND AROUND

Le Châtelain

Map 8, G7. Pl du Châtelain 17. Tram #81.
Mon–Sat 10.30am–2am.

A cheerful café with a well-worn decor serving all the Belgian classics, including *chicons au gratin* and the delicious *stoemp saucisse et lard* – mashed potatoes, carrots and bacon. Although it's a tad pricey at around €13 for the

AVENUE LOUISE AND AROUND

209

stoemp, the friendly atmosphere and great location make up for it.

Conways

Map 2, E7. Ave de la Toison d'Or 10. Ⓜ Porte de Namur. Mon–Wed noon–2am, Thurs–Sat noon–4am, Sun 6pm–2am.

A lively, late-night Irish-American bar frequented by the young, free, and extremely desperate. If you want to get drunk and stand on a barstool playing air-guitar, this is the place to come. But be warned, it's a bit of a meat market.

Tierra del Fuego

Map 8, G4. Rue Berckmans 14. Ⓜ Louise. Sun–Thurs 5pm–12.30am, Fri & Sat 6.30pm–2am.

Just off chaussée de Charleroi, this largely undiscovered Latin American resto-bar in the Maison de l'Amérique Latine is definitely worth a visit. Delicious food and wine, tasteful decor, a lovely candlelit garden and a Moorish ceramics terrace out back make this one of the capital's most relaxing retreats. Live music and barbecues in the summer.

ST GILLES

Living Room

Map 8, F4. Ch de Charleroi 50. Ⓜ Louise. Daily 9pm–3am.

A perfect spot for pre-partying, the *Living Room* has settled down from its early, jam-packed days to a nice, pleasant roar. The very comfortable surroundings – velour walls, soft chairs – live up to its name. A healthy crowd shows up for hot tunes on the weekend and a variety of top-notch house DJs keep your feet busy. You can also grab a bite to eat, although the food isn't great.

Chez Moeder Lambic

Map 8, C7. Rue de Savoie 68. Ⓜ Horta. Daily 4pm–3am.

A small bar in a down-at-heel part of St Gilles, just behind the commune's Hôtel de Ville. Has over 1000 beers available, including 500 Belgian varieties. Not at all expensive and ideal for a quiet drink.

La Porteuse d'Eau

Map 8, C4. Ave Jean Volders 48a. Ⓜ Porte de Hal.

Daily 10am–1am.
This refurbished Art Nouveau café, on the corner of rue Vanderschrick, is one of the few signs of gentrification in this run-down section of St Gilles. The food is not cheap, but it's worth the price of a beer to see the airily ornate interior.

EU QUARTER

Kitty O'Shea's

Map 2, I6. Blvd Charlemagne 42. Ⓜ Schuman.
Mon–Sat noon–3am, Sun noon–3pm.
This large Irish bar, opposite the Centre Berlaymont, is the place to come for Irish food and draught Guinness. Although it gets a bit rowdy when there's a football or rugby international, it's one of the more palatable bars in the area.

The Wild Geese

Map 2, I5. Ave Livingstone

2–4. Ⓜ Schuman or Madou.
Sun–Wed 11am–1am, Thurs 11am–2am, Fri & Sat 11am–3am.
This enormous Irish theme pub is the preferred watering hole of the EU crowd, especially Thursday nights when the Euro-youth strut their stuff en masse. It also serves good-value bar food, including large baked potatoes with salads and fillings for under €5. Occasional live music and a lovely outdoor terrace.

EU QUARTER

Clubs and live music

After a slow start, club culture seems to have finally taken hold in Brussels. The city has a number of established meccas playing anything from acid and techno beats to deep house, including the throbbing Fuse with its regular line-up of big-name house DJs, to the sassy Who's Who Land, which often sees crowds of over 1500 and attracts people from as far away as Paris and Amsterdam.

Most venues are in the **Lower Town**, especially in the area between place St Géry and the Manneken Pis, and in the scruffily hip Marolles quarter just southeast of the Grand-Place. The **Upper Town** has a only few offerings of its own, and there are a couple of places beyond the petit ring that are worth the trip. If you do venture out of the centre, don't forget that the public **transport** system finishes at 12.30am and starts up again at 5.30am, so you may have to get a taxi home. Night buses are fairly infrequent.

As a general rule, clubs are **open** Thursday to Saturday from 11pm until as late as 6am, but it is possible to club every night. **Entry prices** are fairly low: you rarely have to pay more than €10, and many of the smaller clubs have no cover charge at all, although men have to tip the bouncer a nominal fee (€1.25 or so) on the way out.

The **cost of drinks** varies depending on where you are, although shorts and cocktails are expensive across the board. If you're on a limited budget it's worth remembering that the bars which morph into clubs on a weekend, such as *Le Sud* and *L'Acrobat*, tend to have cheaper drinks than ordinary clubs.

Although the city just about holds its own on the club scene, Brussels fares extremely well as a place to catch **live music**. The capital has a vibrant **jazz** scene, with many bars, both in the centre and on the outskirts, playing host to local and international acts. Jazz buffs in particular will be pleased to learn that live jazz has been popular in Brussels since the 1920s – a tradition kept alive today by small atmospheric venues such as *Sounds* and *L'Archiduc,* and by the annual Brussels Jazz Festival (see p.281) – widely regarded as being one of the best in Europe.

Unfortunately the local **rock** and **indie** scene isn't particularly kicking, although if you are prepared to go off the beaten track you can still catch some excellent live music at the *Fool Moon*, *Magasin 4* and *VK*. The good news for mainstream gig-goers is that Brussels is a regular stop on the European tours of major and up-and-coming artists. The biggest **gigs** are held in *Forest National*, although many medium-sized gigs are held in *Le Botanique*, *Cirque Royal* and *Ancienne Belgique*. It's also worth considering going to one of the **music festivals** held regularly outside Brussels, which usually attract a good line-up of rock bands mixed with dance DJs. The Torhout-Werchter Festival (see p.280), held in early July, is the biggest.

For classical music listings, see p.274.

CLUBS AND LIVE MUSIC

For **listings** of concerts and events, check the *What's On* section of the weekly *Bulletin* or the Wednesday pull-out section of *Le Soir*. Flyers for most clubs and raves can be picked up in the trendy bars and cafés in the centre, particularly in the Beursschouwburg – which also has its own events list – *Zebra*, and *Au Soleil*. Tickets for most concerts are available from Fnac in the City 2 complex, on rue Neuve (℡ 02 209 22 11), or from the booking office at the tourist office on the Grand-Place.

CLUBS

THE GRAND PLACE AND AROUND

- -

Butterfly

Map 3, E5. Impasse de la Fidélité 4. Ⓜ Gare Centrale. Thurs & Fri 10.30pm–late. Spread over two floors, with hip pseudo-pub decor upstairs while brilliant house tunes are pumped out over the dance floor below. Gets packed with teens and twentysomethings at weekends. If you're feeling adventurous try out the swings that hang from the ceiling. The "Make it Hot" Thursday nights serve up slabs of funk.

Sonik

Map 3, C6. Rue Marché aux Charbons 112. Ⓜ Gare Centrale. Wed–Sun 10.30pm–late. Despite the tight confines – 250 people are a serious crowd here – *Sonik* plays mainly techno, with some house and breakbeat thrown in for good measure. The ground floor harbours the dark, narrow dance floor, while the brighter upstairs provides you with some room to sit down and take a breather amongst the largely teenage crowd. On Thursdays regular and visiting DJs offer up four-hour sets of music they wouldn't ordinarily play –

CLUBS

the results can be very interesting.

The Sparrow

Map 4, E6. Rue du Duquesnoy 18. Ⓜ Gare Centrale. Fri & Sat 11.30pm–late. Opened in 1998, *The Sparrow* is a welcome oasis from the onslaught of electronica. Blending funk, soul, R n' B, two-step and even zouk, the rhythms are deep and smooth. Nice large, open space for dancing and bar-gazing. Doesn't get moving until around 1am.

THE LOWER TOWN

The Fuse

Map 3, C9. Rue Blaes 208. Ⓜ Porte de Hal. Sat 10pm–7am. Widely recognized as the finest techno club in Belgium, this pulsating dance club has played host to some of the best DJs in Europe, including The Orb, Daft Punk, Carl Cox, Carl Craig and Dave Angel. Three floors of techno, house, jungle and occasional hip-hop, as well as the usual

staple of chill-out rooms and visuals. The acts are slightly oriented towards Belgian DJs, but big international guests are still being pulled in. Entrance is €2.50 before 11pm, €9.90 after. The price goes up if there's a big name spinning the discs.

Who's Who Land

Map 3, C8. Rue du Poinçon 17. Ⓜ Anneessens. Sat 10pm–7am. One of the capital's runaway success stories, this trendy house club (with occasional foam parties) is always packed. Legions of young latex-wearing revellers pile through the doors and make a beeline for the main dance area where classic techno and house anthems are blasted out until the early hours. Entrance around €10.

THE UPPER TOWN

Le Bal

Map 1, E3. Blvd du Triomphe 47. Tram #23 or #90. Fri & Sat 10pm–5am. Large, glitzy and crammed

CLUBS

with tanned bodies and slicked back hair-dos, *Le Bal* is a decent all-round club. Despite the superior airs put on by the bouncers, it provides you with a dollop of dance, punctuated by mainstream favourites, giving enough juice to make the night go on and on.

Le Bazaar

Map 3, C9. Rue des Capucins 63 ☎02 511 26 00. Ⓜ Porte de Hal or Louise.
Tues–Thurs & Sun 7.30pm–1am, Fri & Sat 7.30pm–5am.
Try out the delicious international cuisine in the upstairs bar-restaurant before picking up your drinks and descending to the cellar-like club below for a mixture of funk, soul, rock and indie. Not far from rue Haute, down from the Palais de Justice.

Pitt's Bar

Map 3, D9. Rue des Minimes 53. Ⓜ Louise.
Tues–Sun 8pm–3am.
A popular (it's free) student hangout close to the Palais de Justice, where the music alternates between techno,

garage, house and bangra as well as a regular DJ set at 10.30pm.

EU QUARTER AND ST JOSSE

Mirano Continental

Map 2, H4. Ch de Louvain 38. Ⓜ Madou.
Fri & Sat 11pm–late.
A large, trashy club within staggering distance of Métro Madou, popular with wannabe jet-setters and preppy yuppies. Inside it's more like a second-division catwalk than a house club, with teams of insalubrious, fashion-conscious posers strutting round the place in designer-wear. For sheer tackiness value, the revolving dance floor is worth a go. Entrance will set you back somewhere in the region of €10, and, needless to say, the door policy doesn't favour mere mortals.

KOEKELBERG

Tour & Taxi

Map 1, C2. Rue Picard 5.

CLUBS

Ⓜ Belgica.

Fri & Sat 10.30pm–5am; free entrance before midnight, €8 afterwards.

This huge, industrial site isn't really a club, more of a location where parties are frequently organized. DJs spin a mix of progressive house and ambient dance through the night and the reasonably priced bar means buying a few rounds won't break the bank. The drawback is that it's in a slightly dodgy area so it's worth getting a taxi.

DJ-BARS

THE LOWER TOWN

L'Acrobat
Map 3, C5. Rue Borgval 14–16. Ⓜ Bourse.
Daily 10pm–6am.

A slightly scruffy bar, just round the corner from *Zebra*, which becomes a small club on the weekend (Fri & Sat 10pm–6am). DJs spin disco-house and funk for a clientele who uninhibitedly dance the night away in Latin American kitsch surroundings brightened by fairy lights. There's a great atmosphere, reasonably priced drinks and no entrance fee.

Canoa Quebrada
Map 3, C6. Rue du Marché au Charbon 53. Ⓜ Bourse.
Thurs–Sat 10pm–late.

This lively Latin American bar, close to *Au Soleil*, mutates into a club on the weekend. It's popular with the post-party crowd and other drunken revellers who come to salsa and samba the night away on the small dance floor. If it gets too hectic, head for the small bar at the back where you can down a few delicious Caipirinhas – typical Brazilian cocktails of cachaça (white rum), lemon and sugar. No cover charge, but all the cocktails cost around €8.

Cartagena
Map 3, C6. Rue du Marché au Charbon 70. Ⓜ Bourse.
Fri & Sat 11pm–4/5am.

DJ BARS

217

This enjoyable downtown club is opposite Canoa, and offers arguably the best and certainly the widest range of South American and Latino sounds in town. Attracts the late twenties age-range, and only really gets going around midnight. Entrance €5.

Dali's Bar
Map 4, D3. Petite rue des Bouchers 35. Ⓜ Bourse. Mon–Sat 7pm–late.

As the name suggests, this bar's decor is aptly surreal, with Dali prints, wierd and wonderful-looking furniture and bright colours. Impromptu percussion and didgeridoo concerts can trade off with trip-hop DJs on Friday and Saturday nights, while on Thursdays disco generally rules supreme. The comfortable space and equally relaxed crowd ensure this is a chill-out rather than heat-up session.

Pablo's Disco Bar
Map 4, B4. Rue du Marché au Charbon 60. Ⓜ Bourse. Mon–Thurs 7pm–1am, Fri & Sat 7pm–3/4am.

Small, fashionable, Parisian-style DJ-bar. Good for DJ-spotters who want to admire the techniques. They generally play easy-listening, salsa-Latino, house or drum 'n' bass. The garden terrace is a pleasant chilling area in the summer, though it can get rather crowded.

Le Pacha
Map 3, E5. Rue de l'Ecuyer 41. Ⓜ Bourse. Fri–Sun 11pm–late.

One of Ibiza's most famous clubs has opened up its Brussels campus on the site of the former *Le Siècle*. The result is pretty spectacular, with all the fury and action you'd expect from a crowd that includes Brussels' finest clubbers and skin-barers. Fridays are dedicated to "Flower Power", which includes funk, '60s and '70s rock, soul and house, while Saturday is house music night, with several dance acts thrown in for free. Sundays have a "Cabaret" theme for the gay crowd.

Le Sud
Map 3, E5. Rue de l'Ecuyer 43–45. Ⓜ Bourse.

DJ BARS

Thurs–Sat 10pm–6am.
A large, maze-like hangout with Arabic decor and a slightly Bohemian feel – possibly a hangover from the days when the building was a squat. The front room has a long bar serving the delicious but lethal vodka citron (€13.65 a bottle) especially imported from Bombay, and if you follow the dark and twisting corridors you'll find a DJ pumping out a mixture of rap, jungle and dance. Membership is €2.50 for a year, although if there's a live band (occasionally on Thurs) or guest DJ, you may have to pay more on the door.

LIVE MUSIC VENUES

THE LOWER TOWN

Ancienne Belgique
Map 3, C6. Blvd Anspach 110 ⓣ 02 548 24 24. Ⓜ Bourse. Closed July & Aug.
The capital's premier rock and indie venue with a seating capacity of 2000 (plus 750 standing) and a reputation for showcasing local bands and international acts who perform either in the main auditorium or the smaller space on the first floor (capacity around 400). There are usually around four gigs a week and visiting artists to the AB, as it is known, have included the Buena Vista Social Club, Guru, Roni Size and Roger Hodgson of Supertramp fame. Concert tickets cost around €20.

L'Archiduc
Map 3, C5. Rue Antoine Dansaert 6 ⓣ 02 512 06 52. Ⓜ Bourse.
Daily 4pm–4/5am.
A famous Art Deco jazz café, close to place St Géry, full of thirty-somethingish media types tapping their fingers and wiggling their toes to Blue Note and post-1960s modern sounds. Legend has it Nat King Cole once played here, and music fans will be pleased

to learn the quality of the acts is still high. Live jazz can be heard every Saturday from 1 to 5pm for free and most Sunday evenings from October to April at 5pm with an entrance fee of around €15.

Beursschouwburg

Map 3, C6. Rue Auguste Orts 22 ⓣ 02 513 82 90. Ⓜ Bourse. A great venue next door to and part of the café of the same name (see p.201). It occasionally features live bands and DJ sets, although it's better known for specializing in "the spoken word" - stray musicians give esoteric readings on life, the universe and everything else in between. It's also the annual meeting place of the Belgian hip-hop convention. Look for the Beursschouwburg events calendar available in most of the bars in the area or pay a visit to their events desk. Entrance fees vary, but tend to be under €7.50.

Magasin 4

Map 2, D2. Rue du Magasin 4 ⓣ 02 223 34 74. Ⓜ Yser. This small converted

warehouse is a great place for catching new punk-rock, indie or rap/hip-hop bands and has a reputation for featuring "the next big thing". It's usually worth checking the listings pages. It's a bit of a walk from Métro Yser – head south from the station until you find a turning off rue des Commerçants. Entrance usually sets you back around €7.50.

THE UPPER TOWN

Le Botanique

Map 3, G3. Rue Royale 236 ⓣ 02 226 12 11. Ⓜ Botanique. Housed in the 150-year-old conservatory of the Parc du Jardin Botanique and including an art gallery, two theatres, and a small cinema. Frequent rock and pop concerts, and some good, mostly contemporary, theatre. Tickets €7.50–15.

Le Cercle

Map 3, E8. Rue Ste Anne 20–22 ⓣ 02 514 03 53. Ⓜ Gare Centrale. Daily 8pm–2am.

Just off place du Grand Sablon, a small, unremarkable venue in itself, but people come here for the live music which is on three or four times a week and ranges from jazz and Latino to *chanson française*. The place is not cheap – entrance usually costs at least €7.50 and a small beer will set you back €2 – but there's a relaxed atmosphere and the bands are usually very good. If you have any brain cells left from Saturday night, you might want to pop in on Sunday at 6pm for *Le Cercle*'s regular philosophy discussion.

Palais des Beaux Arts

Map 3, F7. Rue Ravenstein 23 ⓣ 02 507 82 00. Ⓜ Gare Centrale.

With a concert hall holding around 2000, as well as some smaller theatres, the Palais is used for anything from contemporary dance to Tom Jones, though the majority of performances are of classical music – the place is the home of the Orchestre National de Belgique (see p.223).

IXELLES

New York Jazz Café

Map 8, G3. Ch de Charleroi 5 ⓣ 02 534 85 09. Ⓜ Louise. Fri & Sat 10pm–1.30am.

An upmarket bar-bistro just off place Stéphanie. Quality live jazz can be heard Friday and Saturday in the club behind. There's no cover charge and usually a good atmosphere, but the price of booze soars when there's a live band playing.

Sounds

Map 8, I3. Rue de la Tulipe 28 ⓣ 02 512 92 50. Ⓜ Porte de Namur. Mon–Sat noon–4am.

Strangely enough this atmospheric jazz café, close to the place Fernand Cocq, has remained largely undiscovered despite the fact it has been the haunt of both local and internationally renowned jazz acts every weekend for the last twenty or so years. Saturday seems to be the day for the big names and you'll only be charged €5–7.50 entrance fee, although if you pop in midweek it's free and the music is often just as good.

MOLENBEEK

Fool Moon
Map 1, C2. Quai de Mariemont 26 ⓣ 02 410 10 03. Ⓜ Gare de l'Ouest. Tram #18.

A great venue for live music and parties, particularly if you like soul, dub, Latino sounds 'n' drum 'n' bass, but also good for rock and indie bands. Entrance is around €7.50, there are reasonably priced drinks, a good cutting-edge ambience and usually a fair-sized crowd. The upstairs bar with its comfortable sofas is a great place to chill out. The only drawback is the out-of-the-way location.

VK
Map 2, B3. Rue de l'Ecole 76 ⓣ 02 414 29 07. Ⓜ Comte de Flandre.

One of the best cutting-edge "alternative" venues in the capital, VK regularly features top-class hip-hop, ragga, rock and indie acts and occasionally puts on the odd

punk band. The only problem is it's in an area renowned for street crime, so don't hang around after the gig. It's best to get a taxi or one of the shuttle buses which run to the Bourse on the way back. Entrance €7.50–10.

FOREST

Cirque Royal
Map 1, C3. Rue de l'Enseignement 81 ⓣ 02 218 20 15. Ⓜ Madou.

Formerly an indoor circus, this venue has been host to the likes of David Byrne and Lou Reed down the years, although live gigs are randomly scheduled. Now, you can see anything from fashion shows to the Tokyo Ballet perform there.

Forest National
Ave du Globe 36 ⓣ 0900 00 991. Tram #18. Bus #54.

Brussels' main arena for big-name international concerts, holding around 11,000 people. Recent names have included Michael Jackson, B.B. King, Jon Bon Jovi and MC Solaar.

LIVE MUSIC VENUES

The performing arts and film

Despite its reputation as the grey city of Europe, when it comes to the city's cultural scene, Brussels answers, if not confounds, its critics. Domestic talent flourishes, particularly in the **theatre**, which has nurtured a new generation of young playwrights, including Philippe Blasand and Jean-Marie Piemme. The **modern dance** scene is alive and well; one of its major exponents Wim van Dekëybus, artist in residence at Koninklijke Vlaamse Schouwberg, has gained international acclaim for his cutting-edge choreography. Despite serious underfunding over recent years, **classical music** remains strong – the Orchestre National de Belgique continues to thrive under Yuri Simonov, and a number of excellent classical music festivals and concerts is organized by the Philharmonic Society (see "Palais des Beaux Arts", p.227). Sadly, despite Belgians being avid cinema-goers, home-grown film-makers seem something of an endangered species, though, more promisingly, there is a number of first-rate **film** festivals.

THEATRE AND DANCE

Despite underfunding, the Brussels **theatre** scene still remains strong. The city currently has more than thirty theatres staging a variety of productions ranging from Shakespeare to Stoppard. Most theatre is performed in French and Flemish, but there are also various American, Irish and British theatre groups which frequently put on high-quality amateur productions.

Being at the centre of Europe, the city is a stop-off point for many international dance and theatre groups – including the RSC, the Comédie Française and the Israeli dance group Badsheva – and it's quite common for the capital's theatres to stage joint productions with other European theatre companies.

Brussels' **dance** tradition has been impressing visitors ever since Maurice Béjart brought his classical Twentieth Century Ballet here in 1959. However, the city still lacks a proper dance venue, and unfortunately companies have to make do with stages better suited to plays and concert recitals. Commonly used venues are the Palais des Beaux Arts, Théâtre de la Monnaie and the Cirque Royal. The innovative legacy of Béjart lives on, however, with his old company (now called Rosas) regularly performing at La Monnaie.

Listings of theatre and dance performances, concert recitals and films showing, can be found in the "What's On" section of the weekly *Bulletin*, or the Wednesday pull-out section of *Le Soir*. For tickets and information go to either the tourist office on the Grand-Place or the Fnac store in the City 2 shopping complex at rue Neuve.

Cirque Royal

Map 2, F5. Rue de l'Enseignement 81 ⓣ 02 218 20 15. Ⓜ Madou.

This former indoor circus has one of the city's most eclectic programmes. It's best known for dance, classical music, musicals and operettas, but has also staged acts ranging from David Byrne to the Chippendales.

Koninklijke Vlaamse Schouwberg

Map 2, B3. Rue de Launoy 58 ⓣ 02 412 70 70, Ⓦ www.kvs.be. Ⓜ Etangs Noirs.

This Flemish-language theatre has a good reputation for showcasing the works of up-and-coming young playwrights, as well as staging modern classics by the likes of Chekhov, Pinget and Beckett. It's also an excellent place to catch some innovative dance.

Palais des Beaux Arts

Map 2, E5. Rue Ravenstein 23 ⓣ 02 507 82 00. Ⓜ Parc.

The Palais des Beaux Arts' resident theatre company – Rideau de Bruxelles – has been putting on modern theatre productions since its inception in 1943. Performances are in French, and playwrights to have their work performed include David Hare, Paul Willems and Jean Sigrid. It's also an excellent venue for modern dance and classical ballet, and is often one of the first ports of call for touring dance companies, though tickets can rise to €50 for these performances.

Théâtre National

Map 2, E2. Centre Rogier, Pl Rogier ⓣ 02 203 53 03. Ⓜ Rogier.

This French-only theatre performs high-quality productions ranging from

Ticket prices for dance and theatre vary depending on the venue. However, generally speaking, a good seat costs around €17.35–24.80.

THEATRE AND DANCE

Molière to Brecht. It's popular with a wide range of visiting theatre companies including the RSC, the Parisian Théâtre Odéon and the Berlin-based Berliner Scubuhne, who perform classics from their country of origin in the original language.

Théâtre-Poème
Map 2, D8. Rue d'Ecosse 30 ⓉⒹ 02 538 63 58. Ⓜ Hôtel des Monnaies.
A small, avant-garde theatre group, best known for dramatizing excerpts from novels and poems. It's also a place where authors, poets, playwrights and philosophers come to discuss their work – the most notable guest speaker being postmodernist guru Jacques Derrida.

Théâtre Public
Map 2, H4. Rue Braemt 64–70 Ⓣ 0800 944 44. Ⓜ Madou.
The only private theatre in Brussels, Théâtre Public is deservedly acclaimed for bringing the works of young Belgian French-language playwrights – Jean-Marie Piemme and Philippe Blasand to name but two – to the stage, although Chekhov, Molière and Brecht also get a look-in from time to time. Tickets usually cost €18.50. However, for €32.20 you also get wined and dined before the performance at the theatre's very reasonable French restaurant.

Théâtre Royal du Parc
Map 2, G5. Rue de la Loi 3 Ⓣ 02 512 23 39. MO Arts-Loi.
Stage productions are in French only, but even if you don't fancy a play it's worth visiting this glorious theatre for the beautiful architecture alone – the building dates back to 1782. The programme consists mainly of French burlesques and twentieth-century classics – Ionescu, Brecht, Camus – but they also stage more modern pieces, and have been known to put on the odd bit of Shakespeare.

THEATRE AND DANCE

CLASSICAL MUSIC AND OPERA

The **classical music** concert scene in Brussels is impressive. The main venue is the Palais des Beaux Arts, while the Conservatoire Royal de Musique has an excellent reputation for its programme of chamber music and song recitals. **Annual events** include the recently established Ars Musica, held in March, and the prestigious Concours International Musical Reine Elisabeth de Belgique, a competition for piano, violin or voice in May (see p.277), which numbers among its prize-winners Vladimir Ashkenazy, David Oistrakh and Gidon Kremer.

Opera–lovers need go no further than the beautiful and historic Théâtre de la Monnaie, which has enjoyed something of a renaissance of late, first under the musical direction of Gérard Mortier, but more recently with the inspired conductor Antonio Pappano.

Tickets for concerts and opera start from as little as €7.40–12.40, but can zoom up to as much as €154 for a first night at La Monnaie.

Conservatoire Royal de Musique
Map 3, E8. Rue de la Régence 30 ⓣ 02 511 04 27. Ⓜ Louise. Although the Orchestre National de Belgique sometimes plays here, it's more suited to chamber music and song recitals. The acoustics are second to none and there is an impressive, at times highly innovative, programme interspersed with the early rounds of the Concours Musical International Reine Elisabeth de Belgique competition.

Palais des Beaux Arts
Map 3, F7. Rue Ravenstein 23 ⓣ 02 507 82 00, ⓦ www.pskpba.be. Ⓜ Parc. The jewel in the crown of the capital's classical music

scene, the Palais des Beaux Arts is not only the home of Belgium's national orchestra, but also the Philharmonic Society, which organizes classical music performances throughout the city. Visiting orchestras have included the Los Angeles Philharmonic and the Chicago Symphony Orchestra. The season runs from September to June, and the Palais hosts in excess of 350 concerts each year.

Théâtre de la Monnaie

Map 3, E5. Pl de la Monnaie ⓣ 02 229 12 11. Ⓜ de Brouckère.

This is Belgium's premier opera house. Renowned for its adventurous repertoire and production style, it has earned itself glowing reviews over the years. Its policy of nurturing promising singers rather than casting the more established stars ensures that it's a good place to spot potential. It's also of great historical significance. Following the staging of Auber's *The Mute Girl of Portici* in 1830 – an opera based on a revolution – an inspired audience charged out of the building and held an impromptu protest. Belgian independence was declared one month later. Book well in advance: tickets are always difficult to obtain as the house contains only 1200 seats.

CINEMA

Although Belgium's contribution to world **cinema** is modest – *The Sexual Life of the Belgians*, *Man Bites Dog* and the "Muscles from Brussels" himself, Jean-Claude van Damme – cinema-going, particularly in the capital, flourishes. The city's main commercial cinemas are UGC De Brouckère, UGC Acropole and Heysel's Kinepolis, all of which devote their screens to the big US blockbusters. However, the sheer number of cinemas in Brussels means there's a decent range of art-house or classic films being shown.

CINEMA

The city's annual **film festivals** (see "Festivals", p.274) are held in the spring and are highly recommended. They include the impressive Brussels Film Festival in January and the bizarre, but wonderful, Brussels Festival of Fantasy Film, Science Fiction and Thrillers in March.

About half the films shown in Brussels' cinemas are in English (coded "VO" or "version originale"); **subtitles** for non-French or Flemish films are in French and Flemish. *The Bulletin* is the best source for **listings** of the week's movies, which usually change their programmes on Wednesday.

Cinema tickets cost around €7, except on Monday when they are €5.45.

Actors' Studio

Map 2, D4. Petite rue des Bouchers 16 Ⓣ 02 512 16 96. Ⓜ de Brouckère.

This small cinema is probably the best place in the centre to catch art-house or independent films. It's also one of the leading venues for the Brussels Film Festival.

Arenberg Galleries

Map 4, D4. Galerie de la Reine 26 Ⓣ 02 512 80 63. Ⓜ Gare Centrale.

Set in a beautiful Art Deco building converted from a theatre, the Arenberg Galleries is best known for its "Sneak Previews" held every Thursday evening, where you get to see a new film before its official release date. Occasionally they take a poll to gauge audience reaction to the film. An adventurous variety of world films is also screened.

UGC De Brouckère

Map 3, D4. Pl de Brouckère 38 Ⓣ 02 0900 10 440. Ⓜ de Brouckère.

A ten-screen cinema showing the usual Hollywood fare. If you go on Sunday morning you get

CINEMA

a coffee and croissant included in the price of the ticket. Its sister cinema, the UGC Acropole at Galerie de la Toison d'Or 17 screens the same sort of stuff. Both cinemas usually screen in English.

Kinepolis

Map 7, C2. Blvd du Centenaire 20 Ⓣ 02 474 26 00. Ⓜ Heysel. A hi-tech cinema complex with 27 auditoriums and the largest IMAX screen in Europe. The line-up is pretty commercial but the choice of films is unrivalled.

Movy Club

Map 8, A5. Rue des Moines 21 Ⓣ 02 537 69 54. Tram #18. Inconveniently located, but it usually offers a wide range of films in English. The line-up includes modern classics and popular films released within the last year.

Musée du Cinéma

Map 3, F7. Rue Baron Horta 9 Ⓣ 02 507 83 70. Ⓜ Gare Centrale. This small museum-cum-cinema is popular with film buffs who come to watch an excellent selection of old silent movies with piano accompaniment. The museum is pretty interesting as well, especially the early attempts at moving pictures such as the mutoscope and kinetoscope. Children under 16 not admitted.

Nova

Map 2, E5. Rue d'Arenberg 3 Ⓣ 02 511 27 74. Ⓜ de Brouckère. A small, one-screen cinema, popular with students who favour the cheap prices and the art-house programme – anything from obscure Eastern European offerings to Portuguese classics. English-language films are sometimes screened; however, if it's not originally in English, the subtitles will be in French and Flemish. Only two showings per day – 8pm & 10pm.

Styx

Map 8, I4. Rue de l'Arbre Bénit 72 Ⓣ 02 512 21 02. Ⓜ Porte de Namur. A tiny, two-screen repertory cinema, with old moth-eaten chairs, and a smoky atmosphere. Most films are in the original language and there's usually a good selection of English-language movies, as well as midnight screenings.

Vendôme
Map 2, F8. Ch de Wavre 18

ⓣ 02 502 37 00. Ⓜ Porte de Namur.

A trendy, five-screen cinema well-known for its wide selection of arty films as well as more mainstream stuff. They usually have at least two English-language films showing at any one time.

CINEMA

Shopping

Brussels has a wide range and variety of goods on offer although it's not the cheapest of cities in which to **shop**. There are two main shopping areas in the city: the city centre around the **Grand-Place**, and the south part of the **Upper Town**. The city centre's main shopping street is **rue Neuve**, which is home to City 2, the ultimate inner-city shopping mall.

Not far from the Grand-Place, **Galeries St Hubert** accommodates a smattering of conservative boutiques in stark contrast to the **Galerie Agora**, which peddles cheap leather jackets, incense, piercing jewellery and ethnic goods directly opposite. Behind the Bourse, **rue Antoine Dansaert** caters for young, cutting-edge fashion-groupies, housing a number of young designers as well as shops selling clothing ranging from the internationally known to such Belgians as the Antwerp 6 and Raf Simons. Neighbouring **St Géry** contains rue des Riches Claires and rue du Marché au Charbon which have streetwear shops and vintage stores.

Uptown, the **chaussée d'Ixelles** has most of the big stores and a lively feel in the African quarter around the Galerie d'Ixelles. The label-conscious will want to shop at the smartest addresses on avenues Louise and de la Toison d'Or, where shops offer everything from DKNY to Giorgio Armani, as well as Belgian designers.

OPENING HOURS

Shops are generally open from 10am to 6–7pm from Monday to Saturday. On Friday, department stores stay open until 8pm. In some districts, certain shops – mainly those selling booze, news, cigarettes and food – also open at night and/or on Sunday. For instance, the corner shops in St Josse stay open till around 10–11pm. The Grand-Place and the Bourse and St Géry areas have night shops staying open till between 2–5 am. The White Night mini-market chain has central branches at rue du Lombard 8, rue E. Allard 3 and place du Châtelain 43, as well as branches in the outskirts (all open Sun–Thurs 6pm–1am and Fri–Sat 5pm–2am.

The Grand Sablon has a weekend **antiques market** and the surrounding area has a good selection of similar shops. For bric-à-brac, it's best to wander down to the Marolles district – the closest Brussels gets to New York's Lower East Side – and the daily **flea market** at the place du Jeu de Balle. There is a labyrinth of old books in the stores of the **Galerie Bortier** near Gare Centrale.

Belgian beer, chocolate and lace – though found throughout the city – are highly concentrated in the tourist areas around the Grand-Place. Shops catering to another national passion, the comic strip or "bande dessinée" (BD), can be found a little further afield near the Bourse and on the chaussée d'Ixelles near place Fernand Cocq.

We have divided our listings into the following categories: art and antiques p.234; books and comics p.236; chocolate p.238; department stores and galleries p.240; fashion p.242; food and drink p.245; lace p.246; markets p.248; and music p.248.

SHOPPING

ART AND ANTIQUES

Aeroplastics Contemporary

Map 2, E9. Rue Blanche 32.
Tram #93, #94.
Wed–Sat 2–8pm.

Beautiful townhouse with
regular displays of themed
contemporary art, featuring
works by up-and-coming
artists such as Skip Arnold,
Koen Wastijn and Dana
Wyse.

Costermans

Map 2, D6. Pl du Grand
Sablon 5. Tram #92, #93, #94.
Mon–Fri 9am–6pm, Sat
10am–noon & 2–6pm.

Famous Grand Sablon
antiques shop, established in
1839 and now run by Marc-
Henri Jaspar-Costermans. Its
speciality is eighteenth-
century furniture and *objets
d'art* as well as paintings and
beautifully crafted clocks.
There's also an impressive
range of old fireplaces and
wrought ironwork. Prices are
mostly prohibitive, but it's a
lovely place to look around
nonetheless.

De Leye

Map 2, D6. Rue Lebeau 16.
Tram #92, #93, #94.
Tues–Sat 10.30am–12.30pm &
2.30–6.30pm.

Just off place du Grand
Sablon, this newly established
shop specialises in high-
quality seventeenth- and
eighteenth-century silverware
and everything from silver
candlesticks to serving ladles,
mirrors, statuettes, teapots
and gravy boats. Excellent
selection and competitive
prices.

Kanal 11 & 20

Map 2, B4. Bd Barthélemy 11
& 20. Ⓜ Comte de Flandre.
Wed–Sat 2–6pm.

Eight galleries dedicated to
contemporary art.
Particularly interesting is the
Crown Gallery which shows
young Belgian and foreign
artists as well as more
established artists like Liam
Golub and Nancy Spero.
H&R Projects (linked to the
Hussenot Gallery in Paris)
shows Belgians, French and

Americans such as 1960s artist Alain Jacquet or the more contemporary Gregory Crewdson, Karen Kilimnik and George Pardo.

Kenulf Van Bockstade

Map 2, D6. Pl du Grand Sablon 9. Tram #92, #93, #94. Thurs–Fri 2–6pm, Sat 10.30am–6pm, Sun 10.30am–2pm.
Long-established and popular fine art gallery specializing in romantic paintings dating from the nineteenth century, and early twentieth-century Impressionist paintings. Full of portraits, rustic landscapes and seascapes.

Orion Art Gallery

Map 2, D7. Rue aux Laines 19. Tram #92, #93, #94. Wed–Fri noon–6pm, Sat 11am–6pm.
Specialist in modern art, with changing exhibits every six weeks representing young as well as more established artists. Exhibitions have included works by Bart De Zutter, Gerald Dederen and Japan's Masahiro Kanno.

Primitive Art

Map 2, D6. Rue Lebeau 12. Tram #92, #93, #94. Call for opening times on Ⓣ 02 511 78 08.
Sublime assortment of African, Oceanic and Indian art, including a collection of immense two-metre-high wooden figurines from Oceania.

Sabine Wachters

Map 2, B7. Av de Stalingrad 26. Ⓜ Lemonnier. Tues–Sat 11am–7pm.
Gallery specializing in young unknown artists, as well as big names such as Andy Warhol, Donald Judd and Daniel Spoerri.

Euroline, rue du Marché-aux-Herbes 52 (Jan–March Mon–Sat 10am–8pm and Sun 10am–7pm; April–Dec Mon–Sat 9am–11pm and Sun 10am–7pm), is the ultimate in EU kitsch, with flags, car stickers and *objets d'art*, all with the golden stars of the EU insignia.

ART AND ANTIQUES

BOOKS AND COMICS

Le Bande des Six Nez

Map 2, I7. Ch de Wavre 179.
Ⓜ Schuman.
Mon–Sat 10am–7pm.
Stocks a variety of new comics, as well as original editions from the 1940s and 1950s. It also sells original drawings, and those who think cartoon art is kid's stuff might be surprised to learn that a 1930s sketch of Tintin recently sold for €24,780. Fortunately the comics come a little cheaper – anything from €1.50 to €150 – and there's a modest, but interesting, English-language section.

Brüsel

Map 2, C5. Bd Anspach 100.
Ⓜ Bourse.
Mon–Sat 10am–6.30pm.
This well-known comic shop stocks more than 8000 new issues and specialises in French underground editions – Association, Amok and Bill to name but a few. You'll also find the complete works of the famous Belgian comic-book artist Schuiten, most popularly known for his controversial comic Brüsel, which depicts the architectural destruction of a city (guess which one) in the 1960s. Calvin and Hobbes make an appearance, as does Tintin in a babel of language versions. The shop is particularly worth visiting when it hosts a pop-art or comic-book exhibition.

Centre Belge de la Bande Dessinée

Map 2, E5. Rue des Sables 20. Ⓜ de Brouckère, Botanique or Rogier.
Tues–Sun 10am–6pm.
This museum bookstore (see p.40) is definitely worth a visit even if you haven't been to the museum – it contains a wide range of new comics.

Le Dépôt Jonas

Map 2, F8. Ch d'Ixelles 140.
Bus #71.
Mon–Sat 10.15am–2pm & 2.15pm–6.30pm.
Dingy but vast space

containing comics, videos, gaming software, music and collectable prints. Several thousand comics on display.

Espace BD

Map 2, G9. Place Fernand Coq 2. Bus #71.
Mon 1.30pm–7pm, Tues–Sat 10.30am–7pm.

Selling principally adult-themed comics, Espace BD features a beautiful gallery displaying a host of prints and sketches from all sorts of artists, including Dany, Gimenez, Berthet and Alice. Immaculately organized and a pleasant place to spend an afternoon browsing.

Espace Tintin

Map 3, D4. Rue de la Colline 13. Ⓜ Bourse.
Mon 11am–6pm, Tues–Sat 10am–6pm, Sun 11am–5pm.

Set up, no doubt, by someone with an unhealthy obsession with Hergé's quiffed hero. Expect to find anything and everything to do with Tintin – comic books, postcards, stationery, figurines, T-shirts and sweaters – and all Hergé's other cartoon creations, such as Quick & Flupke. Just off the Grand-Place.

Fil à Terre

Map 2, F8. Ch de Wavre 198. Ⓜ Porte de Namur.
Daily 11.30am–8pm.

A comic shop with a fairly wide selection – there are over three thousand – of Belgian and French comics. Fil à Terre also provides customers with a bar in which to read their latest purchase.

Librairie des Etangs

Map 8, J5. Ch d'Ixelles 319. Bus #71.
Mon–Sat 10am–7pm, Sun 10am–2pm.

More than 3000 English-language titles, as well as a good selection of Asian and Caribbean works. They also have occasional prose readings in the basement, and when you get tired of browsing the bookshelves there's a tea-room at the back serving refreshments and a small gallery to wander in.

BOOKS AND COMICS

Pêle-Mêle

Map 2, B6. Bd Maurice Lemonnier 55. Ⓜ Annessens. Mon–Sat 10am–6.30pm.

A maze-like shop with a jumble of second-hand books stacked up against the walls. Thrillers, classics, comics, magazines and even CDs retail at some of the lowest prices in Brussels: a Balzac or a Camus will cost around €0.50. The whole wall devoted to English-language titles houses novels selling at €1–1.50. A good place to unload any unwanted books as they also buy.

Sterling Books

Map 2, D4. Rue du Fossé aux Loups 38. Ⓜ de Brouckère. Mon–Sat 10am–7pm, Sun noon–6.30pm.

This large English-language book shop has more than 50,000 UK and US titles,
including a large selection of magazines, and is much cheaper than Waterstone's – they sell books at the cover price, converted at the day's exchange rate, plus six percent VAT. You can also pay directly in pound sterling. Also has a children's corner with a small play area.

Waterstones

Map 2, E3. Bd Adolphe Max 71–75. Ⓜ de Brouckère or Rogier. Mon–Thurs 9am–6.30pm, Fri–Sat 9am–7pm.

The Brussels branch of the British parent company, selling over 70,000 English-language titles. The premises are a bit cramped, making it far from ideal for browsing, but there's an excellent selection of books and magazines and a good ordering service.

CHOCOLATE

Godiva

Map 2, D6. Pl du Grand Sablon 47/48. Ⓜ Louise. Daily 9am–7pm.

Godiva definitely holds its own against the best of the rest. Jealously-guarded recipes and seasonal, handcrafted

CHOCOLATE

packaging ensure customers keep coming back for more, despite the price.

Léonidas

Map 2, C5. Bd Anspach 46.
Ⓜ Bourse.
Daily 9am–7pm.

Léonidas remains one of the most popular – and cheapest – widespread outlets for Belgian chocolates and pralines, although like some other choc chains they are straight off the production line. They are rather sickly-sweet in comparison to the others but no one will notice the difference back home. Branches all over.

Mary's

Map 2, F5. Rue Royale, 73.
Tram #92, #93, #94.
Tues–Fri & Sun 9am–6pm, Sat 9am–12.30pm & 2–7pm.

A very exclusive and pricey shop, with beautiful period decor, selling handmade chocolates. You can instantly taste the difference between these and those of the chains: these pralines are top-notch, melt-in-the-mouth gourmet delicacies.

Neuhaus

Map 2, D5. Grand-Place 27.
Ⓜ Gare Centrale.
Mon–Sat 9am–6pm.

A chocoholic's paradise, this ludicrously expensive shop stocks some of the best that Belgium has to offer in the chocolate department. Check out their specialities – the handmade Caprices, which are pralines stuffed with crispy nougat, fresh cream and soft-centred chocolate, and the delicious Manons, stuffed white chocolates, which come in fresh cream, vanilla, and coffee fillings. They have branches all over the town, but other central ones are in avenue de la Toison d'Or 27 and in the Galerie de la Reine.

Pierre Marcolini

Map 2, D6. Place du Grand Sablon 39. Ⓜ Louise.
Wed–Sun 10am–6pm.

Considered by many to be the best chocolatier in the world, Pierre Marcolini is a true master of the genre. Try his spice- and tea-filled chocolates as evidence of his

CHOCOLATE

genius. Classy service, beautiful packaging and a wide choice of chocolate cakes that will have you comatose with pleasure.

Planète Chocolat
Map 2, D5. Rue du Lombard 24. Ⓜ Bourse.
Tues–Sat 10am–6.30pm, Sun 1–6.30pm.
Sells standard boxes of delicious Belgian chocolates as well as a whole range of strangely shaped ones. You also get to see how the bonbons are made in their mini-chocolate museum.

When you've had enough of that, pay a visit to their tea-room.

Wittamer
Map 2, D6. Pl du Grand Sablon 6 & 12. Ⓜ Gare Centrale.
Mon 8am–6pm, Tues–Sat 7am–7pm, Sun 7am–6pm.
Brussels' most famous patisserie and chocolate shop, established in 1910 and still run by the Wittamer family, who sell gorgeous if expensive light pastries, cakes, mousses, and chocolates. Also serves speciality teas and coffees in their tearoom at no. 12.

DEPARTMENT STORES AND GALLERIES

City 2
Map 2, E3. Rue Neuve. Ⓜ Place Rogier.
A huge temple to shopping with an abundance of boutiques, restaurants and cinemas, as well as a department store and the massive Fnac store.

Galerie Agora
Map 4, D4. Off rue des Éperonniers. Ⓜ Centrale.

Although near the grandeur of the Grand-Place, this galerie is an exotic bazaar of ethnic clothes, incense, tattooists, piercers and all the tacky accoutrements that make shopping a rush.

Galerie Louise and Galerie de la Toison d'Or
Map 8, H1. Ⓜ Porte de Namur or Louise.
Galleries situated at either

end of the ave du Toison d'Or housing a series of boutiques selling top-of-the-range designer clothing – Armani, Gautier, Helmut Lang – at heart-attack prices: take a peek at the clothes in Ottimo (Mon–Sat 10am–6.30pm). A variety of shoe shops along the same expensive lines, such as Nouchka, are open Monday–Saturday 10.30am–6.30pm. Despite the pretence, the whole sprawl is quite tacky, with red carpet and a glorious golden mock fountain in the centre.

Galeries St Hubert
Map 4, E3–F2. Ⓜ de Brouckère.

Just off rue de l'Ecuyer, this impressive 1846 glass-roofed gallery is divided up into the Galerie de la Reine and the Galerie du Roi, and contains a selection of well-established conservative shops. Those worth looking out for are Longchamps, Galerie du Roi 21, for quality women's accessories; Van Schelle at Galerie du Roi 36; and

Nicholson at Galerie de la Reine 36 – all sell the leading brands in fashion. Neuhaus (see p.239) has one of their poshest shops here and there are various art and philosophy bookshops dotted along the galleries to browse in. For a more highbrow interlude during your shopping day, the excellent art house Arenberg cinema in the Galerie de la Reine has an eclectic film programme, or you could simply relax in one of the cafés.

Inno
Map 3, E3. Rue Neuve 111. MO de Brouckère or Ⓜ Louise.

Brussels' largest department store has four floors peddling goods ranging from perfume and lingerie to home furnishings, clothing and shoes. Prices vary from the high-rise to the bargain basement.

DEPARTMENT STORES AND GALLERIES

FASHION

Elvis Pompilio

Map 4, A6. Rue du Midi 60.
Ⓜ Bourse.
Mon–Sat 10.30am–6.30pm.
From eccentric hats which look like wedding-cakes to simple berets and his trademark cowboy hats, Belgian hatter Elvis Pompilio deserves his high-fashion reputation. The women's shop and the adjacent men's shop at rue des Lombards 24 are unmissable from any window-shopping trip: prices average at €125. He also does made-to-measure and sells accessories such as parasols and specs which are more decorative than useful. Belgian royals Prince Philippe and Princess Mathilde are just some of the store's customers.

Emporio Armani

Map 3, E8. Pl du Grand Sablon 37. Tram #92, #93, #94.
Mon, Wed–Sat 10.30am–7pm, Sun 11am–6pm.
Sleek and smart casual suits, jeans, underwear and accessories for both men and women in the mainstream Armani vein. The store is spacious and the staff are welcoming.

Gianni Versace

Map 8, F2. Bd de Waterloo 64.
Ⓜ Louise.
Mon 1–6.30pm, Tues–Sat 10am–6.30pm.
Everything you expect from a Versace outlet – swish marble decor, stylish clothing and enormous prices. Caters for both men and women.

Hennes & Mauritz (H&M)

Map 3, E3. Rue Neuve 80.
Ⓜ de Brouckère or Rogier.
Mon–Thurs & Sat 9.30am–6.30pm, Fri 9.30am–7pm.
Swedish store with all the high-street fashion trends. Expect to find a mixture of cheap suits, club gear and youthful and casual clothing. There are male, female and kids' sections, as well as underwear and accessories. Items can be exchanged in all the H&Ms in Europe and

FASHION

they accept major European currencies. There are other branches on rue Neuve 36 and chaussée d'Ixelles 41–43.

L'Homme Chrétien
Map 3, D6. Rue des Pierres 27. Ⓜ de Brouckère or Bourse. Mon–Sat 11am–7pm.
Kitsch extravaganza of a store, with a mixture of men and women's vintage and second-hand clothing and shoes, as well as the owner's own designs. These are a combination of quirky fashion-student type ideas – such as customised skirts made out of religious pictures – and stylised versions of high-street fashion. A tad overpriced but there are occasionally jumble-sale type bins worth rummaging through.

Nina Meert
Map 8, I2. Rue Saint Boniface 1. Ⓜ Porte de Namur; bus #71. Mon–Sat 10.30am–6.30pm.
A Flanders-born designer, Meert creates refined and expensive clothes which offer a nice relaxed alternative to other more starchy designers.

She uses silk and knitwear extensively, and at the rear of the store, you'll find an impressive collection of wedding dresses.

Olivier Strelli
Map 8, G3. Ave Louise 72. Ⓜ Louise. Mon–Sat 10am–6.30pm.
One of Belgium's most established designers, Strelli has been creating simple, classic and very modern clothes for years, often with a splash of colour – the rainbow scarves for women are very popular. Prices are on the high side.

Parachute Jump
Map 8, H9. Ch de Waterloo 579. Tram #93 or #94. Mon–Sat 10.30am–6.30pm.
Chic clothes of outstanding quality, whether sportswear or dressy. Pricey, but with polite service and an interesting range of accessories and bags, you're sure to find something you like. Not too far from the Chatelain area.

Peau de Zèbre
Map 4, B3. Rue du Midi 40. Ⓜ Bourse.

FASHION

243

Mon–Sat 10.30am–7pm.
Cool clothes — street wear, urban gear, cargo pants and hooded vests – for kids and teenagers (ages 0–18).

Privé Joke
Map 2, C5. Rue des Riches Claires 8 & 12. Ⓜ Bourse. Mon–Sat 10.30am–7pm.
This shop stocks standard club and streetwear labels such as Carhartt, Ben Sherman and Lady Soul, and they've recently expanded into boyswear and girlswear. It's host to occasional DJs who want to practise in the booth and there are always flyers for clubnights and raves to be picked up.

Smadja
Map 1, D3. Ave Louis Lepoutre 21. Tram #90 or #23. Mon–Sat 10.30am–6.30pm.
Lots of Paul Smith offerings amongst others at this smart, elegant and slightly off-the-beaten-track store.

Stijl
Map 3, C5. Rue Antoine Dansaert 74. Ⓜ Bourse. Mon–Sat 10.30am–6.30pm.

Huge men and womenswear emporium focusing on cutting-edge Belgian designers such as Ann Demeulemeester, Martin Margiela, Dries Van Noten, Dirk Bikkembergs and Raf Simons. They also sell Helmut Lang, John Smedley and Romeo Gigli. Their children's clothing shop, Kat en Muis, is at no. 32.

Zara
Map 3, E4. Rue Neuve 48–50. Ⓜ de Brouckère or Rogier. Mon 10am–7pm, Tues–Thurs 9.30am–7pm, Fri–Sat 9.30am–7.30pm.
This Spanish chain caters for the young professional with lots of smart, conservative suits for both men and women. They also do a wide range of dresses, accessories, jeans and shirts. There are several branches, with another one at avenue Louise 8–10. The same company owns the more upmarket menswear store Massimo Dutti on avenue de la Toison d'Or 22.

FOOD AND DRINK

Au Suisse
Map 2, C5. Boulevard Anspach 73–75. Ⓜ Bourse. Mon–Fri 10am–8pm, Sat & Sun 10am–9pm.
Despite the name, a Belgian-style deli which serves up traditional nosh such as *maatjes* (Belgian herrings), *filet américain* (raw minced meat) or *tête pressée* (brawn), along with a lot more edible options. Two long counters line the deli, and you can eat in, also sampling some of their pastries, ice-cream milkshakes or coffee. The clientele is eclectic, from moustached locals to fashion victims. Their shop next door sells a wide variety of cheeses.

Bière Artisanale
Map 8, J2. Ch de Wavre 174. Ⓜ Porte de Namur. Mon–Sat 11am–7pm.
A drinker's paradise, stocking more than 400 different types of beer. It's quite cheap, too, and you can even buy the correct glass in which to serve your favourite tipple.

To learn more about Belgian beer or to place an order for home delivery, look at their website Ⓦwww.users.skynet .be/beermania or go along to one of the many classes (some given in English) and tasting sessions organized here to spread the word.

Le Caprice des Lieux
Map 1, E2. Rue Bois de Linthout 3. Ⓜ Georges Henri. Tues–Sat 9.30am–7pm, Sun 9am–12.30pm.
A cheese lover's heaven, with hundreds of beautifully presented cheeses set amid tasteful decor. You can also purchase entire cheese platters.

Dandoy
Map 4, C3. Rue au Beurre 31. Ⓜ Bourse. Mon–Sat 8.30am–6.30pm, Sun 10.30am–6.30pm.
This famous shop has been making biscuits since 1829, so it's no surprise they now have it down to a fine art. Their main speciality is known locally as "speculoos", a kind

FOOD AND DRINK

of hard gingerbread biscuit. This shop even has some larger-than-life biccies which are the size of small children and can cost as much as €50. Moreover they come in a weird variety of shapes – the most unappetising one being the life-size biscuit Manneken Pis. They have two branches on the Grand-Place and a tearoom at their rue Charles Buls 14 branch.

De Muynck Regnier
Map 3, D6. Rue du Marché-aux-Herbes 56. Ⓜ Gare Centrale.
Daily 10am–9pm.
This specialist beer shop, handily placed near the Grand-Place, sells over 150 different types of beers, including a number of rare Belgian varieties. Its popularity with tourists explains the slightly inflated prices, but there's a wide selection and the owner will quite happily chat away all day about any Belgian booze you care to mention.

LACE

F. Rubbrecht
Map 4, C3. Grand-Place 23. Ⓜ Gare Centrale.
Mon–Sat 9am–7pm, Sun 10am–6pm.
Traditional lace shop specializing in handmade Brussels lace. They do wholesale and retail, and also valuing and buying.

Manufacture Belge de Dentelle
Map 4, D3. Galerie de la Reine 6–8. Ⓜ Gare Centrale.
Mon–Sat 10am–7pm.
The city's largest lace merchant, in business since 1810. Sells a wide variety of modern and antique lace at fairly reasonable prices. The service is helpfully old-fashioned.

Roses Lace Boutique
Map 4, C5. Rue Charles Buls 30. Ⓜ Gare Centrale.
Mon–Sat 10am–7pm.

LACE

There's a large collection of spooky lace-clad porcelain dolls in the window of this small shop, but it's a good place to go for gifts – they sell everything from parasols to lace crucifixes. It's not cheap however: a tiny lace tea coaster costs €6.80, whereas the tablecloths cost as much as €121.50.

LACE

Renowned for the fineness of the thread and beautiful motifs, Belgian lace is famous the world over. Flanders lace, as it was once known, was worn in the royal courts of Paris and London – Queen Elizabeth I of England alone is said to have had more than 3000 lace dresses, and the famous ruffs of her courtiers were made out of lace, with starch to keep them stiff also introduced from Flanders. Lace reached its zenith of popularity in the mid-nineteenth century when an estimated 10,000 women and girls worked as lacemakers in the capital. By the end of the nineteenth century, though, much of the lace was machine-made.

Masterpieces from that period can still be viewed today – the Musée du Costume et de la Dentelle (see p.29) exhibits an interesting collection, including one of Empress Eugénie's skirts (the Empress owned a lace gown which 600 women had toiled over for ten months) and some of Empress Sissi of Austria's scarves and handkerchiefs.

If you're in the market for some Brussels lace, be warned – much of the lace on sale in the capital is actually made in China, and the authentic handmade stuff can be very pricey, particularly in the much-hyped lace shops in and around the Grand-Place. Your best bet is to head for the flea market at Jeu de Balle where you can usually pick up far nicer pieces for much less money. The shops listed on p.246, although not cheap, offer the pick of the lace in the city.

LACE

MARKETS

The Grand-Place daily **flower market** wins the prize for the most picturesque of Brussels' markets (Mon–Sat 8am–6pm); the Grand-Place also hosts a bird market on Sundays 9am–1pm. Although the swankiest antiques and collectibles market is held at **place du Grand Sablon** (Map 2, D6; Sat 9am–6pm, Sun 9am–2pm), the real bargains can be found at the flea market on **place du Jeu de Balle** (Map 2, C7) in the Marolles quarter. It's held every morning from 7am to 2pm, but it's at its biggest – and most expensive – at weekends, where the eccentric muddle of colonial spoils, quirky odds and ends and domestic and ecclesiastical bric-à-brac give an impression of a century's bourgeois fads and fashions. The largest and most colourful food market is held every Sunday (6am–1pm) at **Gare du Midi** (Map 2, A7), a bazaar-like affair, with traders crammed under the railway bridge and spilling out into the surrounding streets. Stands sell pitta, olives, North African raï tapes, spices, herbs and pulses, among the vegetables and cheap clothes. There's also a picturesque food market at **place du Châtelain** (Map 8, G7) every Wednesday, crampacked with tiny stalls selling fresh vegetables, cheeses, cakes and pastries, as well as fine laces, plants and flowers, and home-made wines.

MUSIC

BCM
Map 3, C6. Plattesteen 6.
Ⓜ Bourse.
Mon–Sat 11am–6.30pm.
If you've come to Belgium to explore the techno scene, this is where to find your vinyl. They also stock lots of drum 'n' bass, speed-garage, and house.

Arlequin

Map 2, G8. Rue de L'Athenee 7 & 8. Bus #71.
Mon–Sat 10.30am–6.30pm.
Small, beat-up second-hand record and CD shop which offers decent collections of almost every type of music you can imagine. The vinyl is in good shape – with some sealed copies around – and the service amiable. The store at no. 8 sells classical and jazz, while no. 7 offers everything else.

La Boîte à Musique

Map 6, D1. Rue Ravenstein 17. Ⓜ Gare Centrale.
Mon–Fri 9am–6.30pm, Sat 9.30am–6.30pm.
Supplier to the Belgian court, owner Bertrand de Wauters is a veritable encyclopaedia of classical music. Not only can he describe differing interpretations of classical works, he can also advise you on the quality of the recordings. Highly recommended.

DiscoSold

Map 2, E3. Bd Adolphe Max 97. Ⓜ Rogier.
Mon–Sat 10.30am–6.30pm.
This small second-hand record shop is well-known for its obscure but cool collection of soul, funk, pop and jazz as well as a large section devoted to classical music. The prices won't break the bank either, most CDs costing under €10.

Fnac

Map 3, E4. Rue Neuve City 2. Ⓜ Rogier or de Brouckère.
Mon–Thurs & Sat 10am–7pm, Fri 10am–8pm.
A store with a fairly wide selection of French and English tapes and CDs, along with books, newspapers and CD players. It's also the place to come to buy tickets for mainstream gigs and concerts in the capital.

Free Record Shop

Map 2, D4. Rue Fossé aux Loups 18. Ⓜ de Brouckère.
Mon–Sat 10am–7pm, Sun noon–6pm.
Huge generic store with an impressive range of CDs, vinyl and tapes. You name it, they have it: techno, house,

MUSIC

easy listening, punk, rock, pop, folk, jazz, rap and classical. They also sell videos and computer games and there's a ticket booth for gigs and official raves.

Music Mania
Map 3, D5. Rue de la Fourche 4. Ⓜ de Brouckère.
Mon–Fri noon–6.30pm, Sat 11am–6pm.

The place to come for the latest release or that elusive vinyl or CD. This independent music store is frequented by rappers, straight-edge skaters and house or drum 'n' bass DJs alike and sells tickets before general sale to large and smaller gigs and parties. It's also a good source for flyers.

Virgin Megastore
Map 3, D4. Bd Anspach. Ⓜ de Brouckère.
Mon–Thurs & Sat 10am–7pm, Fri 10am–8pm, Sun noon–7pm.

Near the junction of rue Grétry. The full range of CDs, listening stands and games as well as the odd piece of vinyl.

Sports

Cycling and football are the nation's top sports, though Belgians also have an ongoing love affair with motorsports, be it motorcross (in which the country has had a number of successes on the international scene), hill climbing or amateur rallying.

Perhaps the most common sports in Brussels, however, are the extremely strenuous "**baby-foot**" (table football), as well as the many versions of **bar billiards**. There's also the traditional sport of **tir à l'arc en hauteur**, found in big parks like the Parc Josaphat, in which contestants shoot down feathers from the top of a very tall pole with a bow and arrow.

ATHLETICS

Two major events dominate the **athletics** calendar of Brussels. The **Ivo van Damme Memorial IAHF Grand Prix** is one of the International Athletic Federation meetings that is held yearly (last fortnight in August) in the Stade Roi Baudouin (Map 7, B2) and attracts many of the stars of the sport. It's named after the Belgian 800m silver-medallist of the 1976 Olympics in Montréal. Call ☎ 02 479 36 54 for tickets and details.

There is also the popular **Brussels 20km Race**, which

takes place in May or June each year, and usually attracts a field of 20,000 runners and more than 50,000 spectators. Although it consists of mostly serious runners, there are lots of festivities along the way and some people semi-walk it. The course takes participants halfway round the city near the EU Quarter, the Palais Royale, the avenue Louise, the Bois de la Cambre and through the tunnels of the Brussels inner ring road. It starts and finishes at the Esplanade du Cinquantenaire, and participants are charged €9 for the privilege of running their socks off for four hours. Call ⓣ02 513 89 40 for details.

FOOTBALL

Brussels' position in European **football** went down several notches following the 1985 Heysel disaster. Not only was the city's reputation in tatters, but Heysel was banned from staging European matches. Even the home club who played in the stadium complex, Racing Jet Brussels, moved out to Wavre, 30km away. However, after being rebuilt and renamed the Stade Roi Baudouin, the new ground was used for several matches in the 2000 European Championship. Despite occasional outbreaks of violence, the championship – hosted jointly by Belgium and Holland – helped restore the country's place as an international football host.

In terms of **league football**, Brussels has been dominated by one club – Anderlecht. Most of the city's other clubs have either folded, migrated or merged to help form the city's poor relation, Racing White Daring Molenbeek (RWDM). Anderlecht's facilities and resources put other Belgian clubs in the shade, but this difference is all the more marked in Brussels, as RWDM attract only a few thousand fans. A third city club, Union Saint-Gilloise, were the Brussels club until their relegation in 1973. They have an identifiable neighbourhood feel and their sardonic Bruxellois humour can still be heard in the club bar. The few fans who still shuffle up the rue du Stade do so now out of duty rather than pleasure.

HEYSEL

The Heysel disaster is synonymous with football violence. The stadium, built in 1930 in the Parc des Expositions in northwest Brussels, was the site for the 1985 European Cup Final between Liverpool FC and Juventus.

Liverpool fans had started drinking early in the day, and were joined by neo-Nazi elements in the stands, as was manifest from the pamphlets later found near the seats. Local policing was disorganised and parts of the stadium were in need of renovation. Shortly before kick-off, a group of Liverpool fans charged through the supposedly neutral block Z and 39 supporters (mainly Italian) were crushed to death when the sector wall collapsed. The match was played out to avoid further pandemonium, resulting in a win for Juventus. English clubs were banned from Europe for five years.

The stadium obviously had to be refurbished, and after various arguments, the Belgian FA agreed to foot the bill. The Stade du Roi Baudouin was built in its place, although some of the original Heysel infrastructure remains. The stadium, with a capacity of 50,000, all-seated, boasts its own new métro station at the end of the 1A line, and can also be accessed from the Heysel métro station. The stadium ticket office, marked Kartenverkoop/Vente Tickets, is along avenue du Marathon by Tribune no. 1 and sells tickets in four different colour-coded price brackets. Call ☎ 02 477 12 11 for ticket details.

FOOTBALL

ROYAL SPORTING CLUB ANDERLECHT

Map 1, B3. Stade Constant Vanden Stock, av Théo Verbeeck 2 Ⓣ 02 522 15 39 for information and tickets. Ⓜ St Guidon.

Founded in 1908, Anderlecht won their first title only in 1947. Two years after that, an England ex-goalie by the name of Bill Gormlie was appointed first team coach, ushering in a decade of seven titles that established Anderlecht as the country's biggest club.

In the early 1960s Real Madrid, CDNA Sofia and Bologna were all beaten, while at home Anderlecht won five titles in a row. In 1964, the Belgian team that beat Holland 1-0 was composed entirely of Anderlecht players. All of Anderlecht's three European successes came during the late 1970s and early 1980s, the club's golden period. Their greatest triumph was their Cup Winners' Cup victory in 1976, with a 4-2 victory over West Ham in the final. Other successes included victory over Liverpool in the European Super Cup in 1978 and an impressive win over Benfica in the UEFA Cup Final in 1983.

After that, the money needed to convert the stadium meant that there was less to spend on players. The Mauves (because of their strip) have thus under-achieved in Europe for most of the 1990s and into the next century – the only highlight being an appearance in the 1990 Cup Winners' Cup Final, which they went on to lose to Sampdoria. Various corruption sagas have also haunted the club. In 1983 the club president Vanden Stock admitted that he had paid a Spanish referee a million francs (€25,000) after a UEFA semi-final with Nottingham Forest.

The only comfort remaining to fans is that they now have a quite classy stadium – it's where the Belgian team practised and played during the Heysel refurbishment.

FOOTBALL

RWD MOLENBEEK

- -

Map 1, B2. Stade Edmond Machtens, rue Charles Malis 61 Ⓣ 02 411 99 00. Ⓜ Beekkant.

RWDM was formed by merging two Brussels clubs, Daring and Racing White, in 1973. Only two years later, a goal from international Jacques Teugels against Anderlecht won the club their first and only title. Key player Johan Boskamp became a local hero – until his move to Anderlecht. Though they were unable to keep their title, the team remained in the top six, and in 1977 they were only one away goal away from a UEFA Cup Final against Juventus. The club have done little since, though coach René Vandereycken did take them back into Europe for 1996–97.

To get there, go to Métro Beekkant, then take bus #85 or a ten-minute walk down rue Jules Vieujant, followed by a left down rue Osseghem.

UNION SAINT-GILLOISE

- -

Map 1, A3. Stade Joseph Marien, ch de Bruxelles 223 Ⓣ 02 344 16 56. Ⓜ Horta.

A more romantic ground would be difficult to imagine. The Stade Joseph Marien, named after a former club president, is bordered by the forest of Parc Duden on one side and by a wonderful old club bar on the other.

People crowded up the hillside in their thousands to see Union in their golden prewar days, when they were the biggest club in Belgium. The last decent Union side, that of the late 1950s and early 1960s, made occasional forays into the Fairs' Cup, beating Roma and Olympique Marseille.

Union were too proud to agree to any of the mergers that swallowed up the lesser Brussels clubs in the 1970s. The result was that the club celebrated their centenary in 1997 by being relegated to the third division. With amateur football and possibly worse looming, the forest is ghostly silent.

To get there, take the tram to Horta and then tram #18, getting off at Van Haelen. From there the stadium is a five-minute walk up rue des Glands.

Young multinational bar lads flock to *O'Reilly's* **(see p.205), which has established itself as the raucous venue for satellite international and particularly English Premiership matches. For big Irish matches, the** *Irish Club* **(☎ 02 231 12 16 or 02 231 12 08) usually organizes big-screen social evenings.**

CYCLING

Cycling is immensely popular in Belgium, both as a sport and a hobby. The country has a great cycling terrain and Brussels plays host to the many national cycling meets, having also been a stop-off point for the Tour de France. In honour of the great Belgian cyclist, the **Eddy Merckx Grand Prix** on the last Sunday of August is a timed event attracting top professionals. Provélo (see below) also organizes an **amateur** version which is an excellent opportunity to take advantage of the car-free 22km circuit within Brussels, starting and ending at the Gare du Nord, via the Botanique, Montgomery tunnel, the canal and Heysel – families are welcome. At other times of the year cyclists can join the joggers to stretch their legs in the Bois de la Cambre and the Forêt de Soignes.

For **bike rental**, go to Provélo (July–Aug Tues–Sun 1–7pm, rue de l'infante Isabelle; Sept–June Mon–Fri 9am–6pm, rue E. Solvay 32; ☎ 02 502 73 55), who also organize bike tours of Brussels and the outskirts. Alternatively, check out the Train-plus-Vélo schemes offered

EDDY MERCKX

Four cyclists have achieved the extraordinary distinction of winning the Tour de France five times: Jacques Anquetil, Bernard Hinault, Miguel Indurain and – the best of them all – Belgium's Eddy Merckx.

In his very first Tour, in 1969, Eddy finished eighteen minutes in front of the runner-up (this in a race in which five minutes is a big gap), destroying the field in a style that was to earn him the nickname "The Cannibal". As strong on mountain climbs as in races against the clock (he set a world record for the greatest distance covered in an hour), and as able in one-day events as in the huge multi-stage tours, Merckx amassed a tally of titles that no rider is ever likely to equal: five victories in the Giro d'Italia (Tour of Italy); three times winner of the Paris–Nice race; three times World Road Champion; five times winner of the Liège–Bastogne–Liège race; three times winner of the Paris–Roubaix (the so-called "Hell of the North"); seven times winner of the Milan–San Remo . . . the list goes on. In the 1974 season he managed to win the tours of Italy and France, then the World Championship, a Grand Slam that only Stephen Roche has matched. Indeed, so complete was his dominance that a disconsolate rival once observed: "If Merckx has decided he wants to win today, then he will."

Merckx retired in 1978, having totalled 525 victories, and has since divided his time between punditry, running his own bike factory, and nurturing the talent of his son Axel, who is now following hot in his father's wheeltracks.

at most railway stations – a bike is thrown in with the price of a train ticket to nineteen destinations in Belgium (☎02 555 25 25 for details). Those who already have their own bike can take it on the train for €4 per single journey, €7.40 for a return. You can also contact the Fédération

CYCLING

Belge du Cyclotourisme, who organize some 600 cycle rides every year throughout Belgium (Ave du Limbourg 34; ☎02 521 86 40).

GO-KARTING

Given the Belgians' infatuation with motorsports, it comes as no surprise that **go-karting** is a popular pastime. There's a track at City Kart, square des Grées du Lou 59 (Map 1, C3; €12 per hour; ☎02 332 36 96, Ⓦwww.citykart.com), or you can head for the Brussels Formula One track, rue de Lusambo 62 (Map 1, C3; €21 per 30min; ☎02 332 37 37), which also has a restaurant attached.

GOLF

Most **golf courses** are outside Brussels and the Fédération Royale Belge de Golf (Map 1, D2; ☎02 672 23 89) can provide information on full-size golf courses in Belgium. The best 18-hole course in Brussels itself is the Royal Amicale Anderlecht Golf Club, rue Scholle 1 (Map 1, B3; ☎02 521 16 87), which has training and driving ranges and is well laid-out in wooded surroundings with lakes. The Brabantse Golf at Steenwagenstraat 11, Melsbroek (Map 1, G1; ☎02 751 82 05), is near the airport and is a pleasant and not too challenging full practice course 5km long. The Golf de l'Empereur near Waterloo (Map 1, E6) is both challenging and beautiful, with the clubhouse in an old farmhouse. It has both 18- and 9-hole courses. You can play **crazy golf** at Parc de Wolvendael on avenue de Wolvendael 44 (Map 1, D3; daily 10am–6pm; tram #92 or #41; ☎02 375 34 62).

SKATING

Ice-skaters will be delighted at the whimsical faerie-atmosphere surrounding the rink on the Grand-Place in December and January. Other public rinks include the Patinoire de Forest, avenue du Globe 36 (Map 1, C1; ☎02 345 16 11), which is open all year round, and Poséidon, avenue des Vaillants 4 (Map 1, E2; Sept–April; ☎02 762 16 33). **Rollerbladers** and **skateboarders** should head for Mont des Arts near Gare Centrale (Map 2, E6), or the Bois de la Cambre on Sundays, when the roads are closed to traffic (Map 1, D3).

SPORTS CENTRES AND GYMS

Winner's at rue Bonneel 13 (Map 1, D2; ☎02 280 02 70) has an inside **climbing**-wall, as well as **squash courts** and a **gym**. The Golden Club at place du Châtelain 33 (Map 8, H7; Mon–Fri noon–10pm, Sat & Sun 10am–4pm; ☎02 538 19 06) has become highly prestigious in beefcake circles since the rise in popularity of that great Belgian export Jean-Claude van Damme – van Damme started off here and his ex-coach is still the manager. It has two thousand square metres of muscle-building machines, plus saunas and sunbeds, and runs aerobics, step and fitness classes, as well as popular **martial arts** classes for all those Hollywood wannabes.

The American Gym at boulevard Général Jacques 144 (Map 1, D3; Mon–Fri 10am–10pm, Sat 10am–3pm, Sun 10am–2pm; ☎02 640 59 92) has similar facilities. The **boxing** and **kick-boxing** on offer are top notch, given the gym's several champions in both categories, and the kung-fu classes are highly recommended. For more martial action, contact the Centre de la Culture Japonaise, rue des Augustines 44 (☎02 426 50 00), which offers English-speaking classes in judo and karate, among others.

The Centre Sportif de Woluwe St Pierre at avenue Salomé 2 (Map 1, E2; ☏02 773 18 20) has a full range of sporting facilities including a multi-sports hall and squash and **tennis courts** (the latter are open till 11pm). The Complexe Sportif du Palais du Midi at rue van der Weyden 3–9 (Map 3, A10; ☏02 279 59 56) is more centrally located and has a sports hall which it rents out to teams including the first-division Brussels basketball team.

There's **skiing** and **snowboarding** available on the artificial slopes of the Parc de Neerpede's Yeti Ski and Snowboard venue, dreve Olympique 11 (Map 1, B3; ☏02 520 77 57, ⓦwww.yeti.ski@pi.com). Lessons are available, and you can rent all the equipment you need; note that wearing gloves is obligatory.

SWIMMING POOLS

The city has a number of **pools** in local sports centres, including an Olympic-sized one at the Centre Sportif de Woluwe St Pierre (Map 1, F3; Mon–Thurs 8am–7pm, Fri 8am–8pm, Sat 8am–7pm). The Ixelles pool at rue de la Natation 10 (Map 1, D3) is open on Sundays from 8am to 5.30pm, while Poséidon, avenue des Vaillants 2 (Map 1, E2), has a separate children's pool, but can get crowded at weekends. Alternatively, both Aqualibi and the Océade water park (see "Kids' Brussels") are great places to go for water slides, wave-making machines and other aquatic havoc.

TENPIN BOWLING

The city has a number of bowling alleys, the biggest, and most centrally located, being the Crosly Super Bowling at boulevard de l'Empereur 36 (Map 2, D6; daily 2pm–2am; ☏02 512 08 74). It has twenty lanes and a late bar.

Kids' Brussels

Although many of the main sights and museums in Brussels (the Manneken Pis, the Grand-Place, the Musée d'Art Moderne) hold little interest for kids, worry not – Brussels can be child-friendly.

In the centre, the **Centre Belge de la Bande Dessinée** museum, **Scientastic**, and the **Théâtre de Toone** are the main attractions for younger and older children alike. Elsewhere, the **Musée des Sciences Naturelles** is host to an impressive display of dinosaur skeletons and is ideal for pre-teens, whereas the **Musée du Jouet**, with its huge collection of toys throughout the ages, seems to be a hit with everybody regardless of age.

Out of town, Heysel gives the impression it was specifically designed for the under-12s, and is home to both **Mini-Europe** and **Océade**, as well as the excellent **Planétarium** which holds regular exhibitions. Further afield, the brand-new **Six Flags Belgium** amusement park and attached **Aqualibi** water park offer enough roller-coasters, amusement rides and water slides to make a day of it.

Most of the city's **parks** have playgrounds – the most popular one is at the lovely Bois de la Cambre. The city also has a summer fun fair – **Foire du Midi** – which is held near the Gare du Midi from mid-July to mid-August. Here you'll find the usual riot of candy floss, amusement arcades and rides, including a large Ferris wheel.

Full listings of children's exhibitions, shows and fairs can be found in the "Jeunes Publics" section of Wednesday's *Le Soir* supplement.

ACTIVITIES

City Kart

Map 1, C3. Sq des Grées du Lou 59 ⓣ 02 332 36 96, Ⓦ www.citykart.com. Tram #52. Childrens' sessions (aged 4–16): Wed noon–5pm, Sat & Sun 9.30am–3.30pm. Wed €37.20 for all-day course, Sat €8.70 per 15min, Sun €12.40 per 15min.

Kids will have a great time tearing around the track at these children-only sessions under adult supervision (lessons available on Wednesdays). Karts can reach speeds of up to 60kph, so you'd better make sure budding Schumachers are up to this first. Reservations necessary.

Océade

Map 7, C2. At Brupark, Bd du Centenaire 20 ⓣ 02 478 43 20. Ⓜ Heysel. Call for times. Adults €12.15 (for 4 hours), children under 1.30m €9.70, children under 1.15m free.

Year-round water park with a number of attractions including high-speed slides, wavepools, whirlpools, solariums and saunas.

THE PICKY CLUB

The Picky Club, Rue de Neerpede 805–807, Anderlecht (Map 1, B3; Sat & Sun 9.30am–7pm; €3.70 1hr, €2.40 half-day, €27.80 one day including meal; ☎02 522 20 84), is a clever solution for parents who want a day to themselves in the city, laying on a number of wildly divergent activities for children aged 3–10. There are inflatable castles, a swimming pool, a go-kart track and even a rock-climbing wall, and the helpful staff can also introduce kids to model-building, archery and mini-golf. The Picky Club can also organize special theme days for birthdays, and has its very own hotel open at weekends.

Six Flags Belgium & Aqualibi
Map 1, F9. 20km from Brussels on autoroute E411 ☎010 42 15 00.
Call for times. Adults €27.25, children under 1.30m €13.65, children under 1m free.
Recently overhauled theme park sporting twenty new attractions – thrillseekers will especially like the Dalton Terror tower, which takes you up to a height of 77m before letting you drop at speeds reaching up to 110kph. The attached water park, Aqualibi, has two 140m-long water slides amongst the usual water park offerings.

CINEMA

UGC De Brouckère
Map 2, D4. Pl de Brouckère 38 ☎0900 10 440. Ⓜ de Brouckère.
Sat 9.30–11.30am. Children €1.50.
Screens children's films – mainly animation – every Saturday morning. Moreover, you can leave your kids in the hands of the supervisors, whilst you go off to watch a film for the grown-ups.

CINEMA

MUSEUMS AND SIGHTS

Centre Belge de la Bande Dessinée

Map 2, F4. Rue des Sables 20 ☏ 02 219 19 80. Ⓜ Botanique or Rogier.

Tues–Sun 10am–6pm. Adults €4.45, under-12s €1.50.

As popular with adults as it is with children, the comic museum documents the illustrious history of the Belgian comic book with numerous displays ranging from Tintin and the Smurfs to comic-book production. There's a comprehensive bookshop attached, as well as a restaurant and brasserie.

Mini-Europe

Map 7, C2. Bd du Centenaire 20 ☏ 02 478 05 50. Ⓜ Heysel.

Daily 9.30am–5pm (check for seasonal variations). Adults €10.65, under-12s €8.20, children under 1.30m free.

Mini-Europe is pure tack, but children love it. All the historic European sights are reproduced in miniature – there are 300 in all – and you can even re-enact the eruption of Vesuvius and the fall of the Berlin wall. Firework displays are held regularly throughout July and August.

Musée des Enfants

Map 8, L9. Rue du Bourgmestre 15 ☏ 02 640 01 07, Ⓦ www.hands-on.nordm.se /old/brussels.htm. Bus #71; tram #90, #23.

Wed, Sat & Sun 2.30–5pm; closed Aug. Adults and children €5.45.

Like Scientastic, this museum's strong point is that it's interactive – there are lots of buttons to press and knobs to turn. It's aimed mostly at under 12s. As well as looking at the many exhibits, children can paint, engage in basic woodwork or even participate in a play.

Musée du Jouet

Map 2, F4. Rue de l'Association 24 ☏ 02 219 61 68. Ⓜ Botanique or Madou.

Daily 10am–6pm. Adults €2.50, children €1.50.

A large toy museum with more than 25,000 toys – dolls, trains, steam engines, pedal cars – with at least 5000 on show at any one time. Some of them date back to 1860, but you can play only with the more modern ones. A small theatre holds occasional marionette shows. The museum is pretty interactive and there's a big play area. Most suitable for 5- to 12-year-olds.

Musée des Sciences Naturelles
Map 2, F6. Rue Vautier 29 ⓣ 02 627 42 38. Ⓜ Trone. Tues–Fri 9.30am–4.45pm, Sat & Sun 10am–6pm. Adults €3.70, children aged 6–17 €2.50, under-6s free.

The centrepieces of this collection are the thirty five-metre-high Iguanadon skeletons, which were found in southern Belgium in 1878, when prospectors were digging for gold. They date back some 65 million years. If Jurassic monsters aren't your thing, there are four more floors covering mammals (stuffed lions, tigers and bears), sea creatures (including a gigantic whale skeleton) fauna, and sections on how people live in the Arctic.

National Planetarium
Map 7, B3. Av de Bouchout 10 ⓣ 02 474 70 50. Ⓜ Heysel. Mon–Fri & Sun 9am–4.30pm. Adults €3, children €2.

A great place for children to take time out and look skyward. Apart from the regular shows such as a "voyage through the cosmos" and "the movement of the stars", there are a number of permanent exhibits on the ground floor including displays on rockets, satellites and astronomical instruments. Temporary exhibitions are held in the entrance hall.

There is a special price combination ticket (adult €19.60, children €19.10) for Mini-Europe, the Atomium and Océade – available from each venue.

MUSEUMS AND SIGHTS

Scientastic

Map 2, D4. Level -1, Métro Bourse station ⓣ02 474 70 500. Ⓜ Bourse.
Easter, July & Aug, Christmas 2–5.30pm; rest of year Sat & Sun 2–5.30pm. Adults €4, children €3.50.
Both younger and older children seem to love the hands-on nature of this small science museum, which has over seventy interactive exhibits including visual illusions such as an impossible box, and sensory games like smelling your way out of a maze, or changing your voice and fusing your image with that of a friend.

PARKS

Bois de la Cambre

Map 1, D3. At the intersection of av Louise and bd de la Cambe. Tram #93, #94.
The capital's largest and most popular inner city park, including lakes and woods. There's plenty of room for the kids to go crazy, and when they get bored of that, you can take them to Halle du Bois – a giant playground in the middle of the park equipped with a bouncy castle and toboggan run. It's open on school holidays and weekends 2–6pm and only costs €2.50 per child.

Parc du Cinquantenaire

Map 2, J6. Entrance av de Cortenberg. Ⓜ Mérode or Schuman.
The main attraction of this spacious park are the child-friendly museums it hosts. See p.104.

The Foret de Soignes (p.120-121) is another green space that's ideal for running around and letting off some steam.

THEATRE

Théâtre de Toone
Map 2, D5. Petite rue des
Bouchers, impasse de
Schuddeveld 6 ☎02 511 71 37.
Ⓜ Bourse or de Brouckère.
Call for times and shows.
Adults €9.90, children €6.20.
World-famous puppet theatre
housed in a seventeenth-
century building a few steps
from the Grand-Place.
Performances are in several
languages (ring in advance)
and range from *The Three
Musketeers* and the *Hunchback
of Notre Dame*, to *Faust* and
Hamlet. There's also a puppet
museum which can be visited
free of charge during the
intermission. Suitable for
children, who love the
puppets, and adults, who
appreciate the sly references
to recent news, politicians
and other salacious titbits.

Also of interest to children are the following: The
Atomium p.117; Autoworld p.106; Musee des
Instruments de Musique; and Espace Tintin p.237.

Gay and lesbian Brussels

Brussels often seems to be lagging a good decade behind the times on gay politics – the city's first gay and lesbian pride event wasn't held until 1996. However, though Brussels can hardly be described as a gay capital like Amsterdam, the actual **gay scene** is reasonably well-developed, with a decent selection of gay bars, clubs and restaurants.

The area just south of the Bourse remains the centre of the action, particularly in the triangle between rue des Pierres, rue du Marché au Charbon, and rue St Géry, which is the closest the capital has to a designated gay quarter. Although many bars in this area aren't specifically gay, no one will bat an eyelid if a gay couple walks in. Gay venues have also been establishing themselves in the Ste Catherine district and around rue des Bouchers, close to place de la Monnaie. The **lesbian scene**, however, continues to remain cloistered. Although a few venues welcome both gays and lesbians equally, there are very few lesbian-only nightspots in the city.

Listings of gay and lesbian events, and a number of useful addresses, can be obtained from Tels Quels (see

"Information Services", below), who also organize events such as the Gay and Lesbian Film Festival held every January at the Botanique (see p.42). *Queensize*, a publication readily available in most bars, lists gay bars, shops and services in most major Belgian cities; email Ⓔ queensize@mailcity.com for more details. An informative English-language website for listings is Ⓦ www.geocities.com/~eggbrussels.

The city's many **gay associations** include Égalité (Ⓣ 02 295 98 87) which, as its name suggests, has a political slant and lobbies the powers that be for equal rights for gays and lesbians, whereas Infor Homo (Ⓣ 02 733 10 24), and the student equivalent Cercle Homosexuel étudiant (Ⓣ 02 650 25 40), both organize regular nights out and gay activity programmes. There are actually more **lesbian associations** in Brussels than there are lesbian venues – the most popular ones being Amazing Grace (Ⓣ 02 218 36 51) and Attirent d'Elles (Ⓣ 02 512 45 87).

Many gay associations in Brussels direct their energies towards educating people about **Aids** and providing support for victims of the disease. The most high-profile ones are Aide Info Sida (Ⓣ 02 514 29 65) and Act Up (Ⓣ 02 512 02 02), which also aims to change government policies towards Aids. Act Together at rue d'Artois 5 (Ⓣ 02 512 05 05) provides support for families of victims, and has an English-speaking helpline.

The age of consent for gay men and women is 16.

INFORMATION SERVICES

Tels Quels
Map 2, D5. Rue Marché au Charbon 81 Ⓣ 02 512 45 87.

Ⓜ Bourse.
Sun–Thurs 5pm–2am, Fri & Sat 5pm–4am.

Gay and lesbian meeting place just round the corner from *Chez Maman*. Although there's a small café, it's best known for its documentation centre which has information on gay and lesbian rights and forthcoming events. It also hosts occasional art exhibitions and group discussions. *Tels Quels*, their monthly French-language publication, includes political reports and a full gay and lesbian listings section for bars, clubs and restaurants, as well as hairdressers, saunas and sex shops.

GAY RESTAURANTS

Le Comptoir
Map 2, D5. Pl de la Vieille Halle-aux-blés 24 Ⓣ 02 514 00 04. Ⓜ Gare Centrale. Daily 7pm–3am.
Well-known gay restaurant and bar, just off rue Chêne, popular with a chic and stylish crowd, who are attracted by the excellent food and decadent candlelit ambience. After you've gorged yourself on the tasty nouvelle cuisine in the restaurant upstairs, head to the dance floor below where you can burn it off to the latest dance, house and techno tracks. Riotous transvestite shows every Sunday.

El Papgayo
Map 2, C6. Pl Rouppe 6 Ⓣ 02 514 50 83. Ⓜ Anneessens. Mon–Thurs & Sun 4pm–2am, Fri & Sat 6pm–2am.
Lively gay restaurant, which gets packed out at weekends when you'll have to wait for a table. The decor is a riot of colour, there's a small dancefloor (salsa music nightly) and the Latin American food is spicy and inexpensive. A healthy blend of people and styles ensures its never dull.

H20
Map 2, D5. Rue du Marché au Charbon 27 Ⓣ 02 512 38 43. Ⓜ Bourse. Daily 7pm–2am.

A fashionable gay restaurant close to the Bourse, popular with late-twenty something couples, who come to sample the simple but tasty world cuisine. Some may find the fantasy theme decor – Tolkien-style sculptures and pictures, and aquamarine-coloured walls – slightly off-putting, but there's always an upbeat atmosphere, the service is friendly and the food is well-priced. Hetero-friendly. Reservations not always necessary.

GAY BARS AND CLUBS

Le Belgica

Map 2, D5. Rue Marché au Charbon 32. Ⓜ Bourse. Thurs–Sat 10pm–3am.

A respected fixture of the Brussels gay scene, *Le Belgica* is arguably the capital's most popular gay bar and pick-up joint. Admittedly it's a tad run-down, with formica tables and dilapidated chairs that have seen better days, but if you're out for a lively, friendly atmosphere, you could do a lot worse. Come at the weekend when the place is heaving – all are welcome, whether male, female, gay or straight – and be sure to slam back a few of the house speciality: lemon-vodka "Belgica" shots.

Le Cabaret

Map 2, D4. Rue de l'Ecuyer 41. Ⓜ Bourse. Sun 11pm–7am.

Good-humoured gay club themed around the kitsch glamour of the 60s and 70s. Open to all, and a welcome respite from the intensity of some of Brussels' other gay clubs.

Chez Maman

Map 2, C5. Rue des Grands Carmes 7. Ⓜ Bourse. Thurs–Tues 9pm–3am.

This tiny bar has achieved an almost cult-like status in Brussels – mainly because of the supremely flamboyant proprietor Maman and his hugely popular half-hour transvestite shows. People flock from all corners of the city to see him strut up and down the bar – which serves as an impromptu stage – singing his heart out Marlene Dietrich-style.

La Démence

Map 3, C9. Rue Blaes 208 ⓣ 02 538 99 31. Ⓜ Porte de Hal.
Sun 11pm–7am.
The city's most popular gay club, held on two floors in *The Fuse* (see p.215) and playing cutting edge techno. The crowd is a bit difficult to pigeonhole – expect to find a hybrid mix of muscle men, transsexuals, trendy fashion victims, and out-and-out ravers. Back rooms available.

L'Homo Erectus

Map 2, C5. Rue des Pierres 57 ⓣ 02 514 74 93. Ⓜ Bourse.
Daily 11am–late.
It's a tight squeeze in this brazenly named gay bar, but the atmosphere is cosy and personal and there's a compact dance-floor, complete with obligatory disco-balls, too. Music ranges from house to disco.

L'Incognito

Map 2, C5. Rue des Pierres 36. Ⓜ Bourse.
Daily 11pm–late.
A popular gay bar, with a lively atmosphere, camp music – Madonna, Celine Dion, disco, and French pop – and a photo gallery of beefy studs and pert behinds lining the walls. It's well situated, not far from the Grand-Place, but can be a bit cliquey.

The Slave

Map 2, D5. Plattesteen 7. Ⓜ Bourse.
Mon–Fri 9pm–4am, Sat & Sun 9pm–6am.
An off-the-beaten-track leather bar, with plenty of back rooms, S&M gear and video pornography. Something of a Brussels underground institution.

The Smart

Map 2, C5. Rue des Pierres 36 ⓣ 02 513 32 13. Ⓜ Bourse.
Daily 3pm–late.
Brand new gay bar, all polished metal and burnished wood, reflecting its clean-cut image and hip, young clientele.

Why Not

Map 2, C5. Rue des Riches Claires 7 Ⓣ 02 512 63 43. Ⓜ Bourse.
Daily 11pm–6am.
Brussels' only nightclub that's open every night of the week, the three-level *Why Not* is absolutely heaving on the weekends with mostly young men dancing to house and dance tracks.

LESBIAN BARS AND CLUBS

Pussy Galore

Map 3, C9. Rue Blaes 208 Ⓣ 02 511 97 89. Ⓜ Porte de Hal.
Second Friday of month.
The lesbian spin-off of *La Démence*, held upstairs in *The Fuse* (see p.215). The music – ambient dance – is a little tamer than most house clubs, and the mixed-age crowd slightly more laid-back.

Le Sapho

Map 3, D4. Rue St Géry 1 Ⓣ 02 512 45 52. Ⓜ Bourse.
Fri–Sat 10pm–late.
One of only two solely lesbian bars in the capital, so it usually attracts a good crowd. The atmosphere is friendly and, unlike in many of the capital's gay bars, members of the opposite sex are not made to feel unwelcome.

Festivals and special events

Music and film feature most prominently in the Brussels calendar of annual **festivals**, although flower lovers and those who appreciate dance and fine art, will not be disappointed. The more traditional festivals – the medieval-style Ommegang and the Planting of the Meiboom – centre on the Grand-Place, while most of the modern ones like the jazz or film festivals take place in various venues around the city and bring the whole of the capital to life. The main annual events are listed below; for information on the dozens of mini-festivals held in Brussels during the year, check *The Bulletin* or ask at the tourist office. Alternatively, it's well worth catching a train to one of the many festivals held in the towns outside the capital. In particular, the Procession of the Holy Blood, held in Bruges, is famous throughout Belgium for its medieval pageant.

JANUARY

Brussels Film Festival

Last two weeks (☎ 02 227 39 80, ⓦ www.brusselsfestival.be) Although not as well known as many European film festivals, this annual event has managed to build up a solid reputation of its own – pulling in actors like Jean-Marc Barr and Jose Garcia along with director Michael Kalesniko at the 2001 event. While you may never have heard of the Crystal Stars and Golden Iris the jury hands out to the best film each year, it's a great occasion to see European or Belgian film premieres. Films are screened at various locations around the city.

FEBRUARY

Antiques Fair

Last two weeks (☎ 02 513 48 31) The meeting point of all dedicated antiquaries, international as well as Belgian, who display their finest wares and choice pieces in the Palais des Beaux Arts. Specialists of Asian, African and South American art also attend and sell everything from antique Indian jewellery to scarred wood fetishes.

Animation and Cartoon Festival

End of February to beginning of March (☎ 02 534 41 25, ⓔ info@folioscope.be) A little-known animation fest which screens as many as 120 new and old cartoons from around the world over the course of the event. Held at Auditorium du Passage 44, boulevard du Jardin Botanique.

MARCH

Ars Musica
Mid-March to end of April
(℡ 02 219 26 60,
Ⓦ www.arsmusica.be)
This contemporary classical music festival regularly features internationally renowned composers, such as Argentina's Mauricio Kagel and France's Pascal Dusapin. The festival organizers are keen to promote interaction between the audience and the musicians and often it's possible to meet the artists before the concert. The festival has built up an impressive reputation for itself on not only a European, but a world-wide scale.

Performances are usually held in the Palais des Beaux Arts or La Monnaie.

Festival of Fantasy Film, Science Fiction and Thrillers
Last two weeks (℡ 02 201 17 13, Ⓦ www.biff.org)
This well-established festival has achieved an almost cult-like status with cult-film lovers, and is the place to see all those entertainingly dreadful B-movies, as well as more modern sci-fi classics, thrillers and fantasy epics. It's held at Auditorium du Passage 44, boulevard du Jardin Botanique.

APRIL

Ghent – Gentse Floralien
End of April (℡ 09 222 73 36)
Held every five years in the Flanders Expo building, Maaltekouter 1, Sint Denijs Westrem, this is one of the world's biggest flower festivals. The one-and-a-half kilometre "inside garden", which is home to a wide range of flowers from around the globe, is also the setting of the main event – the international flower competition. The next festival is scheduled for 2005.

The Royal Glasshouses – Laeken Palace

Ten days from the end of April to beginning of May (☎ 02 513 89 40)

For ten days of the year the Royal Glasshouses (Serres Royales) at Laeken (see p.119) are open to the public. The exquisite glass and iron glasshouses shelter numerous palm trees and tropical plants. It draws thousands each year and you can expect long queues at the entrance.

MAY

Jazz Marathon

Three days in May (☎ 02 456 04 75, Ⓦ www.brusselsjazz marathon.be)

Sometimes regarded as the poor relation of the Jazz Festival (see p.281), the Jazz Marathon is a blast nonetheless. Hip jazz cats can listen to non-stop groove around the city for three cool days, and although most of the sixty-plus bands are little known, the quality of the vibe is usually very high. Entrance fees vary depending on the venue, but you can buy a three-day pass from Fnac or the tourist office for a bargain €13.39. Alternatively head for one of the free jazz concerts on the Grand-Place.

Concours Musical International Reine Elisabeth de Belgique

Beginning of May to late May (☎ 02 513 00 99, Ⓦ www .concours-reine-elisabeth.be)

A world-famous classical music competition founded fifty years ago by Belgium's violin-playing Queen Elisabeth. The categories change annually, rotating piano, voice and violin and the winners perform live in the Grand-Place in July. Tickets for the competition can be difficult to get hold of and can cost as much as €50, but the venues do include the splendid Palais des Beaux Arts and the Conservatoire Royal de Musique.

MAY

JUNE

Couleur Café Festival

End of June (☎ 02 672 12 91)
A trendy three-day live music festival held in a big tent on the site of the Tour & Taxi night-club (see p.216). Expect a fair share of African rhythms, acid-jazz and world music, as well as ragga and hip-hop.

Bruges – The Procession of the Holy Blood

Ascension Day (☎ 05 044 86 86)
This historic Roman Catholic procession was first mentioned in a statute dating back to 1291, and has been held in Bruges on Ascension Day every year since 1970.

Colourfully dressed in biblical and medieval-inspired costumes, the marchers bring to life scenes from both the New and Old Testament, including the legend of how knight and crusader Diederik van den Elzas helped bring back the "relic of the holy blood" (a piece of cloth, said to be stained with the blood of Christ) to Bruges from Jerusalem. The relic itself is displayed in the Chapel of the Holy Blood on place Burg, and can be viewed every Friday. Ascension Day will be May 9 in 2002 and May 29 in 2003.

JULY

Sundays in Bois de la Cambre

July, August and October
A free open-air classical music or jazz concert is held every Sunday in Bois de la Cambre, 11am–1pm. Popular with Belgian families.

Ommegang

First Tuesday and Thursday
(☎ 02 513 89 40)
One of the capital's best-known annual events, the Ommegang is a procession from Grand Sablon to the Grand-Place that began in

the fourteenth century as a religious event, celebrating the arrival of a statue of the Virgin from Antwerp. Nowadays the Ommegang has people in period costumes and the descendants of nobles playing the roles of their ancestors. It all finishes up with a traditional dance on the Grand-Place and is so popular it is now held twice in the same week. If you want a ticket for a seat on the Grand-Place for the finale, you'll need to reserve at the tourist office there at least six months ahead.

Brosella Folk and Jazz Festival

Second weekend (☎ 02 269 69 56)

A small, long-established jazz and folk festival held at Théâtre de Verdure, Parc d'Osseghem near Métro Heysel. The surrounding chaos (things rarely start on time) somehow adds to the attraction and the bands, mostly Belgian, but occasionally international, offer good entertainment.

Bruges – The Cactus Festival

Second week (☎ 05 033 20 14)

This open-air live music festival is held in the beautiful Minnewater Park in central Bruges. The Cactus Festival is a cosy, low-key affair, and you get to hear up-and-upcoming pop, rock and indie acts from Belgium and abroad, as well as blues, reggae and Irish folk. One-day tickets cost €13.63 (€11.15 in advance), whereas a two-day ticket will set you back €24.79 (€19.83 in advance) - they can be purchased from the Fnac store in Brussels at the City 2 complex (Ⓜ Rogier).

Ghent – Gentse Feesten

Mid- to late July (☎ 09 239 42 67)

For ten days every July, Ghent loses its conservative feel and embraces the youth-oriented street festival known as the Gentse Feesten. Local bands perform free outdoor gigs throughout the town, and the place seems to become a haven for every type of street performer in

JULY

the country, buskers, comedians, actors or puppeteers. There's also an outdoor market, selling everything from jenever, a gin-like traditional Ghent liquor, to handmade crafts.

Torhout and Werchter – Torhout-Werchter Festival

First weekend (☎ 01 660 04 06) Belgium's premier rock and pop festival and one of the largest open-air music festivals in Europe. In recent years the all-star line-up has included Massive Attack, Nick Cave and the Bad Seeds, Pulp, Björk, as well as the Beastie Boys, Garbage, Sonic Youth and Tricky. Bands first play at Torhout in West Flanders (Fri–Sat), before moving on to Werchter in Brabant (Sat–Sun). To get to Torhout, take the train from Gare du Midi or Gare Centrale to Bruges (40min), and then the train from Bruges to Torhout (10min). Special buses will take you from Torhout train station to the festival site for free. To reach Werchter, take the train to Leuven (25min), after which a special festival bus will take you to the site for a cost of €3.71.

AUGUST–SEPTEMBER

Planting of the Meiboom
August 9
An annual event in which a *meiboom* (maypole) is planted at the corner of rue des Sables and rue du Marais and involving a procession accompanied by much boozing, food and general partying. The story goes that in 1213 a wedding party was celebrating outside the city's gates when it was attacked by a street gang from Leuven. They were beaten off (with the help of a group of archers who happened to be passing by), and, in thanks, the duke gave them permission to plant a maypole on the eve of their patron saint's feastday.

Tapis des Fleurs
Mid-Aug weekend
If you like flowers and floral designs, head down to the Grand-Place in mid-August. Every two years (2002 is next) its historic cobblestones are covered with a lovely floral carpet made up of over 700,000 begonias from Ghent.

Ghent/Brussels – Festival van Vlaanderen
September to November (☏02 548 95 95, ⊛www.festival-van-vlaanderen.be)
One of the high points of the Flemish cultural calendar, the internationally renowned Festival of Flanders comprises more than 120 classical music concerts and operas held throughout sixty Flemish towns. Most of the festival's international symphony orchestras can be seen in Brussels – in the past these have included the London Symphony Orchestra, the Los Angeles Philharmonic, the Chicago Symphony Orchestra and the Vienna Philharmonic to name but a few. However, it's also worth heading out of the capital, particularly to the Flanders Festival-Ghent, which presents a different theme every year.

OCTOBER

Audi Jazz Festival
Mid-October to November
A month-long jazz extravaganza, featuring a wide range of local and international acts which in the past have included Courtney Pine, Andy Shepherd and Ray Charles. Like the Jazz Marathon, concerts are held in many live music venues (see p.277) around the city. Contact the tourist office for further information.

Europalia
Mid-October to mid-January
(☏ 02 507 85 50)
The Europalia festival focuses

on a different person or country each year and comprises paintings and exhibitions, as well as theatre, dance and live music. Although the Palais des Beaux Arts is at the centre of the festival, a number of venues are used throughout the city.

DECEMBER

Le Marché de Noël
Mid-December (☎ 02 513 89 40)

The capital's traditional Christmas market and fair, held on the Grand-Place for three days every December and featuring food, booze and various wares from EU countries. Admittedly, the piped Christmas tunes are a bit tacky, but it gets even the most cynical humbugs in the Christmas spirit. After the market is over the Christmas tree is put up and a large skating rink is installed.

Directory

AIRLINES British Airways (☏ 02 548 03 36), Aer Lingus (☏ 02 548 98 48) and American Airlines (☏ 02 508 77 11) all have their main offices at rue du Trône 98. Air UK (☏ 02 717 20 70), Cathay Pacific (☏ 02 712 64 48), KLM (☏ 02 717 20 70), Sabena (☏ 02 723 23 23) and Tap Air (☏ 02 720 02 23) have their main offices at Zaventem airport. The main Iberia office is on avenue Louise 54 (☏ 02 548 94 90), as is United Airlines at no. 350 (☏ 02 646 55 88); British Midland is at avenue des Pléiades 1200 (☏ 02 771 77 66).

AIRPORT INFORMATION
For general information at Zaventem call ☏ 02 753 21 11 (24hr). For specific enquiries ring ☏ 02 753 39 13 or 723 31 11 (7am–10pm).

BANKS AND EXCHANGE
Banks are generally open Mon–Fri 9am–4pm, with a one-hour lunch break between noon and 2pm. A few banks are open Saturday mornings. Most banks have a bureau de change, and cash travellers' cheques and Eurocheques. The ATMs at both General Bank and BBL are notorious for running out of money on Saturday night or Sunday morning. Bureau de change offices are widespread, the most central one being the 24-hour Crédit Général Automatic Exchange at Grand-Place 7. However, expect to be charged a flat fee, or lose money on a low exchange rate.

CAR RENTAL Major operators have branches at both Zaventem airport and Gare du

Midi train station. Europcar (Gare du Midi ☎02 522 95 73, Zaventem ☎02 721 05 92); Avis (Gare du Midi ☎02 513 69 69, Zaventem ☎02 720 09 44); and Hertz (Gare du Midi ☎02 524 31 00, Zaventem ☎02 720 60 44). Both Europcar (☎02 640 94 00) and Avis (☎02 524 31 00) have branches in Ixelles, as does Budget (☎02 646 51 30).

CREDIT CARD COMPANIES American Express is based on boulevard du Souverain 100 (☎02 676 21 11 or 24-hour ☎02 676 23 23). If you lose your card (Bankcontact, Eurocard, Visa, Mastercard, or Mr Cash) ring ☎070 34 43 44. For Diners Club, call ☎02 206 79 00.

DISABILITIES, TRAVELLERS WITH Brussels is not easy for the disabled traveller, although the new trams with a low-level platform have improved disabled access, and Braille information panels have been introduced in some métro stations. If you live in Brussels the STIB runs a special low-cost (€1.25), door-to-door mini-bus service within the greater Brussels area – call ☎02 515 23 65. Accommodation-wise,

many of the larger hotels have full disabled access, although smaller and cheaper ones often don't.

ELECTRICITY 220 volts AC. Most European appliances should work, providing you have a standard two-pin plug adapter. North Americans will need this plus a transformer.

EMBASSIES Australia, rue Guimard 6 (☎02 286 05 00); Canada, avenue de Tervuren 2 (☎02 741 06 11); Germany, avenue de Tervuren 190 (☎02 774 19 11); Great Britain, rue d'Arlon 85 (☎02 287 62 11); India, chaussée de Vleurgat 217 (☎02 640 91 40); Ireland, rue Froissart 89–93 (☎02 230 53 37); Japan, avenue des Arts 58 (☎02 511 23 07); New Zealand, boulevard du Régent 47–48 (☎02 512 10 40); South Africa, rue de la Loi 26 (☎02 285 44 00); USA, boulevard du Régent 25–27 (☎02 508 21 11).

EMERGENCIES Dial ☎101 for the police, and ☎100 for the ambulance or fire service. Doctors can be reached 24 hours a day at ☎02 479 18 18.

HEALTH Residents of European Union countries are entitled to free medical treatment and prescribed medicines under the EU Reciprocal Medical Treatment arrangement provided you have a completed E111 form (available from post offices in Britain and Social Security offices elsewhere).

HOSPITALS The main ones are: Brugmann Hospital, Campus Brugmann, place van Gehuchten (☏ 02 477 21 11); Érasme Hospital, route de Lennik 808 (☏ 02 526 34 02); Saint-Luc Hospital, avenue Hippocrate 10 (☏ 02 764 11 11 or 764 16 12) and St Pierre Hospital, rue Haute 322 (☏ 02 535 31 11).

INTERNET ACCESS The Sports Bar, avenue de la Toison d'Or 4, Ixelles (next to MO Porte de Namur) has more than twenty terminals with internet access. Emailing is free, as long as you buy a drink.

LEFT LUGGAGE Major train stations have luggage offices (daily 6am–midnight). Most train stations also have coin-operated lockers.

LOST PROPERTY For property lost on aircraft ring ☏ 02 723 60 11; if lost at the airport contact ☏ 02 753 68 20. The lost property office for the métro, trams and buses is at avenue de la Toison d'Or 15 (☏ 02 515 23 94).

NEWSPAPERS AND MAGAZINES The three main French-language dailies are *Le Soir*, *La Libre Belgique* and *La Dernière Heure*; the main Flemish ones are *De Standard* and *De Morgen*. The only English-language publication is *The Bulletin*. Most English papers are on sale here on the day of publication, though at about double the normal cover price.

PHARMACIES Most pharmacies are open from 8.30am to 6.30pm. There is a rota-system for pharmacies on call at night, Sundays and bank holidays. A list is displayed in the window of all chemists.

POLICE There are two basic types of police: the Gendarmerie Nationale, and the police. The former, who wear blue uniforms with red stripes on their trousers, patrol the motorways and deal with major crime; the latter, in their dark blue uniforms, cover everything else. The central police station is at rue Marché au Charbon 30 (☏ 02 517 96 11).

POST OFFICES Most post

offices are open Mon–Fri 9am–5pm, although the post office at avenue Fosny 48a next door to Gare du Midi is open 24 hours a day, and the central post office on the first floor of Centre Monnaie (place de la Monnaie) is also open on Saturdays.

PUBLIC HOLIDAYS The main holidays when shops and banks will be closed are: Jan 1 (New Year's Day); Easter Monday; May 1 (Labour Day); May 21 (Ascension Day); June 1 (Whitsuntide); July 11 (Flemish Community Day); July 21; Aug 15 (Assumption); Sept 27 (French Community Day); Nov 1 (All Saints' Day); Nov 11 (Armistice 1918); Dec 25 (Christmas Day).

TELEPHONES Local calls cost a minimum of €0.20, but to make an international call you'll need to put in a minimum of €1.20. Many phones accept prepaid cards which can be bought from newsagents, post offices and railway stations for €5 and €10. To make an international call dial Ⓣ 00, wait for the continous tone, and then dial the country code followed by the area code – omitting the initial zero – and then the number. For directory enquiries in English dial Ⓣ 1405. To ring Brussels from abroad dial Ⓣ 00 322, and then the telephone number.

TRAVEL AGENCIES Acotra World Travel Agency (Mon–Fri 8.30am–6pm) at rue du Marché-aux-Herbes 110 (Ⓣ 02 512 86 07) is one of the bigger travel agencies, and specializes in discount train, ferry and plane tickets. Nouvelles Frontières (Ⓣ 02 513 68 15), on chaussée d'Ixelles, just opposite place Fernand Cocq, is also good for cheap flights.

CONTEXTS

A history of Brussels

Early settlement to the sixteenth century

Brussels takes its name from Broekzele, or "village of the marsh", the community which grew up beside the wide and shallow River Senne in the sixth century, reputedly around a chapel built here by St Géry, a French bishop sent here to convert the pagans. A tiny and insignificant part of Charlemagne's empire at the end of the eighth century, it was subsequently inherited by the **dukes of Lower Lorraine** (or Lotharingia – roughly Wallonia and northeast France), who constructed a fortress in 979; the first city walls were added a few decades later. Its inhabitants protected, the village began to benefit from its position on the trade route between Cologne and the burgeoning towns of Bruges and Ghent, and soon became a significant trading centre in its own right. The surrounding marshes were drained to allow for further expansion, and by the end of the twelfth century Brussels had a population of around 30,000.

In 1229 the city was granted its first charter by the **dukes of Brabant**, the new feudal overlords who controlled things here, on and off, for around two hundred years, governing through seven *échevins*, or **aldermen**, each of whom represented one of the patrician families who monopolised the administration. This self-regarding oligarchy was deeply unpopular with the skilled workers who made up the **guilds**, the only real counterweight to the aristocrats. The guildsmen rose in rebellion in 1302 and again in 1356, when the Count of Flanders, Louis de Maele, occupied Brussels during his dispute with Jeanne, the Duchess of Brabant. The guildsmen rallied to the Brabantine cause under the leadership of **Everard 't Serclaes** and, after ejecting the count's garrison, exacted terms from the returning duchess. Jeanne was obliged to swear an oath – the *Joyeuse Entrée* – which stipulated the rights and responsibilities of the ruler and the ruled, effectively a charter of liberties that also recognised the guilds and gave them more political power. This deal between the duchess and her craftsmen led to a period of rapid expansion and it was at this time that a second town wall was constructed, an eight-kilometre pentagon whose lines are followed by the boulevards of today's **petit ring**.

The early decades of the **fifteenth century** proved difficult: the cloth industry began its long decline and there was more trouble between the guildsmen and the patricians. Temporary solutions were, however, found to both these problems. The craftsmen started making luxury goods for the royal courts of Europe, while the city's governing council was modified to contain seven aristocrats, six guildsmen and two aldermen – a municipal compromise that was to last until the late eighteenth century. There was a change of overlord too, when, in 1430, marriage merged the territories of the duchy of Brabant with those of **Burgundy**. Initially, this worked against the interests of the city as the first Burgundian rulers – Philip the Good and his son Charles the Bold – paid little regard to Brussels, and indeed Charles' ceaseless warmongering resulted in a steep increase in taxation. But when Charles' daughter, **Mary of Burgundy**, established her court in Brussels, the city gained political stature and its guildsmen found a ready market for the luxury goods they were already making – everything from gold jewellery and silverware through to tapestries and illuminated books. Painters were drawn to Mary's court, too, and Rogier van der Weyden was appointed the city's first official artist.

Mary married **Maximilian**, a **Habsburg** prince and future Holy Roman Emperor in 1477. She died in a riding accident five years later and her territories passed to her husband, who ruled until 1519. Thus Brussels – as well as the whole of present-day Belgium and Holland – was incorporated into the Habsburg Empire. A sharp operator, Maximilian whittled away at the power of the Brabantine and Flemish cities and despite the odd miscalculation – he was imprisoned by the burghers of Bruges in 1488 – had to all intents and purposes brought them to heel by the end of the century. Maximilian was succeeded by his grandson **Charles V**, whose vast kingdom included Spain, the Low Countries and large parts of Germany and Italy. By necessity, Charles was something of a peripatetic monarch, but he favoured Brussels, his home town, more than any other residence, running his empire from here for a little over twelve years, which made the city wealthy and politically important in equal measure. Just like his grandfather, Charles kept the city's guilds firmly under control.

EARLY SETTLEMENT TO THE SIXTEENTH CENTURY

The Reformation and the Revolt against Spain

The **Reformation** was a religious revolt that stood sixteenth-century Europe on its head. The first stirrings were in the welter of debate that spread across much of western Europe under the auspices of theologians like **Erasmus** (see pp.111–113), who wished to cleanse the Catholic church of its corruptions and extravagant ceremony; only later did some of these same thinkers – principally Martin Luther – decide to support a breakaway church. The seeds of this **Protestantism** fell on fertile ground among the merchants of Brussels, whose wealth and independence had never been easy to accommodate within a rigid caste society. Similarly, their employees, the guildsmen and their apprentices, who had a long history of opposing arbitrary authority, were easily convinced of the need for reform. In 1555, **Charles V abdicated**, transferring his German lands to his brother Ferdinand, and his Italian, Spanish and Low Countries territories to his son, the fanatically Catholic **Philip II**. In the short term, the scene was set for a bitter confrontation between Catholics and Protestants, while the dynastic ramifications of the division of the Habsburg empire were to complicate European affairs for centuries.

After his father's abdication, Philip II decided to teach his heretical subjects a lesson. He garrisoned Brussels and the other towns of the Low Countries with Spanish mercenaries, imported the Inquisition and passed a series of anti-Protestant edicts. However, other pressures on the Habsburg Empire forced him into a tactical withdrawal and he transferred control to his sister **Margaret of Parma** in 1559. Based in Brussels, the equally resolute Margaret implemented the policies of her brother with gusto. Initially, the repression worked, but in 1565 the Protestant workers struck back. In Brussels and most of the other big cities hereabouts they ran amok, sacking the churches and destroying their rich decoration in the **Iconoclastic Fury**.

Protestantism had infiltrated the nobility, but the ferocity of the rioting shocked the upper classes into renewed support for Spain. Philip was keen to capitalize on the increase in support and, in 1567, he dispatched the **Duke of Albe**, with an army of 10,000 men, to the Low Countries to suppress his religious opponents absolutely. Margaret was not at all pleased by Philip's decision and, when Albe arrived in Brussels, she resigned in a huff, initiating a long period of what was, in effect, military rule. One of Albe's first acts in the capital was to set up the Commission of Civil Unrest, which was soon nicknamed the "**Council of Blood**" after its habit of executing those it examined. No fewer than 12,000 citizens went to the block, most famously the counts of **Egmont** and **Hoorn** (see p.75), who were beheaded on the Grand-Place in June 1568.

Once again, the repression soon backfired. The region's greatest landowner, Prince William of Orange-Nassau, known as **William the Silent** (1533–84), raised the Low Countries against the Habsburgs and swept all before him, making a triumphant entrance into Brussels, where he installed a Calvinist administration. Momentarily, it seemed possible for the whole of the Low Countries to unite behind William and all signed the **Union of Brussels**, which demanded the departure of foreign troops as a condition for accepting a diluted Habsburg sovereignty. But Philip was not inclined to compromise. In 1578, he gathered together another army which he dispatched to the Low Countries under the command of Alessandro Farnese, the **Duke of Parma**. Parma was successful, recapturing most of modern Belgium including Brussels and finally Antwerp in 1585. He was, however, unable to advance any further north and the Low Countries were divided into two – the **Spanish Netherlands** and the **United Provinces** –

beginning a separation that would lead, after many changes, to the creation of Belgium and the Netherlands.

The Spanish Netherlands

Parma was surprisingly generous in victory, but the city's weavers, apprentices and skilled workers – the bedrock of Calvinism – still fled north to escape the new Catholic regime, fuelling an economic boom in the province of Holland. The migration badly dented the economy of the **Spanish Netherlands** as a whole, but Brussels – the capital – was relatively immune, its economy buoyed up by the Habsburg elite, whose conspicuous consumption fostered luxury industries like silk weaving, diamond processing and lace making. The city's industries also benefited from the digging of the Willebroek canal, which linked Brussels to the sea for the first time. This commercial restructuring underpinned a brief flourishing of artistic life both here and, in comparable circumstances, in Antwerp, where it was centred on **Rubens** and his circle, including Anthony van Dyck and Jacob Jordaens.

Meanwhile, months before his death in 1598, Philip II had granted control of the Spanish Netherlands to his daughter and her husband, appointing them the **Archdukes Isabella** and **Albert**. Failing to learn from experience, the ducal couple continued to prosecute the war against the Protestant north, but with so little success that they were obliged to make peace – the **Twelve Year Truce** – in 1609. When the truce ended, the new Spanish king Philip IV stubbornly resumed the campaign against the Protestants, this time as part of a general and even more devastating conflict, the **Thirty Years' War** (1618–48), a largely religious-based conflict between Catholic and Protestant countries that involved most of western Europe. Finally, the Habsburgs were compelled to accept the humiliating terms of the **Peace of Westphalia**, a general treaty whose terms formally recognized the independence of the United Provinces and closed the Scheldt estuary, thereby crippling Antwerp. By these means, the commercial pre-eminence of Amsterdam was assured and its Golden Age began.

The Thirty Years' War had devastated the Spanish Netherlands, but the peace was perhaps as bad. Politically dependent on a decaying Spain, economically ruined and deprived of most of its more independent-minded citizens, the country turned in on itself, sustained by the fanatical Catholicism of the **Counter-Reformation**. Literature disappeared, the sciences vegetated and religious orders multiplied to an extraordinary degree. In **painting**, artists – such as Rubens – were used to confirm the ecclesiastical orthodoxies, their canvases full of muscular saints and angels, reflecting a religious faith of mystery and hierarchy; others, such as David Teniers, retreated into minutely observed realism.

The Peace of Westphalia had also freed the king of France from fear of Germany, and the political and military history of the Spanish Netherlands after 1648 was dominated by the efforts of **Louis XIV** to add the country to his territories. Fearful of an over-powerful France, the United Provinces and England, among others, determinedly resisted French designs and, to preserve the balance of power, fought a long series of campaigns beginning in the 1660s. It was during one of these wars, the **War of the Grand Alliance**, that Louis XIV's artillery destroyed much of medieval Brussels, a disaster that led to the construction of the lavish Grand-Place that survives today (see Chapter Two).

The **War of the Spanish Succession** – the final conflict of the series – was sparked by the death in 1700 of **Charles II**, the last of the Spanish Habsburgs, who had willed his territories to the grandson of Louis XIV. An anti-French coalition refused to accept the settlement and there ensued a haphazard series of campaigns that dragged on for eleven years. Eventually, with the **Treaty of Utrecht** of 1713, the French abandoned their attempt to conquer the Spanish Netherlands, which now passed under the control of the Austrian Habsburgs in the figure of the Emperor Charles VI.

The Austrian Netherlands

The transfer of the country from Spanish to **Austrian control** made little appreciable difference: a remote imperial authority continued to operate through an appointed governor in Brussels and the country as a whole remained poor and backward. This sorry state of affairs began to change in the middle of the eighteenth century when the Austrian oligarchy came under the influence of the **Enlightenment**, that belief in reason and progress – as against authority and tradition – that had first been proselytised by French philosophers. In 1753, the arrival of a progressive governor, the **Count of Cobenzl**, signified a transformation of Habsburg policy. Cobenzl initiated an ambitious programme of public works and set about changing the face of Brussels – which had become an urbanised eyesore – by pushing through the grand Neoclassical boulevards and avenues which still characterise the Upper Town (see Chapter Three).

In 1780, the **Emperor Joseph II** came to the throne, determined to "root out silly old prejudices", as he put it – but his reforms were opposed by both left and right. The liberal-minded **Vonckists** demanded a radical, republican constitution, while their enemies, the conservative **Statists**, insisted on the Catholic status quo. There was pandemonium and, in 1789, the Habsburgs dispatched an army to restore order. Against all expectations, the two political groups combined and defeated the Austrians near Antwerp in what became known as the **Brabant Revolution**. In January 1790, the rebels announced the formation of the United States of Belgium, but the country remained in turmoil and when Emperor Joseph died in 1790, his successor, **Léopold**, quickly withdrew the reforming acts and sent in his troops to restore imperial authority.

French occupation and the Kingdom of the Netherlands

The new and repressive Habsburg regime was short-lived. French Republican armies brushed the imperial forces aside in 1794, and the Austrian Netherlands were annexed the following year, an annexation that was to last until 1814. The **French** imposed radical reforms: the Catholic church was stripped of much of its worldly wealth, feudal privileges were abolished, and, most unpopular of all, conscription was introduced. The invaders were deeply resented and French authority had largely evaporated long before **Napoleon**'s final defeat just outside Brussels at the battle of **Waterloo** (see pp.132–134) in 1815.

At the **Congress of Vienna**, called to settle Europe at the end of the Napoleonic Wars, the main concern of the great powers was to bolster the Low Countries against France. With scant regard to the feelings of those affected, they therefore decided to establish the **Kingdom of the Netherlands**, which incorporated both the old United Provinces and the Austrian Netherlands, and on the throne they placed Frederick William of Orange, appointed **King William I**. From the very beginning, the union proved problematic – there were even two capital cities, Brussels and The Hague – and William simply wasn't wily enough to hold things together. Nonetheless, the union struggled on until August 25, 1830, when the singing of a duet,

Amour sacré de la Patrie, in the Brussels opera house hit a nationalist nerve. The audience poured out onto the streets to raise the flag of Brabant in defiance of King William, thereby initiating a countrywide **revolution**. William sent in his troops, but Great Britain and France quickly intervened to stop hostilities. In January of the following year, at the **Conference of London**, the great powers recognized Belgium's independence, with the caveat that the country be classified a "neutral" state – that is one outside any other's sphere of influence. To bolster this new nation, they dug out the uncle of Queen Victoria, Prince Léopold of Saxe-Coburg, to present with the crown.

Independent Belgium

Léopold I (1830–65) was careful to maintain his country's neutrality and encouraged an industrial boom that saw coal mines developed, iron-making factories established and the rapid expansion of the railway system. His successor, **Léopold II** (1865–1909), further boosted industry and supervised the emergence of Belgium as a major industrial power. The king and the reforming Brussels burgomaster Anspach also set about modernizing the capital. New boulevards were built; the free university was founded; the Senne – which by then had become an open sewer – was covered over in the city centre; many slum areas were cleared; and a series of grandiose buildings was erected, the most unpopular of which was the Palais de Justice (see p.77), whose construction involved the forced eviction of hundreds of workers. To round the whole thing off – and turn Brussels into a city deserving of its king – Léopold held the golden jubilee exhibition celebrating the founding of the Belgian state in the newly inaugurated Le Cinquantenaire (see p.104–107), a mammoth edifice he had built just to the east of the old city centre.

The first fly in the royal ointment came in the 1860s and 1870s with the first significant stirrings of a type of **Flemish nationalism** which felt little enthusiasm for the unitary status of Belgium, divided as it was between a French-speaking majority in the south of the country – the Walloons – and the minority Dutch-speakers of the north. The Catholic party ensured that, under the Equality Law of 1898, Dutch was ratified as an official language, equal in status to French – the forerunner of many long and difficult debates.

The twentieth century

At the beginning of the twentieth century, Brussels was a thriving metropolis which took a progressive lead in a country that was determined to keep on good terms with all the great powers. Nonetheless, Belgium could not prevent getting caught up in **World War I**. Indifferent to Belgium's proclaimed neutrality, the Germans had decided as early as 1908 that the best way to attack France was via Belgium, and this is precisely what they did in 1914. They captured almost all of the country, the exception being a narrow strip of territory around De Panne. Undaunted, the new king **Albert I** (1909–34) and the Belgian army bravely manned the northern part of the Allied line. It made Albert a national hero.

The Germans returned in May 1940, launching a blitzkrieg that overwhelmed both Belgium and the Netherlands. This time there was no heroic resistance by the Belgian king, now **Léopold III** (1934–51), who ignored the advice of his government and surrendered unconditionally and in great haste. It is true that the Belgian army had been badly mauled and that a German victory seemed inevitable, but the manner of the surrender infuriated many Belgians, as did the king's refusal to form

THE BELGIAN LANGUAGE DIVIDE

The Belgians are divided between two main groups, the Walloons, French-speakers who account for around forty percent of the population, and the Flemish, or Dutch speakers, who form about sixty percent, out of a total population of some ten million.

The Flemish-French language divide has troubled the country for decades, its historical significance rooted in deep class and economic divisions. Prosperity has shifted back and forth between the two communities over the centuries: in medieval times Flanders grew rich on its textile trade; later Wallonia developed mining and steel industries. However, Francophones have always dominated the aristocracy, and, since the Middle Ages, the middle classes as well. The setting-up of the Belgian state in 1830 crystallized this antagonism, with the final arrangements favouring the French-speakers. French became the official language, Flemish was banned in schools (the Belgian Civil Code was only translated into Flemish in 1961), and the industries of Wallonia were regarded as pre-eminent. Nowadays, however, Flanders is the industrial powerhouse of Belgium, and the heavy industies of Wallonia are in decline, an economic change of fortunes which has made the Flemish-speakers more assertive in their demands for linguistic and cultural parity. However, Flemish "parity" is often perceived as "domination" by Walloons.

In recognition of the differences, the Language Frontier between the two groups – effectively cutting the country in half, west to east – was drawn in 1962. This did not, however, improve relations and, in 1980, the constitution was redrawn on a federal basis, with three separate communities – the Flemish North, the Walloon South and the German-speaking east around the towns of Eupen and Malmédy – responsible for their own cultural and social affairs and education. At the same time, Belgium was simultaneously divided into three regions – the Flemish North, the Walloon South and Brussels (which is officially bilingual, although a majority of its population is French-speaking), with each regional authority dealing with matters like economic development, the environment and employment.

Although the niceties of this partition have calmed troubled waters, in bilingual Brussels and at national government level the division between Flemish and French speakers still influences many aspects of working and social life. Schools, political parties, literature and culture are all segregated along linguistic lines leading to a set of complex regulations which can verge on the absurd. Government press conferences, for example, must have questions and answers repeated in both languages. Across Belgium as a whole, bitterness about the economy, unemployment and the government smoulders within (or seeks an outlet through) the framework of this linguistic division, and individual neighbourhoods can be paralyzed by language disputes. The communities of Fourons/Voeren, for instance, a largely French-speaking collection of villages in Flemish Limburg, almost brought down the government in the mid-Eighties when the Francophone mayor, Jose Happart, refused to take the Flemish language exam required of all Limburg officials. Dismissed, he stood again and was re-elected, prompting the prime minister at the time, Wilfred Martens, to offer his own resignation. The Fourons affair was symptomatic of the obstinacy that besets the country to this day. Jose Happart could probably have passed the exam easily – indeed rumour has it that he is fluent in Flemish – but he simply chose not to submit, giving succour to the political extremists on both sides – namely the Vlaams Blok on the Flemish side, and, for the French-speakers, the Front des Francophones (FDF).

The casual visitor to Belgium will rarely get a sniff of these bilingual tensions. Although it's probably better to speak English rather than Flemish or French in the "wrong" part of Belgium, if you make a mistake the worst you'll get is a look of glazed indifference.

THE BELGIUM LANGUAGE DIVIDE

a government in exile. It took time for the Belgians to adjust to the new situation, but by 1941 a Resistance movement was mounting acts of sabotage against the occupying forces – and **liberation** by the Allies came three years later.

After the war, the Belgians set about the task of economic **reconstruction**, helped by aid from the United States, but hindered by a divisive controversy over the wartime activities of King Léopold. Many felt his surrender to the Germans was cowardly and his subsequent willingness to work with them treacherous; others pointed out his efforts to increase the country's food rations and his negotiations to secure the release of Belgian prisoners. Inevitably, the complex shadings of collaboration and forced co-operation were hard to disentangle, and the debate continued until 1950 when a referendum narrowly recommended his return from exile. Léopold's return was, however, marked by rioting in Brussels and across Wallonia, where the king's opponents were concentrated, and Léopold abdicated in favour of his son, **Baudouin** (1951–1993).

The development of the postwar Belgian economy follows the pattern of most of western Europe – reconstruction in the 1950s; boom in the 1960s; recession in the 1970s; and retrenchment in the 1980s and 1990s. In the meantime, Brussels, which had been one of the lesser European capitals, was turned into a major player when it became the home of the **EU** and **NATO** – the latter organization was ejected from France on the orders of de Gaulle in 1967. But, above all, the postwar period has been dominated by the increasing **tension between the Walloon and Flemish communities**. Every national institution is now dogged by the prerequisites of bilingualism – speeches in parliament have to be delivered in both languages – and in Brussels, the country's one and only

bilingual region, every instance of the written word, from road signs to the yellow pages, has to be bilingual as well. Brussels has also been subtly affected by the **Linguistic Divide** (or Language Frontier), which was formally delineated in 1962. Bilingual Brussels is now encircled by Flemish-speaking regions and, partly as a result, many Francophones living in the city have developed something of a siege mentality; the Flemish, on the other hand, can't help but notice the prevalence of French in what is supposed to be their capital city.

Bogged down by these linguistic preoccupations – the current Prime Minister (Guy Verhofstadt) and his cabinet squeeze in four hours of language classes every week – the federal government often appears extraordinarily cumbersome. In addition, much of the political class is at least partly reliant on the linguistic divide for their jobs and, institutionally speaking, has little incentive to see the antagonisms resolved. A rare moment of national unity came in 1996 when communities from both sides of the linguistic divide rose up in protest at the Belgian police, which proved itself at best hopelessly inefficient, at worst complicit in, the gruesome activities of the child murderer and pornographer **Marc Dutroux.** Over 350,000 people took to the streets, demanding the police and justice system be overhauled. This outburst of public protest peaked again two years later when, amazingly enough, Dutroux escaped his police guards, stole a car and headed out of the city. Although he was subsequently recaptured, most Belgians were simply appalled.

The Dutroux affair dented the national psyche, and few Belgians believe that the reforms imposed on the police have made much difference. Into this psychological breach rode the **royal family**, one of the few institutions to bind the country together. In 1999, the heir to the throne, Prince Philippe, broke with tradition and married Mathilde

THE TWENTIETH CENTURY

303

d'Udekem d'Acoz – a Belgian of non-royal descent, with family on both sides of the linguistic divide. The marriage may well have healed a few wounds, but its effects should not be over-estimated. Over 400,000 people snapped up the free travel tickets offered by the Belgian railways, but only around twenty percent were used to come to Brussels, and out of them one can only speculate as to how many loyal subjects chose to wave the flag on a cold December day rather than head for the nearest bar.

Top twenty Belgian beers

Belgium's beer-making history goes back centuries and from whatever bar of the world you come from you'll know that this is serious beer country. Official estimates suggest that there are more than 700 **beers** to choose from, with the rarest and most precious given all the reverence of a fine wine. The professional beer drinker will already know the brews listed below, but for the tippling amateur we have produced this top twenty to get you started. Every bar in Brussels has a beer menu and although it's unlikely that any one establishment will have all those listed, all of them should have at least a couple. Cheers!

DON'T DRINK THE WATER!

In the eleventh century, a Benedictine monk dipped his crucifix into a Belgian brewer's kettle to encourage the populace to drink beer instead of plague-contaminated water: the plague stopped. The monk was later beatified as St Arnold and he became – logically enough – the patron saint of brewers.

Bush Beer (7.5% and 12%)

A Wallonian speciality, it is claimed that the original version is – at 12% – the strongest beer in Belgium, but it's actually more like a barley wine, and has a lovely golden colour, and an earthy aroma. The 7.5% Bush is a tasty pale ale with a zip of coriander.

Brugse Straffe Hendrik (Blond 6.5%, Bruin 8.5%)

Straffe Hendrik, a smart little brewery located in the centre of Bruges, produces zippy, refreshing ales. Their Blond is a light and tangy pale ale, whereas the Bruin is a classic brown ale with a full body.

Chimay (red top 7%, blue top 9%)

Made by the Trappist monks of Forges-les-Chimay in southern Belgium, Chimay beers are widely regarded as being amongst the best in the world. Of the several brews they produce, these two are the most readily available, fruity and strong, deep in body, and somewhat spicy with a hint of nutmeg and thyme.

La Chouffe (8%)

Produced in the Ardennes, this distinctive beer is instantly recognizable by the red-hooded gnome (or *chouffe*) which adorns its label. It's a refreshing pale ale with a hint of coriander and it leaves a peachy aftertaste.

Corsendonk Pater Noster (5.6%)

The creation of Jef Keersmaekers, this bottled beer is easily the pick of the many Corsendonk brews. It is known for its Burgundy-brown colour and smoky bouquet.

See Chapter Eleven for good places to drink. If you fancy bringing a couple of bottles home with you, head for any supermarket or, for a greater range, the specialist Bière Artisanale (see p.245).

Delirium Tremens (9%)

Great name for this spicy amber ale that is the leading product of Ghent's Huyghe brewery.

Gouden Carolus (8%)

Named after – and allegedly the favourite tipple of – the Habsburg emperor Charles V, Gouden Carolus is a full-bodied dark brown ale with a sour and slightly fruity aftertaste. Brewed in the Flemish town of Mechelen.

De Koninck (5%)

Antwerp's leading brewery, De Koninck, is something of a Flemish institution – for some a way of life. Its standard beer, De Koninck, is a smooth, yellowish pale ale that is better on draft than in the bottle. Very drinkable and with a sharp aftertaste.

Gueuze (Cantillon Gueuze Lambic 5%)

A type of beer rather than an individual brew, Gueuze is made by blending old and new lambic (see below) to fuel re-fermentation, with the end result being bottled. This process makes Gueuze a little sweeter and fuller bodied than lambic. Traditional Gueuze – like the brand mentioned above – can, however, be hard to track down and you may have to settle for the sweeter, more commercial brands, notably Belle Vue Gueuze (5.2%), Timmermans Gueuze (5.5%) and the exemplary Lindemans Gueuze (5.2%).

Hoegaarden (5%)

The role model of all Belgian wheat beers, Hoegaarden – named after a small town east of Leuven – is light and extremely refreshing, despite its cloudy appearance. It is brewed from equal parts of wheat and malted barley and is the ideal drink for a hot summer's day. The history of wheat beers is curious: in the late 1950s, they were so unpopular that they faced extinction, but within twenty years they had been taken up by a new generation of drinkers and are now extremely popular. Hoegaarden is as good a wheat beer as any.

Kriek (Cantillon Kriek Lambic 5%, Belle Vue Kriek 5.2%, Mort Subite Kriek 4.3%)

A type of beer rather than a particular brew, Kriek is made from a base beer to which is added cherries or, in the case of the more commercial brands, cherry juice and perhaps even sugar. It is decanted from a bottle with a cork, as with sparkling wine. The better examples – including the three mentioned above – are not too sweet and taste simply wonderful. Other fruit beers are available too, but Kriek is perhaps the most successful.

Kwak (8%)

This Flemish beer, the main product of the family-run Bosteels brewery, is not all that special – it's an amber ale sweetened by a little sugar – but it's served in dramatic style with its distinctive hourglass placed in a wooden stand.

Lambic (Cantillon Lambik 5%, Lindemans Lambik 4%)

Specific to the Brussels area and representing one of the world's oldest styles of beer manufacture, lambic beers are tart because they are brewed with at least thirty percent raw wheat as well as the more usual malted barley. The key feature is, however, the use of wild yeast in their production, a process of spontaneous fermentation in which the yeasts of the atmosphere gravitate down into open wooden casks over a period of between two and three years. Draught lambic is extremely rare, but it is served in central Brussels at *À la Bécasse* (see p.198). The bottled varieties are often modified, but Cantillon Lambik is authentic, an excellent drink with a lemony zip. It is produced at the Cantillon brewery, in Anderlecht, which is home to the Gueuze Museum (see p.113). Lindemans Lambik is similar and a tad more commonplace.

Leffe (Leffe Brune 6.5%, Leffe Blond 6.6%)

Brewed in Leuven, just to the east of Brussels, Leffe is strong and malty and comes in two main varieties. Leffe Blond is bright, fragrant, and has a slight orangey flavour, whereas Leffe Brune is dark, aromatic and full of body. Very popular, but a little gassy for some tastes.

Orval (6.2%)

One of the world's most distinctive malt beers, Orval is made in the Ardennes at the Abbaye d'Orval, which was founded in the twelfth century by Benedictine monks from Calabria. The beer is a lovely amber colour, refreshingly bitter and makes a great aperitif.

Rochefort (Rochefort 6 7.5%, Rochefort 8 9.2%, Rochefort 10 11.3%)

Produced at a Trappist monastery in the Ardennes, Rochefort beers are typically dark and sweet and come in three main versions: Rochefort 6, Rochefort 8, and the extremely popular Rochefort 10, which has a deep reddish-brown colour and a delicious fruity palate.

Rodenbach (Rodenbach 5%, Rodenbach Grand Cru 6.5%)

Located in the Flemish town of Roeselare, the Rodenbach brewery produces a reddish brown ale in several different formats, with the best brews aged in oak containers. Their widely available Rodenbach (5%) is a tangy brown ale with a hint of sourness. The much fuller – and sourer – Rodenbach Grand Cru is far more difficult to get hold of, but is particularly delicious.

Verboden Vrucht, or Forbidden Fruit (9%)

Forbidden Fruit is worth buying just for the label, which depicts a fig-leaf clad Adam offering a strategically covered Eve a glass of beer in the garden of Eden. The actual drink is dark, strong and has a spicy aroma, and has something of a cult following in Belgium. Produced by Hoegaarden.

Westmalle (Westmalle Dubbel 7%, Tripel 9%)

The Trappist monks of Westmalle, just north of

Antwerp, claim their beers not only cure loss of appetite and insomnia, but reduce stress by half. Whatever the truth, the prescription certainly tastes good. Their most famous beer, the Westmalle Tripel, is deliciously creamy and aromatic, while the popular Westmalle Dubbel is dark and supremely malty.

Westvleteren (Special 6° 6.2%, Extra 8° 8%)

Made at the abbey of St Sixtus in West Flanders, Westvleteren beers come in several varieties. These two are the most common, dark and full-bodied, sour with an almost chocolate-like taste.

Books

Most of the following books should be readily available in the UK, US and Canada. Where titles are published by different **publishers** in the UK and US, we've given both, separated by an oblique slash (UK/US); where only one publisher is given, this covers both the UK and US unless specifically stated. Out-of-print tiles are marked "o/p".

History and politics

Neal Ascherson *The King Incorporated* (Granta). You'd never guess from Brussels' Musée de la Dynastie (see p.70), but King Léopold II was responsible for one of the cruellest of colonial regimes, a savage system of repression and exploitation that devastated the Belgian Congo. Ascherson details it all.

J. C. H. Blom (ed.) *History of the Low Countries* (Berghahn Books). Belgian history books are thin on the ground, so this incisive, well-balanced volume is very welcome. A series of historians weigh in with their specialities to build a comprehensive picture of the region from the Celts and Romans through to the 1980s. Highly recommended, though hardly sun-lounge reading.

Paul van Buitenen *Blowing the Whistle* (Politico's Publishing,

UK). All your worst fears about the EU confirmed. Buitenen was an assistant auditor in the EU's Financial Control Directorate in Brussels and this book, published in 1998, exposed the fraud and corruption. Needless to say, the EU was far from grateful for his revelations and forced him to resign, but even so the scandal stories became so widespread that the entire Commission was obliged to resign en bloc. Since then, there have been earnest declarations that things would be much better.

Martin Conway Collaboration in Belgium (Yale UP). Detailed analysis of wartime collaboration and the development of Fascism in Belgium in the 1930s and 1940s. Authoritative and well-written, but something of a special interest text.

Pieter Geyl The Revolt of The Netherlands 1555–1609 (Littlefield Adams, US). Geyl presents a concise account of the Netherlands during its formative years, chronicling the uprising against the Spanish and the formation of the United Provinces. Without doubt the definitive book on the period.

Christopher Hibbert Waterloo (Wordsworth, UK). Hibbert is one of Britain's leading historians, an astute commentator who writes in a fluent, easily accessible style. This book is divided into three parts. The first examines Napoleon's rise to power, the second looks at Wellington and his allies, the third deals with the battle. Hibbert is also responsible for editing The Wheatley Diary (Windrush), the journal and sketchbook of a young English officer, who fought his way across Europe during the Napoleonic Wars.

Adam Hochschild King Leopold's Ghost (Macmillan/Houghton Mifflin). Harrowing and detailed account – a little on the long side – of King Leopold's savage colonial regime in the Congo. Particularly good on Roger Casement, the one-time British consul to the Congo, who publicised the cruelty and helped bring it to an end. Hochschild's last chapter – "The Great Forgetting" – is a stern criticism of the Belgians for their failure to acknowledge their dreadful colonial history.

B. H. Liddell Hart (ed.) *The Letters of Private Wheeler* (Windrush/Interlink Pub). A veteran of World War I, Liddell Hart writes with panache and clarity, editing up the letters penned by the eponymous private as he fought Napoleon and the French across a fair slice of Europe. Wheeler fought at Waterloo, but the section on the battle is surprisingly brief. As a whole, the letters are a delight, a witty insight into the living conditions and attitudes of Wellington's infantry.

Geoffrey Parker *The Dutch Revolt* (Penguin, UK). Compelling account of the struggle between the Netherlands and Spain. Probably the best work of its kind. Also *The Army of Flanders and the Spanish Road 1567–1659* (Cambridge UP), a fascinating insight into the Habsburg army which occupied "Belgium" for well over a hundred years – how it functioned, was fed and moved from Spain to the Low Countries along the so-called Spanish Road.

Geoffrey Wootten *Waterloo 1815* (Osprey). About one third of the length of Hibbert's *Waterloo* (see above) – this 96-page book focuses on the battle, providing a clear, thorough and interesting account.

Art and architecture

Kristin Lohse Belkin *Rubens* (Phaidon Press). Too long for its own good, this book details Rubens' spectacularly successful career both as artist and diplomat. Belkin is particularly thorough in her discussions of technique and the workings of his workshop. Extensive reference is made to Rubens' letters. Excellent illustrations.

Robin Blake *Anthony van Dyck* (Ivan R Dee). Whether or not van Dyck justifies 448 pages is a moot point, but he did have an interesting life and certainly thumped out a fair few paintings. This volume explores every artistic nook and cranny.

David Dernie *Victor Horta* (John Wiley & Sons). Perhaps surprisingly, this is the only book in print dedicated to that pioneer of Art Nouveau, Victor Horta (see pp.83-86). It's a competent effort too, describing his milieu and lingering on his architectural legacy, but it does cost an arm and a leg.

R. H. Fuchs *Dutch Painting* (Thames & Hudson). Thoughtful and well-researched title which tracks through the history of its subject from the fifteenth century onwards. Highly recommended.

R. H. Fuchs et al *Flemish and Dutch Painting (from Van Gogh, Ensor, Magritte and Mondrian to Contemporary)* (Rizzoli, US). Excellent, lucid account giving an overview of the development of Flemish and Dutch painting.

Suzi Gablik *Magritte* (Thames & Hudson). Suzi Gablik lived in Magritte's house for six months in the 1960s and this personal contact informs the text, which is lucid and thoughtful. Most of the illustrations are, however, black and white. At 208 pages, much longer than the Hammacher version (see below).

Walter S. Gibson *Bosch* (Thames & Hudson). Everything you wanted to know about

Bosch, his paintings and his late fifteenth-century milieu. Superbly illustrated. Also, try the beautifully illustrated *Bruegel* (Thames & Hudson), which takes a detailed look at the artist with nine well-argued chapters investigating the components of Pieter Bruegel the Elder's art.

A M Hammacher *René Magritte* (Thames & Hudson/Harry N Abrams). Thames & Hudson produce some of the finest art books in the world and this is an excellent sample, beautifully illustrated and featuring a detailed examination of Magritte's life, times and artistic output. One of the "Masters of Art" series. Very competitively priced too. First printed 1986; 128 pages.

Craig Harbison *Jan van Eyck: the Play of Realism* (Reaktion Books). Not much is known about van Eyck, but Harbison has done his best to root out every detail. The text is accompanied by illustrations of all of Eyck's major paintings.

Hergé *The Calculus Affair* (Mammoth/Little Brown); *The*

Making of Tintin: Cigars of the Pharaoh & the Blue Lotus (Methuen UK, Little Brown US). Tintin comic strips come in and out of print at a rapid rate and there is a wide selection of audio cassettes too. The two anthologies listed here are as good a place as any to start.

Benoit Peeters *Tintin and the World of Hergé: an Illustrated History* (Methuen/Joy St Books). Examines the life and career of Hergé, particularly the development of Tintin, and the influences on his work. No less than 300 illustrations.

Philippe Roberts-Jones *Brussels: Fin de Siecle* (Benedikt Taschen Verlag, UK). Specialist text describing – and illustrating – the fizz of architectural and artistic endeavour that swept Brussels at the turn of the twentieth century. Art Nouveau and Symbolism are the two leading protagonists.

Peter Weiermair *Eros & Death: Belgian Symbolism* (Oehrli/Art Books). Great title and an original book exploring the nature of Belgian symbolism with reference to drawings, prints, paintings and sculptures. Artists featured include James Ensor and Felician Rops.

Christopher White *Peter Paul Rubens: Man and Artist* (o/p). A beautifully illustrated introduction to both Rubens' work and social milieu.

Travel and specialist guides

Charlotte and Emily Brontë (ed. Sue Lonoff) *The Belgian Essays* (Yale UP). The Brontë sisters left their native Yorkshire for the first time in 1842 to make a trip to Brussels. Charlotte returned to Brussels the following year. This handsome volume reproduces the twenty-eight essays they penned (in French) during their journey and provides the English translation opposite. It makes a delightful read with particular highlights being "The Butterfly", "The Caterpillar" and "The Death of Napoleon".

S. A. Delta (ed.) *Guide Delta Bruxelles 2001*. Over five hundred pages of detailed and perceptive hotel and restaurant reviews – ideal if you're moving to Brussels. Only in French; available at leading bookshops in Brussels.

Ernest Gilliat-Smith *The Story of Brussels* (Periodicals Services, US). Quirky, good-humoured account of Brussels written in 1906. In the UK, pick it up at the library or a second-hand bookshop.

Michael Jackson *The Great Beers of Belgium* (Prion/Running Press). Belgium produces the best beers in the world. Michael Jackson is one of the best beer writers in the world. The result is cheeky, palatable and sinewy with just a hint of fruitiness.

Luc Sante *The Factory of Facts* (Granta/Vintage). Born in Belgium but raised in the US, Sante returned to his native land for an extended visit in 1989 – at the age of 35. His book is primarily a personal reflection, but he also uses this as a base for a thoughtful exploration of Belgium and the Belgians – from their art to their food and beyond. Highly recommended.

Marianne Thys *Belgian Cinema* (Ludion). This authoritative volume has reviews of every Belgian film ever made. Published in 1999, it's 992 pages long.

San van de Veire *Belgian Fashion Design* (Ludion, UK). The staggering success of Flemish fashion designers is chronicled in this well-illustrated book. The centre of the action is Antwerp, but Brussels also gets a look-in.

Tim Webb *Good Beer Guide to Belgium, Holland & Luxembourg* (CAMRA Books/Storey). Detailed and enthusiastic guide to the best bars, beers and breweries. A good read, and extremely well informed to boot. Undoubtedly, the best book on its subject on the market.

Literature

Mark Bles *A Child at War* (Warner/Mercury House). This powerful book describes the tribulations of Hortense Daman, a Belgian girl who joined the Resistance at the tender age of fifteen. Betrayed to the Gestapo, Daman was sent to the Ravensbruck concentration camp, where she was used in medical experiments, but remarkably she survived. This is her story, though the book would have benefited from some editorial pruning.

Hugo Claus *The Sorrow of Belgium* (Penguin, US). Born in Bruges in 1929, Claus is generally regarded as Belgium's foremost Flemish-language novelist, and this is generally regarded as his best novel. It charts the growing maturity of a young boy living in Flanders under the Nazi occupation. Claus' style is somewhat dense to say the least, but the book gets to grips with the guilt, bigotry and mistrust of the period, and caused a minor uproar when it was first published in the early 1980s. His *Swordfish* (Dufour) is a story of an isolated village rife with ethnic and religious tensions. The effects of this prove too much for a boy in his spiral down to madness. Also *Desire* (Penguin, UK), the strange and disconcerting tale of two drinking buddies, who, on an impulse, abandon small-town Belgium for Las Vegas, where both of them start to unravel.

Amelie Nothomb *Loving Sabotage* (New Directions). English-language translations of modern Belgian writers (in both French and Dutch) are a rarity, but Nothomb, one of Belgium's most popular writers, has made the linguistic leap. This particular novel deals with the daughter of a diplomat stationed in Peking in the 1970s, a rites-of-passage story with a Maoist backdrop. *The Stranger Next Door* (Henry Holt), perhaps Nothomb's most successful translated work, deals with weird and disconcerting happenings in the Belgian countryside, while *Fear and Trembling* (St Martins, US) is a sharply observed tale of the shoddy

LITERATURE

treatment meted out to a young Western businesswoman in a big corporation in Tokyo.

Jean Ray *Malpertuis* (Atlas, UK). This spine-chilling Gothic novel was written by a Belgian in 1943. It's set in Belgium, too, where the suffocating Catholicism of the Inquisition provides a perfect backcloth.

Georges Rodenbach *Bruges la Morte* (Atlas). First published in 1892, this slim and subtly evocative novel is all about love and obsession – or rather a highly stylised, decadent view of it. It's credited with starting the craze for visiting Bruges, the "dead city" where the action unfolds.

Glossaries

French terms

Abbaye Abbey or group of monastic buildings.

Aéroport Airport.

Auberge de la Jeunesse Youth hostel.

Beaux Arts Fine arts.

Beffroi Belfry.

Béguinage Convent occupied by béguines, ie members of a sisterhood living as nuns but without vows and with the right of return to the secular world.

Bicyclette Bicycle.

Bourse Stock exchange.

Chapelle Chapel.

Château Mansion, country house, or castle.

Cour Court(yard).

Couvent Convent, monastery.

Dégustation Tasting (wine or food).

Donjon Castle keep.

Eglise Church.

Entrée Entrance.

Etage Floor (of a museum etc).

Fermeture Closing period.

Fouilles Archeological excavations.

Gare Railway station.

Gîte d'Etape Dormitory-style lodgings situated in relatively remote parts of the country which can house anywhere between ten and one hundred people per establishment.

Grand-Place Central town square and the heart of most Belgian communities.

Halles Covered, central food market.

Hôpital Hospital.

Hôtel Either hotel, or – in its earlier sense – (private) town house

Hôtel de Ville Town hall.

Jardin Garden.

Jours Feriés Public holidays.

Maison House.

Marché Market.

Moulin Windmill.

Municipal Civic, municipal.

Musée Museum.

Notre Dame Our Lady.

Palais Palace.

Place Square, market place.

Pont Bridge.

Porte Gateway.

Quai Quai, or station platform.

Quartier District of a town.

Rue Street.

Sortie Exit.

Syndicat d'initiative Tourist office.

Tour Tower.

Trésor Treasury.

Flemish terms

Abdij Abbey or group of monastic buildings.

Beiaard Carillon (ie a set of tuned church bells, either operated by an automatic mechanism or played by a keyboard).

Begijnhof Convent occupied by

béguines (*begijns*), ie members of a sisterhood living as nuns but without vows and with the right of return to the secular world.

Belfort Belfry.

Beurs Stock exchange.

Botermarkt Butter market.

Brug Bridge.

Burgher Member of the upper or mercantile classes of a town, usually with civic powers.

Fietspad Bicycle path, and fiets — bicycle.

Gasthuis Hospital.

Gemeente Municipal: eg Gemeentehuis – town hall.

Gilde Guild.

Gerechtshof Law Courts.

Groentenmarkt Vegetable market.

Grote Markt Central town square and the heart of most Belgian communities.

Hal Hall.

Hof Court(yard).

Huis House.

Ingang Entrance.

Jeugdherberg Youth hostel.

Kaai Quai.

Kapel Chapel.

Kasteel Castle.

Kerk Church; eg Grote Kerk – the principal church of the town;

Onze Lieve Vrouwekerk – church dedicated to the Virgin Mary.

Koninklijk Royal.

Korenmarkt Corn market.

Kunst Art.

Kursaal Casino.

Lakenhalle Cloth hall. The building in medieval weaving towns where cloth would be weighed, graded and sold.

Luchthaven Airport.

Markt Marketplace.

Molen Windmill.

Ommegang Procession.

Paleis Palace.

Poort Gate.

Plein A square or open space.

Rijk State.

Schepenzaal Alderman's Hall.

Schouwburg Theatre.

Sierkunst Decorative arts.

Schone Kunsten Fine arts.

Spoor Track (as in railway) – trains arrive and depart on track (as distinct from platform) numbers.

FLEMISH TERMS

Stadhuis Town hall.

Station (Railway or bus) station.

Stitching Institute or foundation.

Stedelijk Civic, municipal.

Stenn Fortress.

Toren Tower.

Tuin Garden.

Uitgang Exit.

Volkskunde Folklore.

Art and architectural terms

Ambulatory Covered passage around the outer edge of the choir of a church.

Apse Semicircular protrusion at (usually) the east end of a church.

Art Deco Geometrical style of art and architecture especially popular in the 1930s.

Art Nouveau Style of art, architecture and design based on highly stylized vegetal forms. Particularly popular in the early part of the twentieth century.

Basilica Roman Catholic church with honorific privileges.

Baroque The art and architecture of the Counter-Reformation, dating from around 1600. Distinguished by its extreme ornateness, exuberance and by the complex but harmonious spatial arrangement of interiors.

Carillon A set of tuned church bells, either operated by an automatic mechanism or played by a keyboard.

Caryatid A sculptured female figure used as a column.

Classical Architectural style incorporating Greek and Roman elements – pillars, domes, colonnades, etc – at its height in the seventeenth century and revived, as Neoclassical, in the nineteenth century.

Clerestory Upper storey of a church, incorporating the windows.

Flamboyant Florid form of Gothic (see below).

Fresco Wall painting – durable through application to wet plaster.

Gable The triangular upper portion of a wall – decorative or supporting a roof.

Gobelins A rich French tapestry, named after the most famous of all tapestry manufacturers, based in Paris, whose most renowned period was in the reign of Louis XIV. Also loosely applied to tapestries of similar style.

Gothic Architectural style of the thirteenth to sixteenth century, characterized by pointed arches, rib vaulting, flying buttresses and a general emphasis on verticality.

Misericord Ledge on choir stall on which occupant can be supported while standing; often carved with secular subjects (bottoms were not thought worthy of religious ones).

Nave Main body of a church.

Neoclassical Architectural style derived from Greek and Roman elements – pillars, domes, colonnades, etc – popular in the Low Countries during French rule in the early nineteenth century.

Rococo Highly florid, light and graceful eighteenth-century style of architecture, painting and interior design, forming the last phase of Baroque.

Renaissance Movement in art and architecture developed in fifteenth-century Italy.

Retable Altarpiece.

Romanesque Early medieval architecture distinguished by squat forms, rounded arches and naive sculpture.

Stucco Marble-based plaster used to embellish ceilings, etc.

Transept Arms of a cross-shaped church, placed at ninety degrees to nave and chancel.

Triptych Carved or painted work on three panels. Often used as an altarpiece.

Tympanum Sculpted, usually recessed, panel above a door.

Vault An arched ceiling or roof.

ART AND ARCHITECTURAL TERMS

INDEX

100 Essential CDs

Eight titles,
one name

ROUGH
GUIDES

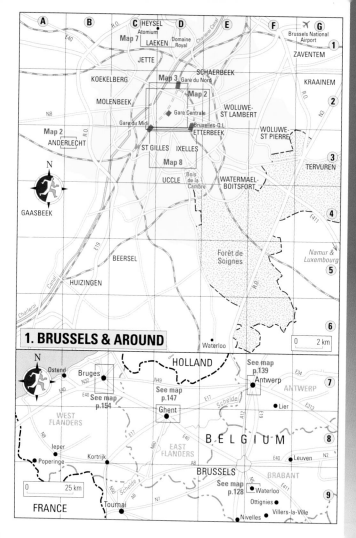

1. BRUSSELS & AROUND

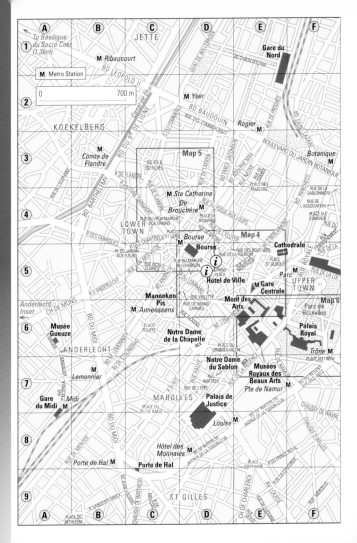

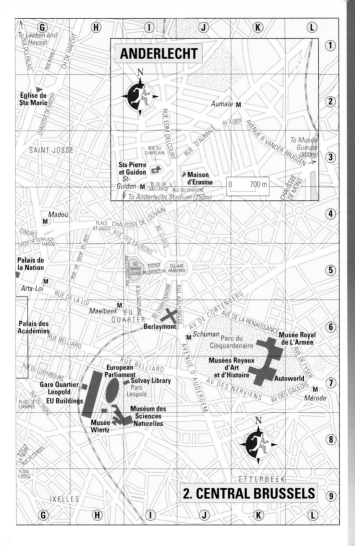

G H I J K L

1

ANDERLECHT

N

To Laeken and
Heysel
RUE DES PALAIS
RUE DE FACH
CH. DE FACH

Église de
Ste Marie

CHAUSSÉE DE FACH

SAINT JOSSE

Aumale M

AV AUBER AVENUE R VANDER BRUGGEN

To Musée
Gueuze
(800m)

RUE EDM DE COURT

RUE D'AUMALE

RUE DU CHAPELAIN

Sts Pierre
et Guidon
St-Guidon M

Maison
d'Erasme

CHAUSSÉE DE MONS

0   700 m

PL DE LA
VAILLANCE   RUE DU CHAPITRE

To Anderlecht Stadium (250m)

Madou
M

PLACE   CHAUSSÉE DE LOUVAIN
ST JOSSE   RUE DES EBURONS

CONGRÈS

CROIX DE FER
PLACE
MADOU

Palais de
la Nation
M

SQ
MARIE
LOUISE

AVENUE
PALMERSTON

SQUARE
AMBIORIX

RUE DE DEUX ÉGLISES

Arts-Loi   RUE DE LA LOI

RUE DU TACITURNE

RUE DE LA LOI FACITURNE

Palais des
Académies

Maelbeek M   EU
QUARTER

RUE ARCHIMÈDE

BD CHARLEMAGNE

AV DE CORTENBERG

AVE DE LA RENAISSANCE

RUE BELLIARD

Berlaymont

M Schuman

Parc du
Cinquantenaire

Musée Royal
de L'Armée

RUE DU LUXEMBOURG

RUE BELLIARD

European
Parliament

Solvay Library

Musées Royaux
d'Art
et d'Histoire

AVENUE DE L'YSER

Gare Quartier
Leopold
EU Buildings

Parc
Leopold

Autoworld

AVENUE D'AUDERGEM

AV DES NERVIENS

AV DES GAULOIS

M
Mérode

RUE DU TRÔNE

PLACE DE
LONDRES

Muséum des
Sciences
Naturelles

Musée
Wiertz

PLACE
LA HULPE

RUE DU CONSEIL

N

PLACE
F. COCQ

IXELLES

ETTERBEEK

2. CENTRAL BRUSSELS

9

G H I J K L

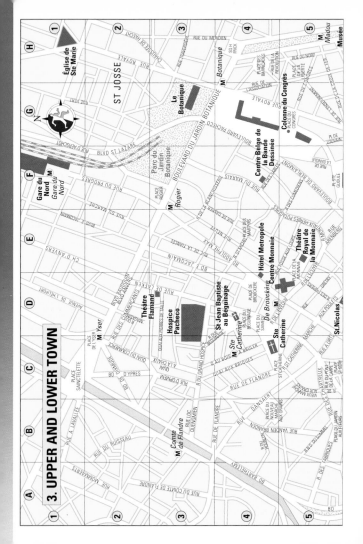

3. UPPER AND LOWER TOWN

Église de Ste Marie

ST JOSSE

Gare du Nord

Le Botanique

Parc du Jardin Botanique

Centre Belge de la Bande Dessinée

Colonne du Congrès

Hôtel Metropole

Théâtre Flamand

Hospice Pacheco

St Jean Baptiste au Béguinage

Ste Catherine

De Brouckère

Théâtre Royal de la Monnaie

Centre Monnaie

St.Nicolas

Comte de Flandre

Musée

Madou

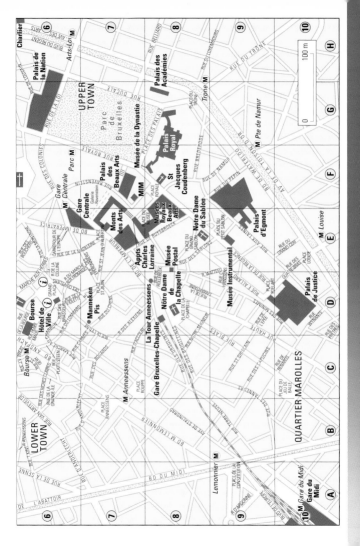

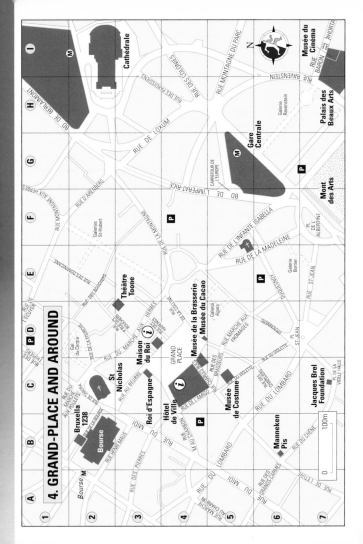

4. GRAND-PLACE AND AROUND

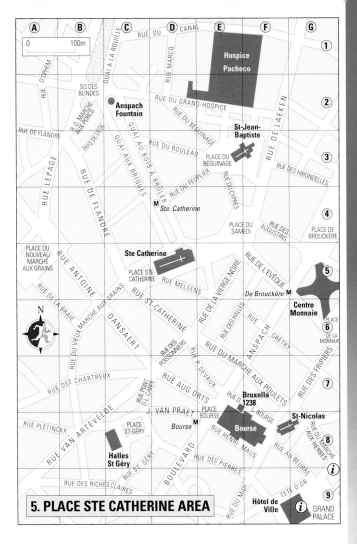

5. PLACE STE CATHERINE AREA

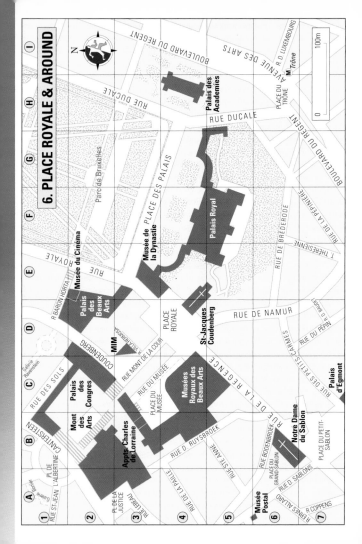

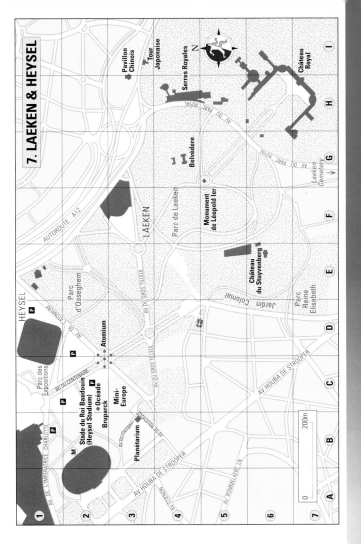

7. LAEKEN & HEYSEL

Pavillon Chinois
Tour Japonaise
Serres Royales
Château Royal
Belvédère
Laeken Cemetery
Parc de Laeken
Monument de Léopold Ier
LAEKEN
AUTOROUTE A12
Parc d'Osseghem
HEYSEL
Parc des Expositions
Stade du Roi Baudouin (Heysel Stadium)
Océade
Bruparck
Mini-Europe
Atomium
Planétarium
Château du Stuyvenberg
Jardin Colonial
Parc Reine Elisabeth

AV DE L'IMPÉRATRICE CHARLOTTE
BD DU CENTENAIRE
AV DE MIRAMAR
AV DU GROS TILLEUL
AV DU PARC ROYAL
AV HOUBA DE STROOPER
AV DE MADRID
AV DE BOUCHOUT
AV DE L'ATOMIUM
AV ROMMELAERE
AV TENBOSCH

N

200m
0

A B C D E F G H I
1 2 3 4 5 6 7

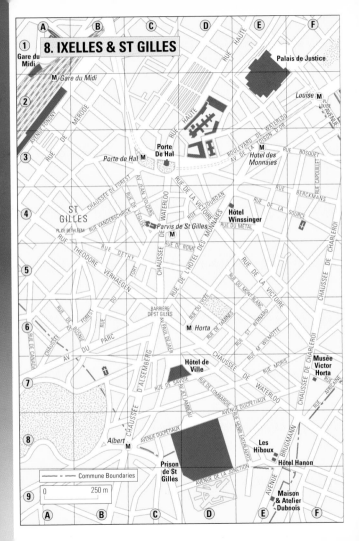